HARVARD ECONOMIC STUDIES

VOLUME XCVI

ECONOMICS AND LIBERALISM

COLLECTED PAPERS

❦

O. H. Taylor

HARVARD UNIVERSITY PRESS
Cambridge, Massachusetts
1967

PREFACE

Kind friends and colleagues at Harvard — as it happened, two of them in particular, S. E. Harris and E. H. Chamberlin — first suggested to me that I should publish this book of reprints of my previously scattered writings, and persuaded me to do so. Allowing their faith to supplement my own, I bring out this volume in the hope that its contents may be of some interest and value to a perhaps small but varied group of readers: former students of mine, friends and colleagues, and others, having interests similar to mine in "mixed" inquiries in the "border zones" between or among the fields of economics, other social sciences, philosophy, political thought, and intellectual history. Substantially all of the writings I have ever published hitherto, are here; only a few short book reviews and other, similar, unimportant items have been omitted.

For help in the steps leading to the publication of this volume I wish to thank, besides the two friends already mentioned: the Harvard Department of Economics as a whole, for authorizing publication in this Series; John Kenneth Galbraith, editor of the Series, for his helpful suggestions; the publishers and editors of the journals or books in which the now assembled items first appeared, for their permission to republish in this form; and the always coöperative Harvard University Press.

O. H. T.

CONTENTS

ECONOMICS AND LIBERALISM

Introduction

THE CHARACTER AND DEVELOPMENT

OF THE IDEAS EXPRESSED IN THE PAPERS

IN THIS VOLUME

❧

As of possible interest to some readers I offer the remarks which follow about the origins and development of my intellectual interests, studies, reflections, and point of view or fundamental convictions, and about the diverse and always mutable, particular interests behind, and positions taken in, the diverse, successive papers in this volume. This collection presents my writings in the chronological order of their dates of first publication, since that seems an order as logical as any, and reflects certain stages in the development of my outlook, knowledge, and opinions. It is about those stages that I now want to speak.

Various internal tendencies and external influences seem to have combined long ago to make me a belated specimen of a now nearly extinct intellectual "species." That is, I am not, or am hardly, "an economist" in the now most usual meaning of the term; but am instead an old-fashioned, philosophical, political economist, with interests extending far beyond the limits of "economics" as now commonly conceived, into all the surrounding fields or parts of all social science, history, and philosophy. Perhaps the right descriptive designation may be even — though this *sounds* immodestly ambitious — a political philosopher *and* economist. And in that very wide field of reflection, my particular point of view or pattern of convictions undoubtedly had its first sources in two not unrelated, early phases of my education in the widest sense. The first source was my initial "upbringing" which made me on the whole I think a very typical American, with a deep commitment to the most common American moral-political faith in liberal democracy and liberal capitalism or "the system of free enterprise," as — when and where attainable in this world — the ethically and pragmatically best, general form or kind of human "social order" and way of life. And a somewhat later, second, reinforcing, clarifying, and slightly modifying influence in shaping my adult point of view was my college and graduate school education in — rather centrally among other things — the classical (or neoclassical) political economy which still pervaded the instruction in "economics" that I received at Harvard in the 1920's, in my graduate school training.

The teachers who did the most — after my earlier upbringing — to form my outlook were F. W. Taussig and Allyn A. Young. The latter's course, at Harvard in the middle to late 1920's, in "modern schools of economic thought," exerted on me a particular, strong influence by directing my attention to the historic intellectual background of the classical liberalism and economics in the philosophical and social thought of the eighteenth-century "enlightenment," and to the continuing disagreements and issues in dispute among (1) the more modern heirs of the eighteenth- and nineteenth-century liberal-and-scientific intellectual tradition, and (2) the different groups of exponents of the diverse, opposed philosophies of romanticism, positivism, historicism, socialism, and institutionalism. It was under Young's direction and influence, also, that I wrote my doctoral dissertation, on eighteenth-century ideas of "natural law" and their contributions to the basic substance of the classical-economic-liberal philosophy. And ever since I wrote that dissertation and received my doctorate (in 1928) my subsequent intellectual life and work have been largely dominated by my continuing interests in the entire range of fundamental questions and historic viewpoints related in any way to the general subject of that dissertation. My later studies have turned partly to other parts of intellectual history, before and since the eighteenth century, and partly to efforts to apply my own basic views, as formed or modified by my appreciative and critical studies of historic and modern modes of thought, to or in reflections on contemporary (twentieth-century) problems of public policy.

In my on-going search for wisdom, I have tried to learn to do justice to the major, "other," pre- and post-eighteenth-century general and social, moral, and political philosophies, offering contrasts with the basic philosophy of the classical liberalism; and to use the "other" — to my mind valid — insights I have found in those "other" philosophies, to modify and supplement the liberal "faith" which in the main has remained the one most attractive and persuasive to me. But to a great extent I have remained, in my personal convictions, a liberal in the now old, classical meaning of the word, of the general "school" of Grotius, Locke, Quesnay, Adam Smith, J. S. Mill, etc. Substantially this same outlook, of course, was also that of the principal founding fathers of the United States — especially Thomas Jefferson, James Madison, and others. I hope I am not, and have never been, a blind devotee of this one tradition of philosophical, social, economic, moral, and political thought; and certainly I do not always see eye to eye on particular issues with those American businessmen of today who preach "free enterprise." But while I have in some ways modified my early adherence to the strict creed of liberal individualism — making some concessions to more "social" or (in a very loose sense) "socialistic" views — I have done so only to a limited extent. Hence in present-day American politics I am stranded in about the middle of the no-man's land between the positions of the A.D.A. on my left and the central bulk of the Republican Party on my right. Such a statement, however, suggests only the general locus of my views on the mass of relatively specific political or policy questions; whereas my strongest interests have been always not in just these questions only, but rather in the search for the broadest and deepest intellectual foundations on which to build my over-all economic, social, moral and political philosophy. And this concern undoubtedly is the most antiquated, "obsolescent" feature of my outlook. I simply cannot do as others now do — jump directly into special problems of economic policy, with only an economist's equipment and my basic, personal predilections *left in the state of being merely unexamined prejudices.* Impelled by an inner need, I go on forever, trying again and again to reformulate, reconsider, and re-revise all my opinions and all their ultimate or primary and intermediate grounds, and bring them all into line or make them consistent with all of the knowledge and the best, reflective judgments that I can attain, in the very wide range and variety of — at least to my mind — relevant fields or intellectual disciplines. Thus economic theory is not, to me, an isolated, self-sufficient, independent inquiry at all, but one of many integral parts of the all-embracing philosophy that is forever in the making — in flux, ever growing and changing — in my mind. The diverse writings assembled in this volume express diverse, small fragments of that philosophy, as they stood at the times when the several, individual writings or pieces in question were first perpetrated. Turning now to the latter, I offer a few brief explanations about each one in turn.

The early (August 1927) "review-article" on R. H. Tawney's *Religion and the Rise of Capitalism* is not, strictly speaking, a real "review" of that book, but a response only to one theme in it, and a response conditioned by my own preoccupations as they were at the time when I wrote this article. It was written at the request of Professor Taussig, then editor of the *Quarterly Journal of Economics,* at a time when I was in the midst of the work of producing my doctoral dissertation, and the materials and thoughts which were to become the contents of the latter and already filled my mind controlled my response to the part of Tawney's book pertaining to the same (my) subject matter. The main things in Tawney's book — the direct fruits of his research into sixteenth- and seventeenth-century English Puritan thought on economic ethics and its relation to "the rise of capitalism" — largely passed me by at that time. I reacted only to his expression, chiefly in his concluding chapter, of his own personal, unfavorable interpretation and appraisal of the late eighteenth- and nineteenth-century economic-liberal philosophy, as the "creed" of established laissez-faire "capitalism." The purpose of my article was to state and support, with the aid of my eighteenth-century materials, my own more favorable interpretation of that philosophy, and to defend the latter against Tawney's misinterpretation and ill-founded criticism, and to demonstrate its superiority (in my belief) to his odd blend of neomedievalism and Christian socialism. I would not now defend everything that is said in this old "juvenile" article of mine, but in the main I do still hold the views expressed in it.

The pair of articles on "natural-law" ideas and economics (published in the *Quarterly Journal of Economics*, November 1929 and February 1930) represents a condensation and rewriting of the main substance of my doctoral dissertation, and the only version of the latter that I ever published or would care to publish. These two articles need to be read together in their sequence as the successive halves of a continuous, single discourse. I think of them now as representing about the best writing I have ever done, but that does not mean I am entirely satisfied with them. In my present opinion, they perhaps separate a bit too sharply the two "ideas" respectively considered in them: the "idea" of "natural laws" of economics supposedly analogous to those of physics, and the "idea" of a body or code of ethical "natural law" to be embodied in the legal system of the ideal liberal society. My later studies in the history of philosophy have since further enlarged and deepened my understanding of the old, intelligible, close interfusion of the natural-and-social-scientific and ethical-normative sides of the "idea" of an all-embracing "system of natural law" which pervaded most pre-modern and early-modern European thought. I will not here attempt, however, to explain my present understanding of this matter, or suggest the revisions that I would now make in these articles if I were to rewrite them. Their somewhat too sharp separation of the two "ideas" is more congenial and thus more readily intelligible to most modern minds than a more accurate interpretation of the historic pattern of thought examined in them would be, and the slight inaccuracy is not, I think, of serious importance.

The main contributions made in these articles to understanding

— and correction of the usual misunderstandings — of the special, two-sided philosophy of "natural law" which originally underlay the classical liberalism-and-economics are contributions that I think stand up all right. The two main points may be summarized as follows: (1) that philosophy did include, *along with* its conception of the *descriptive* "natural laws" of the operation of the market "mechanisms" of the liberal economy, a further conception of the *prescriptive* principles of ethical "natural law," or justice, to be made effective in and through the legal framework around that economy; and (2), while the ethico-legal side of the philosophy indeed mainly stressed the "natural rights" of all individuals, it also recognized as implied therein equitable limitations of each person's rights by those of all other persons, and the duty of all to respect the rights of all, and thus a full set of social or civic moral duties *as well as* rights for everyone. In other words, the authentic, classical liberalism never was the crude endorsement of an amoral or unsocial, absolute individualism, which diverse opponents have so often falsely accused it of being. It would be a further and false claim, however, which I never have made in these articles or elsewhere, to say that the old liberalism *adequately* recognized or conceived *all* of the moral and legal regulations of economic conduct that would ever be required for due protection of the common welfare. But it would mislead the reader of these articles to fix his whole attention in advance solely upon this one theme in them. They consider also a number of other interesting *facets*, not here mentioned, of the complex, early liberal-and-economic philosophy of explanatory-and-normative "natural laws"; and without any further extension of the present remarks, I leave it to the reader to find what he may of interest in the articles.

On the first occasion on which I turned my attention away from intellectual history to contemporary problems of public policy, I produced the not-too-good essay "Economics Versus Politics," for inclusion as the final chapter in the little book *The Economics of the Recovery Program* (McGraw-Hill, New York, 1934), which was written jointly by seven of us, all then teaching at Harvard, in the fall of 1933. "We seven" authors of that book were the members at that time of a long-active "shop club" or discussion group in which Professor Schumpeter was the central figure and the rest of us were younger scholars "sitting at his feet." Our monthly dinners and long evenings of high intellectual discussion were lively, memorable affairs. And during that fall we used them, and our spare time in the intervals between them, to collaborate in producing that small book — a symposium of our individual, critical essays on diverse, selected, major parts or aspects of the then current early New Deal and body of popular thought involved in it. For readers unfamiliar with the book a few words about its other parts may usefully precede the self-critical comment that I want to make on my part of it, the final chapter, alone reproduced in the present volume.

The seven authors, named here in the order of their chapters in the book, were E. H. Chamberlin, E. S. Mason, J. A. Schumpeter, W. Leontief, Douglass V. Brown, S. E. Harris, and myself. Chamberlin's chapter was a critical discussion of the then current, popular ideas — in their vulgar form, not in the new, superior form in which Keynes was about to elevate them to a new level of respectability — about a too-small flow of money or "purchasing power" as the immediate "cause" of the continuing depression, and the alleged needs for re-inflationary monetary, price and wage policies as the appropriate "remedies." Mason wrote in criticism of the "philosophy" of the National Industrial Recovery Act. Schumpeter applied his theory and historical knowledge of business cycles to or in a general diagnosis of the current depression, i.e., discussion of its causation, meaning, comparative severity, prospective duration and results, recovery prospects, and the expected effects on the latter of the New Deal policies. Brown, as our "expert" on labor economics and industrial relations, judicially examined that forerunner of the then still unborn Wagner Act, Section 7A of the N.I.R.A. And Harris wrote about the New Deal's problems and efforts in the field of monetary and fiscal policies, overlapping with Chamberlin's opening chapter and not entirely agreeing with that, but showing already more sympathy than the rest of us at that time felt with the point of view — soon to be so brilliantly supported by Keynes — which underlay that part of the "Recovery Pro-

gram." Thus all contributors to the book except myself wrote
their chapters simply as economists and remained within the
limits of the subject indicated by the book's title — the economics
of the Recovery Program as such. But I, for my part, tried in
the final chapter to round out or supplement the combined work
of the others with a broader essay discussing not only economic
but also political and ethical considerations, and attempting on
that more adequate basis a general evaluation of the New Deal
as a whole.

But alas! the result was this essay or chapter which is not to
me, now, a source of much pride. Though I include it in this
volume, for whatever interest it may have for some readers, I
must briefly indicate and disavow the worst, false notions advanced in it — strange aberrations from my usual views of both
earlier and later dates. In my previous writings I had tried to
rescue the authentic, old or classical, liberal philosophy of economic life and policy from the always too frequent perversions
and misunderstandings responsible for the common, false antithesis between it and all efforts by or through democratic governments to make the business economy a better servant of the
common welfare. And in various later writings I was to go beyond the authentic, classical, liberal position, and approve other,
positive, public measures in addition to the ones it sanctioned.
But in my first reaction to and against the New Deal, I somehow
fell below the level of my own best insights — even those already
expressed in my previous writings — and took a position too near
to the common, crude, extreme, and unauthentic laissez-faire
position of the modern pseudo-classical-liberal "reactionaries."
And what is even worse, in arguing for the position taken I
argued in terms of a scheme of three ill-conceived and misused
abstractions — abstract conceptions of the "pure" economic, political, and ethical ingredients of the over-all social process and
problem — which betrayed me into adoption of the wholly
pessimistic, cynical view of all political and governmental action;
a view that belongs not to liberal thought of any variety, but
instead to fascism and other ancient and modern forms of antiliberal authoritarianism. I will not take space here to say any
more about this essay, which the reader is welcome to read and

evaluate in his own terms but not to regard as at all representative of my present, or my normal, opinions.

In a sense, the potentially sound element of that unfortunate essay, "Economics Versus Politics," which I have just discussed, reappears in a somewhat improved or rectified shape, and not in application to policy issues and polemics but on the level of more objective, fundamental theory, as part of the content of the next essay in this volume, "Economic Theory and Certain Non-Economic Elements in Social Life," which I wrote in the winter of 1934–35 as my contribution to the Taussig Memorial volume, *Explorations in Economics* (McGraw-Hill, New York, 1936). But another influence that by then was operating on my thinking also helped to shape this later essay. My colleague and friend Talcott Parsons was then finishing his now justly famous book, *The Structure of Social Action*, and at his request I read the manuscript — an early draft — of that work, and gave him, and discussed with him, my criticisms and suggestions. Parsons and I, in fact, had by then already had a good many oral discussions of many of the ideas and problems treated in his book and lying equally in my own field of interest, and I cannot even swear that I had not already partially absorbed his development of Max Weber's analysis of the subject matters and relations of the different social sciences, even as early as 1933 when I wrote "Economics Versus Politics." It seems to me, however, that my own independent fumbling in the same direction had produced the idea involved in the structure of *that* essay — and mishandled there — viz., the idea of viewing all concrete social phenomena as "joint products" or "compounds" of several diverse, abstract or pure "elements," such as "economic-rational action" (to use the Weber-Parsons term), and "power politics" (pursuit of ends through pursuit and use of power over others), and the ethical value-systems' ingredient in the cultures of particular societies-and-epochs, etc. At all events, though my effort to think in such terms in writing "Economics Versus Politics" had largely gone wrong — through a tendency to fall into what A. N. Whitehead called "the fallacy of misplaced concreteness" (confusing abstractions with concrete realities, e.g., pure economic-rational action with actual business behavior, and sheer power-politics with the total process of democratic determination of governmental policies) — in writing the new essay for the Taussig volume I did a different and much better job, both because I was discussing Parsons' book with him through the same time-period and getting the full if not the first benefit of the Weber-Parsons scheme of analysis, and also because I was now dealing only with methodology and basic theory, not "applied" discussion of the New Deal or any policy-program evocative of my emotional "bias."

One other novel ingredient of the essay contributed to the *Explorations* volume is the inclusion in it of discussion of "technology" as a fourth "element of action," along with "economizing," and the power-struggles within and power-structures of societies, and the value-systems pervading their cultures and normatively affecting their members' choices of their ultimate ends and routes toward them. And here, in my approach to the special topic of technological versus economic efficiency, etc., I shared with Parsons an old (with both of us) aversion to the "Veblenian" error, of blindness to the real economic "element" and problem, and over-absolute idealization of technological efficiency alone as though it could be the full "economic" goal, and acceptance of the analyses made long ago by "Austrian School" economists, Weber, and others, as revealing the truth corrective of that error. My chapter, then, in the *Explorations* volume, endeavors to suggest a view of the interrelations of four "factors" in the "lives" of societies, viz., pursuit of technical efficiency in all activities taken singly, pursuit of economy in the use of resources by (for the ends of) all activities together, the power-politics of intra-societal group struggles, and communal value-systems. The discussion is not wholly "objective" in one sense of the word, i.e. "neutral, but reveals my own belief in one particular — the classical-liberal — communal value-system; and resembles, in a measure, the earlier essay, "Economics Versus Politics," in assigning to that value-system (where achieved or accepted) the role or function of "freeing," furthering, and facilitating the pursuit of economy and economic welfare for all, and limiting development of destructive intergroup struggles and power politics. But I think that this later essay is free of the tendency of its forerunner to preach, or even imply, an extreme and dogmatic laissez-faire "gospel," and that it contains suggestions of or toward a "universal," objective, theoretical analysis, applicable to all societies, liberal or not. The value that it may have for economists as such lies, if anywhere, in its suggestion of one way of seeing the "economic" subject matter not apart from but *in* the context of a more inclusive view of "social realities" and the subject matters also included therein, of the other social sciences.

Between the composition of the essay just discussed and that of the one to be discussed hereafter, there intervened a ten-year hiatus in my writing activities about which I must say a word. The fact that I published nothing in that long interval resulted from my absorption in an effort of very large scope, which failed, to produce a "great" book. The project was a history of and commentary on many broad developments of varieties — composite patterns — of philosophical and social, economic, moral, and political thought, from the systems of Plato and Aristotle down through all the history of the West to the present time. It is hardly surprising that I was never able to carry out this project, or write and complete such a book and make its quality good enough to satisfy me. What would need the explanation and apology that would be out of place here is the fact that a project so vast and visionary not only seemed practicable to me at first, but enthralled me so long and prevented me from doing any other feasible, productive work. It is possible, but not certain, that I may yet in the future renew the effort and succeed, eventually, in cutting the project or parts of it down to manageable proportions and producing one or more books in that area. In the meantime, from 1945 on to the present, I have resumed the writing, at intervals, of short pieces or articles, as my only current productive activities apart from teaching. But while I published nothing in the decade 1935–1945, I did do in that time a great deal of reading and thinking in great parts of the vast field of the intended book, and this all contributed to or affected all that I have written since 1945.

Most of that work went into studies concerned with portions

of ancient, medieval, and early-modern (pre-eighteenth-century) "intellectual history," and with philosophy in the strict sense and its history. I became associated with — a sort of honorary member of — the Department of Philosophy at Harvard, and developed there first, under the auspices of that department, a college course on economic and social philosophies, which later became the course that I still give — in the offering, in more recent years, of the Economics Department — on Economics and Political Ideas in Modern Times. But back in the decade I now speak of, I profited a great deal intellectually from my intimate association, and frequent discussions of all sorts of subjects, with my friends in the philosophy department, especially Raphael Demos, John D. Wild, and Donald Williams. Also I read and studied all the Platonic dialogues, works of Aristotle, some medieval philosophic literature and modern literature about that, etc. The main part of my activities continued to be in the Economics Department and the study of historic and modern (including new) economic literature, but the work in philosophy and intellectual history absorbed nearly half of all my time and attention, and, for the time being, nearly all of my real, enthusiastic interest. Besides the work pertaining to ancient philosophy already mentioned, I also was studying fully modern philosophical literature, including here, above all, the works of A. N. Whitehead, who impresses me more than all other philosophers of our own epoch. And in the latter part of this same — as to published writing, sterile — decade, I also thought a good deal about general problems concerning the proper ends and means of all undergraduate education. These meditations merged with or into my participation in the early evolution of the Conant-sponsored, Harvard College, "general education program," and the faculty debates which immediately preceded the inauguration of that program. And the first new piece of writing that I published, to mark the end of my non-writing decade, originated in that last connection. It has no bearing at all on economics but appears in this volume because I am making the latter a complete collection of my writings, of whatever sort, down to its date of publication. At the same time this next essay, "Liberal Education and Liberalism," now to be introduced with a few further remarks here, does contain some reflection also of my 1935–1945 studies in all philosophy and intellectual history, and may perhaps deserve its place in this volume for that reason also.

I was never a member of the Harvard Faculty's original Committee on General Education, which produced the famous "red book" *General Education in a Free Society* (Harvard University Press, 1945) — the original charter, or bible, of the subsequently inaugurated "general education program." But I had friends on that Committee, and sat in on a few of its meetings, and was stimulated by its discussions, and those in general meetings of the entire faculty, to write the paper that became the essay or article, "Liberal Education and Liberalism." At the outset I had no thought of publishing the paper as an article, but wrote it for the Committee as a statement of views that might interest members of the Committee and contribute something to their own deliberations and decisions. It was circulated, in typewritten form, through the Committee, and received favorably by at least some of its members, and one of them, my old, close friend Raphael Demos, urged and persuaded me to submit it to the journal, *Ethics* (published at the University of Chicago), for publication. *Ethics* accepted it and brought it out in the April 1945 issue. Only one rather incidental part of it needs any further comment here: the included remarks on the history, meaning, and valid content of the age-old conception of a system of ethical as well as positive-scientific "natural law," explaining all phenomena and implying the "right," normative, fundamental ideals for all human life. Going distinctly further than I had gone in my long-previous doctoral dissertation and "natural law" articles, into outright, full agreement with the antique "natural law" philosophy or doctrine in that (double) sense, this new discussion of my old, "pet" subject went, I now think, *too* far in that direction, and is not to be read as expressing precisely the views I would now defend.

The "excess" of commitment to a less than fully sound position was a temporary effect of my studies of Platonism, Aristotelianism, Stoicism, and Scholasticism — related philosophies, all supporting the "natural law" doctrine or variants of it, and tending at first to over-persuade me, until at a later time I again became more critical of them. The error involved was that of acceptance of the ancient, complete or absolute "rationalism" — belief in the power of human, intuitive-and-logical "reason" to reveal or apprehend all truth and solve all problems, including those in the sphere of ultimate values and the practical decisions to be made in life, in the choice of ends as well as of means. Metaphysical and ethical beliefs, of all kinds, involve not only the discoveries of "reason" but also those extra-rational decisions of the spirit and fruits of all experience in the widest sense, which belong in part to the different domain of religion, or faith. As a matter of faith I do still, personally, believe in a really, objectively ordered, law-abiding, and moral universe, and one, moreover, in which the particular morality implicit in the pattern of the universal natures of things and of men has been most nearly humanly grasped and expressed in the ethical spirit of the authentic, classical liberalism. But I know now that this faith is not demonstrable by or to human "reason"; it really is a faith, persuasive I believe to the combined, universal "reason" *and* best or finest feelings of mankind, but needing to be described in the scholastic phrase as "above reason though not contrary to reason." The ancient "natural law" doctrine in its full rigor always sought to formulate and "prove" a complete, final system of morality, and this mistaken effort always led to authoritarian dogmatisms inconsistent with the liberal ideal of never-ending, free inquiry, discussion, and revision of all traditionally accepted truths and precepts. My wholly approving comments on this ethical rationalism, in the course of the "Liberal Education" essay, are inconsistent with its concluding stand against moral-political indoctrination of any kind, even in or with any principles of liberalism, as any proper part of education. My real, continuing stand is the latter one, not the one implied in the too full defense of the "natural law" tradition. But this does not mean that I favor the kind of "objective, neutral" scholarship and teaching which tries to avoid all moral issues and/or expressions of the scholar's and teacher's own moral judgments. Discussion, not indoctrination, is the substance of education, and the process should be one in which all participants — pupils as well as teach-

ers, and "lay" citizens as well as learned "experts" of all kinds —
collaborate and contribute, in the liberal-democratic way, to the
never finished or perfected but forever changing and improving
fund of relative "wisdom," in current use to enlighten and guide
all private and public actions.

I returned to economic-and-political writing only in the spring
of 1947, with the review-article entitled "Economic Theory and
the Age We Live In," and reviewing A. G. B. Fisher's excellent
book *Economic Progress and Social Security*. This I wrote for
the May 1947 issue of *The Review of Economics and Statistics*,
and at the request of its editor, S. E. Harris. Almost from the
time of its first appearance in print, and ever since, I have
regretted the never intended and slight but noticeable touches
of an unwarranted and unbecoming, almost offensive tone in this
review-article, its mixture of unduly harsh criticism with rather
patronizing (!) praise of an admirable and lovable scholar's
excellent book, and the touch of arrogance and condescension involved in that. There might well have been some justified complaint from an author more sensitive and less magnanimous than
Alan Fisher, but thanks to his good nature, my "perpetration"
of this unfair review of his book led only to a later, entirely
friendly meeting (I had never met him before) and discussion
between us and the beginning of what I still hope may ripen
into an active friendship. In the main I still think well of the
substance of this review-article, apart from the mode of expression and resulting "tone" already described, but it may be of
some interest to note what underlay the latter, in my state of
mind at the time.

In the business of perpetually revising all my own opinions,
along what is generally a zig-zag route of successive over-correc-
tions and re-correction of my just previously held positions, I
was then "swinging" a bit too far, as I now think, away from
my earlier devotion to the classical liberalism and economics,
into a temporary mood of rather full agreement with the basic
orientation of "New Dealism," or the latter day American "liberalism" which (a) responds more fully to mass-popular desires
for "security" than to desires for economic and general, in-

dividual freedom, opportunity, and progress; and (b) prefers the "Keynesian" to the "classical" part of the truth in the technical field of economic analysis and policy. Two different judgments, in fact, were involved together in my then current attitude to the latter outlook as a whole: a judgment that its predominant influence on all public feeling, thought, and action in the modern world had come to stay a good while, or grown so strong and durable as to make continuing opposition to it on old-liberal lines futile and foolish, and also a further judgment that, anyway, it deserved and indeed required acceptance in the main as — under present day conditions — reasonable and right. Also I was feeling a bit annoyed with myself for having arrived belatedly, only, at those new judgments — having clung so long to my earlier opinions while the world around me moved on and made them "obsolete"; and hence I was similarly annoyed with the other political economists, like Fisher, who continued to express and stand for the old position I was "giving up." I have since returned a good part of the way, as the last essays in this volume will show, toward the classical-liberal position, though I still "modify" that, substantially, with the class of "concessions" to more "modern" views which I advocated, too intemperately, in the review-article on Fisher's book. But before returning at all toward the classical-liberal position, I first went on still further, in the meantime, into the "New Dealing" camp — in the next piece of writing which now calls for notice.

The essay entitled "Free Enterprise and Democracy" was written, and appeared, as a chapter in the political symposium book called *Saving American Capitalism* (Knopf, New York, 1948), which was published under the editorship of S. E. Harris, who assembled the contributions (chapters) from a large, varied group of pro-New-Deal economists and other "intellectuals." Both through my willingness to appear in that company, and through the contents and character of my own essay or chapter in that book, I at that time fully aligned myself, temporarily, with the all-out "crusaders" for the "revolution" led by Franklin D. Roosevelt. I had moved all the way from the opposite extreme stand recorded in my 1933 essay "Economics Versus Politics" to this extreme, and in retrospect now I like the later as little as I like the earlier one of these two essays, though their faults are of different kinds. It is probably significant that the faults of "method" in these two unlike arguments or "studies" are of opposite kinds or represent opposite extremes, and are paired as they are with the oppositely extreme positions taken and defended. In 1933 I reached extreme laissez-faire conclusions, by a route that involved much mere juggling with a few very abstract, general notions, and much too little reference to the richly various and ever-changing, detailed, concrete, empirical and historical backgrounds of the different constellations of desires and views widely prevalent in diverse, particular societies and times, and supporting the policy-programs favored within them. And in 1948, *per contra*, I arrived at a full *apologia* for the New Deal's revised "liberalism" and great enlargement of the role of government, by reviewing the histories of forms of "liberalism" and "conservatism" in prevailing public thought and action in different countries and historical periods, and appraising all creeds, severally, in their "settings," with *too little* examination of the intrinsic, intellectual and moral merits of the "creeds" themselves — of their general principles — and *too much* of the tendency to merely "explain" each one as a "natural" product of the special, local and transitory circumstances and desires behind it, *and to judge* it in each case merely through sympathy, or the reverse, with the motives I ascribed to its supporters. The philosophizing relied on in my early, unfavorable appraisal of the New Deal was too unhistorical, and the account of history relied on in my later, favorable appraisal, was too unphilosophical. Moreover, while in the 1933 essay I went to one extreme in representing all political and governmental action as (necessarily) amoral in nature, i.e., controlled by sheer power-politics, in the concluding part of the 1948 essay I went to the other extreme of optimism about the potential, high ethical quality of all the governmental action desired by full-fledged New Dealers, and over-minimized the dangers in that program to individual liberties and the best functioning of the enterprise economy. Attaining a perfectly "well-balanced" point of view on these broad issues seems to me extremely difficult, and I am not sure that I ever have attained it, even down to the present moment, but I am sure, in retrospect, that in these two essays I took positions about equally far removed from it, in opposite directions.

To explain the origins and character of the next, long essay — "Philosophies and Economic Theories in Modern Occidental Culture" — I must again refer back to my 1935–1945 period of trying, vainly, to write a great book in the vast field of "intellectual history," and reading very widely with that in view. The fruits of that reading and the concomitant thinking never got book-length expression, but they did get a later, condensed, partial expression in this strange essay — a virtual précis of the intended but unwritten book — which came into being in the following way. One day in the fall or winter of either 1947 or 1948 — I can't remember the date any more exactly — Yale University's original, brilliant, bold, erratic, and very engaging, likable philosopher, F. S. C. Northrup, paid me an unexpected personal visit and asked me to contribute an essay or chapter of just this kind to the symposium book which he, as editor, was then preparing to assemble and produce, and did bring out a year or two later, under the title *Ideological Differences and World Order* (Yale University Press, 1949). I had never before met Northrup and knew little about him, though I had just read — with equally great amounts of interest and dissent — his then new, current, and already famous book, *The Meeting of East and West.* Also I had read one or two articles by him pertaining to problems of economic theory as well as philosophy, and knew that he had much real knowledge and understanding — such as few modern philosophers or other scholars in fields other than economics have — of economics and the history and literature of economic theory. And Northrup had learned of the nature of my interests in studying, together, philosophy, intellectual history, and economic theory and its history, and decided that I was the man he wanted as author of the chapter in that area, which he wanted to include in his projected, symposium book. As he explained to me what he had in mind for the plan of the book and of the chapter he wanted me to write, it became evident that a condensation of my main ideas for my own intended book, if I could achieve this, would exactly meet his requirements. So I undertook to fill his order, and did so with this essay.

Ideological Differences and World Order is a strange or odd, and to me exciting, book containing a "wild" diversity of independent essays (chapters) by diverse authors chosen to represent at once a wide variety of intellectual disciplines, and of "cultures" oriental and occidental, capitalist and communist, etc. The idea or purpose behind the design of the book — to contribute something to the growth of a more harmonious, future intellectual community of all mankind, and thus to the necessary cultural basis for world peace and order, and to do this by explaining to all and sundry the diverse existing local cultures and their native modes of thought in all kinds of inquiries — is to my mind highly visionary and probably chimerical, but I do not scorn it. And however little faith one may have in the value of that effort, the book itself is full of interest. But the number of economists — or scholars in any other one specialty — who have ever read or will ever read the book, or even see or hear of it, must be extremely small. So by making this essay of mine a chapter in that book, I effectually "buried" it in a place where extremely few of my colleagues would ever see it. Republication in the present volume is therefore, in this case, particularly necessary to make this piece of my work accessible in the right quarters.

I must grant, however, that it is perhaps a piece of work as strange or odd as the book in which it first appeared. For one thing, its substance is so very greatly condensed or compressed — it covers so vast an amount of ground so very briefly and superficially — that it is a perhaps outrageous *tour de force* and string of sweeping assertions all unexplained, unsupported, and undocumented. Moreover, the particular "bird's-eye view" that it tries to give of the immense panorama of historic combined political philosophies and type-systems of economic theory by no means seems to me now at all points the "correct" view, even within its space-limitations. But I must resist the temptation to elaborate here the many adverse criticisms that I would now make of it and the extensive revisions that would be needed to bring it into line with any present views. It does outline or suggest, however faultily, my general vision of the general, historic evolution of Western culture and of economic thought in that wider context, and I think some readers may find it a piece of stimulating, suggestive, provocative reading, whatever their dissents from many things in it.

Turning my attention once more from historic to current literature and problems, I next wrote, for the *Quarterly Journal of Economics* (November 1948), the review-article on four different books — "The Economics of a 'Free' Society: Four Essays." This article reviews in turn: *Ordeal by Planning*, by John Jewkes, *Economic Policy for a Free Society* (the collected papers of the late Henry Simons), J. M. Clark's *Alternative to Serfdom*, and David McCord Wright's *Democracy and Progress*. It introduces that series of reviews with a discussion of the nature of the class of problems treated in all four books, and of the broad or multiple approach through many disciplines that is ideally required, in my view, for full or adequate treatment of such problems. On the whole this article still seems to me, as it has seemed to some of my friends, to be one of my best productions, but one friend, Frank Knight, after reading it, sent me in a letter some adverse criticisms, which I later came to see as largely valid, of some positions taken in it.

As Knight rightly protested, the introductory section takes too extreme a position in demanding that economists, whenever they approve or condemn general programs of public policy, should *always*, to arrive at their verdicts, canvass *all* the relevant considerations in the fields of all the social sciences, history, and philosophy, and that they should *never* argue from knowledge of economics alone. Evaluating policy programs from the standpoint of economics alone, though this can never yield a conclusive judgment, is of course often a quite important, and quite sufficiently large and difficult, and semi-independent task, such that a good performance of this and no more may deserve full praise and no reproach, if the limited significance of what it "proves" is recognized. Then, too, in the body of this article — the reviews of the four books — there are reflections of attitudes which deserved Knight's criticisms, and have since undergone new revisions in my mind. Thus he not unjustly resented the "tone" of my commentaries on the books by his friends, Jewkes and Simons, for here, as in my earlier review of Fisher's *Economic Progress and Social Security*, I was unduly severe on exponents of the relatively "pure," "strict" economic liberalism which formerly had been, but at this time was not, my own point of view. And finally — but without associating Knight or anyone else with *this* point — let me add simply my own acknowledgment that this article now seems to me too enthusiastic in its praise of David M. Wright's *Democracy and Progress*. Though I still think very well indeed of that book, I would now a little moderate the praise bestowed on it and add a few criticisms not suggested in this article; on what lines, I will not attempt to say in this place.

After producing, during 1947 and 1948, the last four pieces of writing that have just been discussed here, I became so absorbed for a time in studies in a largely new field for me that I wrote nothing for publication in the next two to three years. I was reading and thinking my way into more knowledge and understanding than I had possessed of (1) socialist thought and its history, (2) intellectual Marxism, and (3) most of the (published) work and thought of Professor Schumpeter, whose complex mixture of agreement and disagreement with the teachings of Karl Marx, which he knew so well, became the subject of my next article. The reader will find in the first few paragraphs of this article — "Schumpeter and Marx," *Q.J.E.* (November 1951) — a full explanation of the occasion which evoked it, and which thus enabled me to utilize some main results and to fulfill some of the purpose of my reading and thinking over the just preceding years. It is, of course, both less comprehensive than the full, comparative study which its main or general title might suggest, and a good deal more than just a "review" of the Schumpeter essays on imperialism and social classes. There is in it, perhaps, less of my own opinions than in most of my other writings; in the main it tries to say, not what I think, but only what Marx and Schumpeter, as I understand them, seem to have thought on the subjects considered. Thus it gives no indication of the wide divergence of my own position *both* from Marx's *and* from Schumpeter's position, e.g., on the questions at issue in their similar and different "economic interpretations of history." If it interests anyone to know this, I accept no form of full or strict historical determinism and do not believe that the "evolution" of "modes of production," or of economic systems and conditions, is either "autonomous" — in any full or unique sense or measure — or has any greater or more "fundamental" causative importance than that which probably belongs to each of the several major, non-economic components to be viewed as interacting with (upon) each other and the economic complex within complete, "evolving" civilizations. Intellectual and spiritual-cultural configurations, political-and-power organizations, activities, and struggles, and perhaps some other "factors" that might be named, may well — it seems to me — "evolve" with degrees of partial "autonomy," and exert amounts of influence on everything in the whole movement or course of history, not at all inferior to what may inhere in and grow out of "economic development." And there goes with this — my preference for a view of history of this kind — much more of dissent from both Marxian and Schumpeterian views on many other questions, also, than is at all suggested in this article. Basically, of course, my entire perspective is radically unlike either Marx's or Schumpeter's for the following reasons. (1) My interests center more in normative moral-social philosophy than in explanatory-predictive economic and social science, and I neither, like Marx, submerge the former in the latter nor, like Schumpeter, try to banish it in favor of the latter. And (2) the particular moral-social and political philosophy which has my adherence — liberalism — not only is profoundly unlike and opposed to both Marxian socialism and Schumpeter's old-European conservatism, but by its nature involves or requires and carries with it a philosophy of all existence, history, and science, equally alien to those two great minds. Nevertheless I have learned much from both, and I hope that this article, which suppresses or omits my own dissenting views and tries to offer "objective," fair interpretations of their main positions, may be of interest and of value to some readers.

There remains the final essay in this volume — "The Future of Economic Liberalism" — which was first presented as a paper at the annual meeting of the American Economic Association in December 1951 and published in the May 1952 *American Economic Review* (*Papers and Proceedings*). I had an extraordinarily difficult time endeavoring to write that paper to my own satisfaction, and remained deeply dissatisfied with it in the form in which it finally emerged. It is not well written as to style, and does not resolve the complex multiplicity of lines of thought suggested in its different parts into any fully coherent and well-balanced whole. The version of "economic liberalism" which it outlines and defends, and about the prospects of which it inquires, is or seems a shade more "conservative" as that political word is commonly used today — closer to agreement with the usual ideals of American businessmen — than (on the average over any long run) I really am or like to be. The reader of these pages who has reached this point will know how I have vacillated back and forth in this respect through many years. In composing this paper I "swung back" from the "New Deal liberalism" I had embraced a few years earlier, not all, but much of the way toward the classical-economic-liberal position espoused in my earliest, youthful writings. Yet the impression to that effect is partly false, because in fact the argument suggested in the small part toward the end of the essay, which touches on the non-economic defects of the civilization of "liberal capitalism," and the need to ameliorate them, really implies support of more extensive departures from *laissez faire* and "free competition," than is indicated. With all its inconsistencies and faults, however, this essay does perhaps suggest, fairly well, the main elements of my over-all position or outlook in about the latest phase of its "evolution" thus far; and it may stand, appropriately enough, as the last item in this serial collection of the writings of one who is perhaps less truly an economist than a perpetually troubled, mind-changing moralist.

1

TAWNEY'S RELIGION AND CAPITALISM,

AND EIGHTEENTH-CENTURY LIBERALISM

❧

Mr. Tawney's book[1] deals with the influence of religious thought in England in the sixteenth and seventeenth centuries upon economic ideals, practices, and institutions. It begins with an account of the economic philosophy of the medieval church, which substantially agrees with such familiar accounts as those of Ashley and of Cunningham. It ends with a very brief description of that new philosophy of encouragement, rather than restraint, of acquisitive ambition and enterprise, which had definitely displaced the medieval outlook by the beginning of the eighteenth century. Intervening chapters describe the slow conversion of the mind of the nation from the medieval to the modern point of view, giving special attention to the evolution and influence of Puritan ideals. The thesis is very similar to that of Max Weber's essay, "Die protestantische Ethik und der Geist des Kapitalismus," to which Mr. Tawny acknowledges his indebtedness. He criticizes Weber, however, for exaggerating the influence of Puritanism, and the simplicity both of Puritanism and of "the spirit of capi-

[1] Richard H. Tawney, *Religion and the Rise of Capitalism* (New York: Longmans, 1926). This review-article was first published in the *Quarterly Journal of Economics* for August 1927, and is reprinted here with the kind permission of the editor.

talism." [2] Throughout his own treatment, he carefully emphasizes qualifications and complexities; at least, until he reaches the period of the definite emergence of that new philosophy whose genesis he has been tracing. Here it seems possible to suspect some serious oversimplification and onesidedness. It may be best to summarize the argument of the book, before dealing with this possible deficiency.

The medieval church, we are told, tried to impose upon the population of Europe a moral discipline, which included within its sphere the economic side of life, and restrained the acquisitive desires of individuals, in the interest both of their own spiritual health and of justice and the common welfare. The restrictions were often unwise in their details, and often ineffective; but they embodied a noble and sound ideal, and did mitigate, though they could not eradicate, the harsher forms of exploitation and oppression. The Reformation, in its earlier stages, brought no abandonment, but rather a more vigorous preaching, of the traditional code of Christian economic ethics. The rising bourgeoisie, however, became increasingly impatient with the restraints imposed by this code. Conditions of the times required some change; and various intellectual currents converged in the seventeenth century to produce a new philosophy. Puritanism in its old age evolved an ethic that sanctified acquisitive ambition, and nearly summed up the Christian's duty in the "economic virtues."

This new gospel not only stimulated industry, thrift, and the accumulation of wealth, but also gradually weakened, and eventually destroyed, the medieval scruples which had restrained the greed of traders in the social interest. The entire liberal, or anti-traditionary and anti-authoritarian movement of the time, which in politics produced modern democracy, had as its outcome in the economic sphere simply the unfettering of capitalists and business men, and an amoral or non-moral theory of economic relations. Its crowning intellectual achievement was the new economic science, which taught that the business man's actions are inevitable products of a social mechanism whose motions can be scientifically explained, but cannot be criticized. In the atmos-

[2] See his Notes on chap. 4, pp. 315–316, note 32.

phere of such ideas, modern capitalism, or the organization and direction of the nation's economic life by self-seeking members of a rich commercial class, could flower and flourish.

I will not venture to discuss this argument in its entirety. The subject has been too much neglected by English and, especially, by American economists; and a readable yet erudite contribution such as this would be welcome, even if its faults were many. It may be desirable, however, to suggest the possibility of a different interpretation of the liberal movement and of the economist's notion of a social mechanism. To do this, it will be necessary to refer mainly to writers whom Mr. Tawney neglects or ignores, above all, to eighteenth-century writers. These may perhaps be regarded as lying outside of his chosen period; but they are not irrelevant to his thesis. He professes to trace for us the transition from the medieval to the modern attitude toward economic life.[3] His assumpion that the essential part of the transition was complete by 1700, and that its outcome is adequately seen in the writings of some late seventeenth-century Puritan divines and pamphleteers, requires to be tested by reference to the writings of other leaders in the wider intellectual movement, not only of the seventeenth century but of the eighteenth as well. Even for his narrower special purpose, of exhibiting the influence of Protestant religious and ethical ideas upon economic theories and arrangements, the views of orthodox Anglican and Puritan clergymen are surely no more relevant than those of Grotius, Locke, Shaftesbury, and Hutcheson. Though the two last mentioned, like many later philosophers of liberalism, were perhaps not technically Christians, their "natural religion" was hardly a shade different from the liberal Christianity of Locke; and their whole social outlook was probably about as much (or as little) a product of the Reformation, as was the social outlook of the Puritans of an earlier generation.[4] On all accounts its seems permissible, without

[3] See his Introduction, paragraph 1, last 3 sentences; and his concluding chapter (5).

[4] For the religious and ethical views of Shaftesbury and Hutcheson, and their relations to Locke, and to Adam Smith, see L. Stephen, *English Thought in the Eighteenth Century.* A good study by an economist, which emphasizes the influence of Shaftesbury upon the eighteenth century in general and Adam Smith in particular, is Hasbach's *Die philosophischen*

questioning Mr. Tawney's interpretations of his own chosen materials, to ask whether a wider survey would bear out his conception of the liberal movement as simply a progressive stripping off of legal and moral restraints upon the anti-social greed of individuals.

Medieval restraints upon activities and contracts motivated by acquisitive ambition had originally been formulated in the name of the moral Law of Nature, which prescribes to individuals their duties and sets just limits to their claims. But the liberal protest against these restraints was formulated in the name of that same Law of Nature. And while the morality that was summed up in the Natural Law of Locke and the physiocrats was not the same morality that was embodied in the Natural Law of Aquinas, one must hesitate to pronounce it a less noble or less generous morality. Aquinas and his contemporaries talked mainly of the *duties* of men; Locke and his successors emphasized their *rights*. Yet it is a commonplace observation that A's right against B is the other aspect of B's duty toward A, and vice versa. If all men did their duties, all would enjoy their rights; if rights are universally respected, certain duties are thereby recognized.

The significant question is, which formulation of the moral law is more conducive in practice to a healthy social situation, and is least easily perverted to the selfish uses of a dominant class? And this is not so easy to determine. A priest who talks to men about their duties seems to be inculcating a high and unselfish morality. A philosopher who talks to them about their rights is accused of flattering selfish interests, and encouraging an anarchistic and immoral individualism. But it is noteworthy that men in positions of power and authority often prefer to talk the language of duties, though it involves their paying at least lip-service to the idea that they themselves have duties toward their inferiors. This is the language of paternalism. When a submerged class rebels, its leaders generally prefer to talk the language of rights, even if they must

Grundlagen der von F. Quesnay und A. Smith begründeten politischen Ökonomie, in vol. X of Schmoller's *Forschungen.* An old work, interesting and valuable because of its author's close relation to Adam Smith in time and environment, is Dugald Stewart's *Dissertation* on the history of philosophy since the Renaissance; published as vol. I of Sir W. Hamilton's edition of Stewart's *Works.*

recognize, at least in theory, that *all* men have rights and that rights limit one another. This is the language of democracy. Traders in the seventeenth century, and laborers in the nineteenth, claimed new rights, and were rebuked by conservative churchmen and statesmen for casting aside and denying old duties. Can we conclude, from this alone, in either case, that all of the moral idealism was on the side of conservatism, and all of the selfishness on the side of rebels and innovators?

It is true that seventeenth- and eighteenth-century liberals accorded to the self-regarding desires and ambitions of individual men a measure of moral approval which medieval Christians had denied to them. But it does not follow that they wished to discard all moral restraints that might protect the community against the overweening greed of individuals. The new leniency toward individual desires was closely connected with a new faith in the moral faculties of individuals, and in the goodness of normal human nature. Self-centered desires were trusted to promote the general welfare, because reason and the moral sense were trusted to restrain them wherever their indulgence would be inconsistent with that welfare. Evidence upon this point could be multiplied *ad infinitum*, if there were space. It may suffice for the present purpose to note some important writers whose general positions bear out the assertion.

To begin at the beginning, Grotius once for all founded the whole liberal theory of natural rights upon the doctrine that men are endowed with a disinterested love of society, and a capacity to know and a tendency to do what is right or just toward their neighbors.[5] The British philosopher who most roundly denied this, and asserted the complete selfishness of men, was logical enough to plan a state which, with its absolute power, should ruthlessly curb the lusts of individuals.[6] Once Hobbes had written, every liberal who dared to advocate a measure of *laissez faire* in any department of life had first to defend the old doctrine

---

[5] Grotius, *De Jure Belli ac Pacis*, Prolegomena, secs. 5 to 10 inclusive. In W. Whewell's edition, with accompanying translation, pp. xl to xlv.

[6] See *Leviathan*, and any commentary. Croom Robertson's *Hobbes*, pp. 138–159, is good.

of Grotius against Hobbes.[7] The group of religious philosophers known as the Cambridge Platonists, who were all in the liberal movement, led the attack upon Hobbism, declaring that all men may intuitively recognize the eternal moral truths which bind us to subordinate our own good to the good of mankind.[8] Locke held, with Grotius, that moral axioms are known by an "internal sense"; that from these axioms, the whole moral law may be deduced with a precision approaching that of mathematics; and that thus the Law of Nature was knowable, and binding, even before the establishment of government.[9] Shaftesbury, the father of the school of Scotch moral philosophers that bred Adam Smith, endowed man with an innate "moral sense," and a complete outfit of "benevolent affections"; and taught that self-regarding desires are legitimate, and even virtuous, so long, but only so long, as they are duly controlled and limited by these other propensities.[10] Mandeville revived against Shaftesbury the doctrine of Hobbes, that men are completely selfish; made selfish economic appetites (called vices, in true medieval spirit) the springs of all progress beyond savagery; taught, like Rousseau, that such progress is inseparably connected with many evils, injustices, and forms of misery; and seemed to prefer to have men

[7] This is still true in a measure even of the physiocrats, a century later. See Quesnay's article on "Droit Natural," in Oncken's edition of Quesnay's works. While opposing Grotius also on some points, Quesnay plainly has Hobbes in mind as his chief antagonist; and emphatically holds, against him, that natural right is grounded, not in the egoistic calculations of a *non-social* individual, but in (*a*) man's dependence on his fellows, and (*b*) his innate knowledge of moral axioms, both of which show that he was designed for society. And the implication is that, because his nature is social, he can and should be free.

[8] The best account of this interesting group is the Rev. J. Tulloch's *Rational Theology and Christian Philosophy in England in the Seventeenth Century*, vol. II. For their influence on Shaftesbury, see Leslie Stephen, *English Thought in the Eighteenth Century*, II, 23.

[9] Sidgwick, *Outline of the History of Ethics*, pp. 172–175; and Seth, *English Philosophers and Schools of Philosophy*, p. 112.

[10] Stephen, II, 27–32; and Hasbach, pp. 103–108. Hasbach makes Shaftesbury's preaching of the natural goodness of man a main source of all eighteenth-century individualism. "Locke had taught that man had a *right* to freedom; Shaftesbury taught that he was *fit* for it." But Locke believed the second doctrine, too. See note 8 above.

wisely governed and deceived by autocrats, who should restrain their "vices" partly but not wholly.[11] Francis Hutcheson, disciple of Shaftesbury and teacher of Adam Smith, defended his master's doctrine against Mandeville, and went so far as to make the pure, disinterested love of mankind the *only* virtuous motive in our natures.[12] Finally, Adam Smith himself, before writing the *Wealth of Nations,* wrote upon our *Moral Sentiments;* and in the earlier book analyzed the mental processes by which we build up out of our experience a knowledge of the moral rules, obedience to which yields conduct conducive to the common welfare; finding in this social beneficence of our moral faculties the same proof of providential design of our natures, which he afterward saw also in the social beneficence of economic (acquisitive) ambition.[13] If the two books are read together, it is clear that Smith agreed with Shaftesbury, that self-centered economic ambition is socially beneficent, *so long as* it is limited, as it normally is, by the beneficent dictates of our moral faculties.

The whole movement, then, for freeing acquisitive enterprise, along with the other activities of individuals, from the old restraints of medieval law and custom, was greatly aided by the faith that, wherever restraints are really necessary in the social

---

[11] An excellent commentary on Mandeville is in Höffding, *History of Modern Philosophy,* I, 400–402.

[12] Sidgwick, *Outline,* pp. 195–200; Albee, *History of English Utilitarianism,* pp. 58–63.

[13] The general doctrine of the *Moral Sentiments* can be appreciated only by one who carefully reads the book through from beginning to end. On the beneficence of our moral faculties, see especially part III, chap 5. On the relation of Smith's ethical to his economic theories, see Hasbach, *Die philosophischen Grundlagen,* and G. W. Morrow, *The Ethics and Economics of Adam Smith.*

Cf. also Professor Jacob Viner's interesting article on "Adam Smith and Laissez Faire," in the *Journal of Political Economy* for April, 1927. I cannot agree with Professor Viner's opinion that the *Moral Sentiments* embodies an early, uncritical, enthusiastic outlook which Smith had abandoned before writing the *Wealth of Nations;* nor with his dictum (p. 210) that "benevolence or sympathy" was made a prominent quality of human nature in the early book, and a negligible quality in the later one. The "sympathy" of the *Moral Sentiments* is not "benevolence," but is equally the foundation of this, and of the sense of justice, which, as Professor Viner admits (p. 203), always limits the action of self-interest, in both treatises.

interest, they will normally be supplied by a moral sense as native to the individual as his selfish appetites. The function of "positive law" should be the limited one of merely declaring so much of natural law as could be formulated in precise general rules, and could be enforced by the courts against exceptional persons with an abnormally weak moral sense.[14] The objections to the medieval regulations were that they imposed many restraints *not* necessary to the general interest, and often harmful to it; and that much was embodied in inflexible law and custom which was better entrusted to individual consciences.

There was one chief reason for believing that, at least under seventeenth- and eighteenth-century conditions, the surviving medieval rules of conduct and regulations were more often harmful than beneficial to the general interest. Mr. Tawney admits[15] that many of the regulations, such as those of the guilds regarding apprenticeship, quality of work, and prices, either created or fortified monopoly privileges, and were welcomed by the privileged parties partly for this reason; though they also purported to protect the public against bad work and excessive charges. The prohibition of loans at interest, which in Mr. Tawney's view seems to be about the most important regulation of all, must have had a similar effect. That is, it limited the supply of loan funds to that provided by those persons and organizations that were favorably situated either to evade the prohibition or — like the church itself, or its financial agents, and rich religious orders — to take full advantage of the exceptions, legalizing interest in special circumstances; and meant for them a high, "monopoly" rate of return, and a vested interest in supporting the restrictive law. Mr. Tawney rightly insists that medieval artisans, merchants, and their spiritual advisers be given credit for a degree of sincere moral idealism,

---

[14] See the numerous passages in the *De Jure Belli*, in which Grotius distinguishes between the full moral duty of the Christian, and the minimum portion of that duty which is strictly required by Natural Law (here juristically conceived as the ideal or norm of positive law). Also A. Smith's distinction (in the *Moral Sentiments*) between the rules of justice, exactly definable and hence fit to be written in statute books, and the vaguer rules of prudence and of wise benevolence, which are best left to private discretion.

[15] Page 27.

even where protection of their own monopoly privileges and gains
supplied a part of the motive for adherence to the regulations.[16]
Why, then, should not seventeenth-century Puritan business men
and *their* spiritual advisers be given credit for an equal degree of
idealism, when they sought to throw off regulations; even though
new opportunities of private gain proved to be created by reforms perhaps primarily designed to open new sources of supply
of loan funds and of wares? The pamphleteers who urged removal
of restrictions upon loans seem generally to have been, not lend-
ers, but borrowing traders, whose cry was for reduction of the
interest rate.[17] And certainly it must be clear to careful readers
of the physiocrats and Adam Smith, that *their* belief in *laissez
faire* and free competition was not a belief in the absolute right
of individuals to make as much money as possible, regardless of
social consequences, but, on the contrary, a belief that the public's right to good service at fair prices could be best protected
by universalizing the right to pursuit of the best profits obtainable.[18] They preferred to trust the individual's moral sense, plus
his fear of competitors, rather than a law which prescribed the
quality of his output and his prices but made him a sheltered
monopolist.

The medieval regime of regulated monopolies quite possibly
was well suited to medieval conditions. Early modern liberals
believed that a regime of free competition would be better suited
to the only conditions with which they were familiar; and they
may have had too great a tendency to assume its universal superiority. Much depends upon whether we wish merely to preserve
an established system of "fair" prices and group standards of living, or to stimulate economic progress, a constant lowering of
the real costs of goods, a raising of all standards of living. But
the essential point to be made here is merely that a concern for
justice and the general welfare may be, and has been, as much
the motive and ground of advocacy of one regime as of the other.

[16] Pages 27, 28.

[17] See articles in Palgrave's *Dictionary of Political Economy* on Mun,
North, Child, the Culpeppers, etc.

[18] See the many strong passages in the *Wealth of Nations* on the monopolistic spirit among merchants, and the resulting evils.

I shall not take space to discuss further the general spirit of the liberal movement. Enough has perhaps been said to raise some doubts of the justice of treating it as essentially a glorification of private selfishness. But something may be added, in conclusion, about the implications of the economists' conception of economic society as a mechanism, whose processes (made up of human actions) are to be causally explained. The intricate logical problems here involved cannot, of course, be gone into; but a way out of the difficulty of scientifically explaining and morally criticizing the same human actions may be suggested.

By way of approach to this topic, it may be pointed out that Mr. Tawney's criticism of traditional economic theory is an example of one of two contrasting types of criticism, which get curiously combined and confused in much current controversy. From Carlyle onward, there have been moralists who tended to denounce economists as atheists, materialists, and "mechanistic" fatalists, and to accuse them of teaching that men and societies are mere machines. They are supposed to maintain that all actions, events, and conditions are inevitable; that prices and incomes, in particular, are governed by "inexorable laws"; and that "interference" with these laws, in the interest of justice, is impossible.[19] On the other hand, at least from Auguste Comte onward, there have been persons with a leaning to "naturalistic" or "positivistic" types of philosophy, who have accused these same economists of being antiquated and pious thinkers, theologically or metaphysically minded, who confuse the causal "laws" of modern science with the beneficent ordinances and moral precepts of a deified "Nature."[20] The fullest statement of this second accusation is contained in Thorstein Veblen's well-known essays.[21] Here is a

[19] Others of the "English romanticists" besides Carlyle took this line. See an amusing essay by the poet Southey, attacking Malthus, written in 1818, and published in Southey's collected *Essays*. Ruskin in *Unto This Last* and *Munera Pulveris* is more explicit than Carlyle in attacking the supposed inexorability of economic laws.

[20] See, for instance, chap. 4 of Ingram's *History of Political Economy* (Ingram was a disciple of Comte); and Cliffe Leslie's essay on "The Political Economy of Adam Smith," in his *Essays, Moral and Political*.

[21] Thorstein Veblen, *The Place of Science in Modern Civilisation, and Other Essays* — especially the three connected essays on Preconceptions of Economic Science.

contrast! According to Tawney, the classical economists and their seventeenth- and eighteenth-century predecessors used the ideas of physical science to explain economic actions and events in a way that logically precluded the application to them of ethical criteria. According to Veblen, they used theological, metaphysical, and ethical ideas to describe the economic order planned by "Nature," in a way that made objective economic science impossible until this pious structure was demolished. Both interpretations assume a conflict, or at least a hiatus, between moral philosophy and explanatory science as applied to human behavior. The suggestion offered here is that for the founders of economic science no such conflict or hiatus existed; and that when their conception of a social mechanism, and the uses they made of it, are fully understood, they will be seen to have opened a way to causal explanation of economic behavior without abdication of the right of criticizing it or the hope of reforming it.

If competition generally prevails in a community, and the dominant motive of its members in their business activities is the desire to make as much money as they can make honestly, then the best guide to explanation and prediction of the actions of masses and classes of men will be found in the assumption that, other things being equal, they will do, in any given circumstances, whatever promises to be most profitable to them financially. If the effects of a war, a crop failure, a gold discovery, a law, a tax, or any other phenomenon, upon men's opportunities of gain, can be predicted, its effects upon their conduct can be predicted, with a greater or less approach to certainty. Each man's action, in turn, will affect his neighbors' opportunities of gain, and hence his neighbors' actions, in a roughly predictable manner. This is the whole simple secret of the method of economic theory. The business man draws from his partial foresight of the reactions which his customers, competitors, and employees manifest to their opportunities of gain, working rules for the efficient conduct of his own quest of gain. The economist seeks to draw, from a somewhat more complete and accurate foresight of the reactions of all, working rules for public policy designed to promote large production and just distribution of wealth.

Now, any whole composed of parts so interrelated that, when

one part moves, the movements of the other parts can be predicted, is a "mechanism." Hence a society composed of individuals and groups whose opportunities of gain are so interrelated that, when some of them act, the profitable and therefore probable actions of the others can be predicted, is, by analogy, a "mechanism." But though this analogy points a way to explanation and prediction, it in no way precludes concomitant attempts to criticize, reform, or control economic behavior. Here, as elsewhere, prediction makes possible control. We can often get men to do what we want them to do, by creating situations that will make the desired actions profitable. But that is not all. The *ceteris paribus* phrase that qualifies our fundamental assumption must never be forgotten. Men do not pursue financial gains only, to the exclusion of other objects of desire. The number, quality, and strength of the non-pecuniary motives that interplay with the desire for gain, and check or modify it, may be indefinitely modified by legal, religious, intellectual, and moral influences. Actions can be induced by making them respectable or honorable or pious, as well as by making them profitable. "Mechanistic" economists have not generally denied this. Their use of "laws" of most-profitable-action to explain prices and other economic phenomena, therefore, does not prove that they ever wished to put economic life outside of the sphere of the moralist.

We may go further. The working rules which individuals use in their pursuit of gain, *can* be regarded as *moral* rules, forming part of a wider system of rules for the wise governance of human behavior. These working rules are rules of "prudence," and prudence is generally conceded to be one of the virtues, albeit one of the humbler ones.[22] Prudence in the *acquisition* of one's income consists in the use of intelligence and foresight to make it as large as possible, consistently with concurrent practice of the other virtues. Prudence in *spending* an income is a deeper matter, involving in the end about all that the Greeks included under "temperance," or the preservation of a reasonable balance among one's interests, such as may make life most worth living

[22] Smith's picture of the "prudent man" in the *Moral Sentiments* is famous. It is a prudent *business man* he is depicting; but how different from his pictures of business men in the *Wealth of Nations!*

on the whole. Now the physiocrats and Adam Smith seem to
have believed that, if the state will enforce the rules of justice
and set all individuals free to observe the rules of prudence as
they see them in their private affairs, the nation will secure a
larger production, juster distribution, and wiser consumption of
wealth than it would be likely to secure under a regime of pa-
ternalistic state regulations. The moral Law of Nature therefore
prescribed "the system of natural liberty" as the wisest legal
order; and under it, those causal or mechanical "laws of nature,"
in accordance with which both our economic appetites and our
moral sentiments arise and function in society, will generally
ensure individual behavior conducive to the general welfare.

I would not be understood as being in complete agreement
with either the philosophy of liberalism or the doctrines of the
early economists. "The system of natural liberty" is not a clear
and complete definition of an eternally wise legal order. The
reforms introduced in its name have bred new evils, even though
removing old ones. Mr. Tawney may be right in believing that
we need to revive, in our present day, some parts of the medieval
philosophy which the seventeenth- and eighteenth-century radicals discarded. But it is not always necessary to castigate the
prophets of one religion in order to be open-minded toward
those of another. Mr. Tawney has given us another version of
the socialist myth, that all capitalists are conscienceless and greedy
and that liberals and "bourgeois economists" are their flatterers
and apologists. Those dour and grim old seventeenth-century
Puritan controversialists often talked in a vein like that of the
Hobbists whom they execrated. But one hardly believes, after
reading Grotius and Locke and Adam Smith, that their temper
was the main temper of the liberal movement. If modern capitalism, modern liberalism, and modern civilization in general are
to be regarded as products of a new religion that arose in the
seventeenth century, that religion has inculcated humanitarianism as well as "the economic virtues." When some one writes
the real history of the liberal movement, from Grotius to J. S.
Mill, we may possibly find that its leaders were, in greater measure than we had supposed, the prophets, not of an "acquisitive"
but of a "functional" society.

2

ECONOMICS AND THE IDEA OF

NATURAL LAWS*

❧

I

Economic theory of the traditional type has always purported
to be a "scientific" statement of the most general "laws" of society's economic life. Not long ago, respectable economists were
still boldly calling these "laws" of their science "natural laws"
or "laws of nature." But the idea of natural laws, which so largely
dominated scientific and philosophical thought in the eighteenth
and nineteenth centuries, has in recent decades lost something of
its former freight of meaning, and perhaps of its former prestige.
Philosophers have been criticizing the notion which the phrase
conveyed to the nineteenth-century mind, and especially the uses
that were made of it in psychological and social "sciences"; and
even physical scientists have been revising their conceptions of
the nature and significance of scientific "laws." [1] The laws which

---

* This article first appeared in the *Quarterly Journal of Economics* for
November 1929.

[1] P. Struvé, in his article "L'idée de loi naturelle dans la science économique" (*Revue d'économie politique*, 1921), refers to Windelband and
Rickert, and the earlier work of Renouvier, as having specially contributed
to the modern critical revaluation of the idea of scientific "laws." Windelband and Rickert have been especially concerned with criticism of attempts
to apply it in historical and social studies. E. Boutroux, working in the

the natural sciences discover are still called "laws," but there is
a disposition, perhaps growing, to stop calling them "laws of nature," on account of the dubious inherited connotations of that
phrase.[2] At all events, whatever terminology is employed, there
is at least a new scepticism toward some of the notions which
the general idea of laws of nature carried with it in the mid-
nineteenth-century mind. The tendency of present-day economists, even of the more "orthodox" type, to speak with more
modesty and caution about the "laws" of their own science, and
to drop all rhetorical language about the "natural laws" of economic life is thus in harmony with current tendencies in other
sciences.

But the matter still needs a more definite clearing up. What is
the exact nature and significance of the "laws" at which economic theory arrives? Exactly what and how much of all that
was involved in or suggested by the old idea of them as real
"laws of nature" do we need to discard? A clear answer to this
last question, if it could be given, would do much to put an end
to the controversy that has dragged on for a century, between
the adherents of "theory" of the more "orthodox" type and the
"rebels" who have wanted to turn economic inquiries in some
wholly different direction. The latter have generally been men
who were alienated by some of the apparent implications of the
traditional idea of "natural" economic laws. They have regarded
that idea, and the scheme of thought bound up with it, as the
unalterable essence of "orthodox" theory, and hence have wished

---

general tradition of Renouvier, has written keenly on the nature of laws
in science generally. A. N. Whitehead, Bertrand Russell, and some other
English philosophers have, I believe, attacked the problem on rather
different lines. An indication of the present state of the discussion in physical science may be obtained from A. S. Eddington's *The Nature of the
Physical World* (1928).

The article by Struvé, referred to here, and again below in the text,
discusses brilliantly some aspects of the problems considered in the present
article. But my approach is different, and my indebtedness to him is not
great. I should perhaps apologize for the accidental similarity of my
opening remarks to his, which seemed inevitable.

[2] "The conception of the 'working hypothesis,' provisional, approximate,
and merely useful, has more and more pushed aside the comfortable 18th-
century conception of 'laws of nature.'" — Bertrand Russell, in Preface to
H. Poincaré's *Science and Method*, trans. Maitland, p. 6.

to abandon such theory entirely. But the majority of modern adherents of "theory" of this type are ready to concede that its "laws" are not all that the older economists, who called them "laws of nature," thought they were. The way would seem to be open for an attempt to "get together" on the basis of a clearer separation of the valid from the invalid or dubious elements in the philosophy of the older economists.

The best way to solve the problem would probably be to make a thorough philosophical and critical study of the historic evolution of the theory of economic laws. Criticism of the notions of the older economists must be based upon a real knowledge and comprehension of them; and this can come only from a study of their origins and development and of their setting in the life and thought of the times. This approach is all the more indispensable because of the fact that the notions here in question — namely, those connected with the particular significance then attached to the idea of "natural laws," in the minds of both economists and contemporary workers in other sciences — were not adequately thought out and expressed by anyone, but were merely an elusive part of the "mental climate" or "atmosphere."[3] The student must undertake the dangerous task of making fully "explicit" ideas which in part are merely "implicit" in the writings of the physiocrats, of Adam Smith, and of the classical economists; for without making them more fully explicit than they are in those writings, it is impossible to criticize them intelligently. This undertaking would be a dangerous one in any case; but a sufficient knowledge of the development of the whole outlook and philosophy of the epoch might make it possible to penetrate to the half-hidden foundations of its theory of the

[3] Whitehead (*Science and the Modern World*, pp. 4, 5, 10, 11, and *passim*) emphasizes the importance of the "climate of opinion" and the "secret imaginative background" which colored the fundamental conceptions of the creators of modern physical science. Possibly this was even more important in the case of the pioneers in economics, who were less closely tied down, so to speak, to perfectly definite facts, and who were not yet thinking in terms of mathematics. But I do not think this influence of half-hidden "preconceptions," to use Veblen's term, upon a writer's theories, means that they are *wholly* a mere product of an historically transient intellectual and social environment, and contain no elements of permanently valid "truth."

"natural" organization and laws of society's economic life, and then to separate what was soundly "scientific" in that theory, according to modern standards, from what was merely dubious and misleading speculation.

Numerous scholars have, of course, made historical studies covering some of the ground that needs to be covered. Some American readers will think at once of Thorstein Veblen's contribution.[4] But this, brilliant as it is in its way, can hardly be supposed by any one to rank as a serious piece of historical and critical scholarship. It is an impressionistic and polemical sketch, and is, I believe, biased by a serious misunderstanding of the ideas of the older economists. Of more importance are the studies of several European writers. The work of Neumann[5] is, of course, a classic in the field; but its historical part is subordinate to his critical discussion of the relation (of resemblance or difference) of economic laws to the laws of the natural sciences; and this, I think, is only a part of the problem. Hasbach's monograph on the "philosophical foundations" of the teachings of Quesnay and of Adam Smith,[6] reflects much careful research; but is concerned with other problems in addition to the special one of understanding and criticizing their conceptions of "natural laws," and therefore does not deal as directly or as adequately with that problem as could be wished. P. Struvé, a Russian scholar, in a brilliant article in the *Revue d'économie politique*,[7] has applied the ideas of neo-Kantian philosophy to a critique of "l'idée de loi naturelle dans la science économique," whose historical development he

[4] I refer, of course, to *The Place of Science in Modern Civilisation, and Other Essays,* especially the essay on "The Preconceptions" of the older economists.

[5] F. J. Neumann, "Naturgesetz und Wirtschaftsgesetz," in *Zeitschr. für die ges. Staatswiss.* (1892). Also "Wirtschaftliche Gesetze nach früherer und jetziger Auffassung," in *Jahrbücher für Nationalökon. u. Statistik,* 3rd series, vol. XVI (1898). The former of these monographs is praised by Marshall, *Principles of Economics,* footnote, p. 33.

[6] W. Hasbach, *Die allgemeinen philosophischen Grundlagen der von F. Quesnay und A. Smith begründeten politischen Ökonomie* (Leipzig, 1890). I owe a good deal to this work, and something also to the same author's *Untersuchungen über A. Smith.*

[7] See note on p. 37 above.

outlines. Other studies might be mentioned.[8] But no one seems to me to have dealt with *all* of the important aspects of the history and meaning of the idea, or to have attained the point of view from which all of its aspects can be simultaneously grasped, and therefore properly criticized.

The present article attempts no more than to make suggestions in this field of inquiry. It does not, of course, pretend to be even a part, however small, of the adequate historical study which I have called for. It is rather a preliminary survey of the ground and the problems, and an effort to indicate some very tentative conclusions.

II

The belief that all events, including human actions, are subject to strict "laws of nature" can be traced back to antiquity, and has played an important role in the philosophies of at least some leading thinkers in nearly every epoch in the history of European thought.[9] But in the seventeenth century it attained a somewhat new prominence, a new and more definite shade of meaning, and a new fruitfulness for scientific thought, which have made it a main element in the scientific mentality of the last three centuries. In the eighteenth century, the idea pervaded all disciplines, including the "moral" or psychological and social

[8] The *Revue d'économie politique* has published a number of good articles on this subject, and others close to it, of which I note the following: B. Raynaud, "Les discussions sur l'ordre naturel au xviiie siècle," vol. XVIII (1905); E. Allix, "Le physicisme des Physiocrates," vol. XXV (1911) — a particularly excellent article; and the same author's "Destutt de Tracy, Économiste," vol. XXVI (1912), which has little on economic laws, but shows how this ideologist connected a quite orthodox type of theory with his system of psychology and its mental "laws."

[9] A good brief survey of the history of the notion, from antiquity down, is given by R. Eucken in *Main Currents of Modern Thought*, trans. M. Booth (New York, 1912), art. "B. 3-Law." Windelbrand's *History of Philosophy* has brilliant sections on the roles it played in ancient, medieval, and seventeenth- and eighteenth-century thought. The first chapter of Whitehead's *Science and the Modern World* is suggestive on the probable nature of the debt of modern science, for its conception of strict laws of nature, to ancient philosophy and even to medieval theology.

as well as the "natural" sciences.[10] In the course of the nineteenth century, its sphere gradually became limited in effect, for
many minds, to the natural sciences. Students of the social sciences became conscious of difficulties in the way of its use in
their field, of which the eighteenth-century mind had been less
acutely aware.[11] This was due, I believe, to an important change
in the connotations of the idea.

Even in the history of the natural sciences, since the early seventeenth century, the content of the general belief in "laws of
nature" has been slowly changing. Throughout the whole period of three centuries, it is true, the idea in this field has implied
the doctrine of determinism; and it is almost certain that a "mechanistic" metaphysics or cosmology has lurked somewhere in the
background, when not explicitly accepted as the starting-point, of
scientific thought.[12] The seventeenth-century pioneers who created classical physics conceived the physical universe as almost
literally a "machine," a mass of particles of matter spread through
space and perpetually moving and impelling one another to move,
in accordance with the laws of mechanics. Robert Boyle, the
great pioneer chemist, adopted the "mechanical hypothesis" as
the basis also of his own science, and defended it in voluminous

[10] I cannot crowd much evidence in support of this statement into a footnote. Some evidence is given in the text and notes below. Standard histories
of philosophy that deal extensively with the seventeenth and eighteenth
centuries recognize the prevalence, especially in the latter, of efforts to
discover and formulate, and of the belief in, natural (causal) laws of human
action (psychological and social laws): Windelbrand, Höffding, Lévy-Bruhl,
and others. Condillac in France, and Hartley in England, started the most
definite systems of psychology, on this basis, on lines suggested by Hobbes
and Locke. All the French *philosophes* — Diderot, D'Alembert, Condorcet,
Helvetius, Holbach, and the rest — were full of the idea; and Hutcheson,
Hume, Adam Smith, and others had it, though they did not parade it so
much.

[11] I do not mean that talk of "social laws," historical laws, and the like,
became less prevalent; it became steadily more prevalent. But I think the
efforts which this came to involve, to assimilate social science more completely to the character of natural science, and the simultaneous decline of
the old religious "humanization of nature" as it has been called, combined
to produce an increasing dissatisfaction with the whole proceeding. This
is not the kind of thing that one can prove by a few citations in a footnote.

[12] Windelband, Whitehead, and many others stress the importance of the
"mechanistic" assumption.

essays.[13] Most of the students who were advancing the various biological sciences also adopted it, and regarded the bodies of animals and men as "machines." [14] In the eighteenth century, the idea was almost universally accepted. The whole universe, including living organisms, was pictured as a vast "machine," whose operations are all explainable and predictable by the laws of mechanics.[15] And the doctrine of mechanistic determinism has remained until very recently a first article in the creed of the natural scientist.

In the eighteenth century, however, this idea was still combined with the theological idea of an harmonious "Order of Nature," in which every thing or being has a definite, ideal function to fulfill in the wisely planned economy of the cosmos. The world-machine was admired as a wise contrivance of the Deity for causing every part of the whole to fulfill its function. Hence the "laws of nature," though conceived as laws of mechanical causation, were also and at the same time conceived as "canons of conduct" providentially imposed upon things. E. Mach, the great historian of the science of mechanics, has shown how eighteenth-century physicists, who followed up and completed the work of Newton, were often actually led to their formulations of the laws of mechanics by setting out from theological postulates about the wisdom, simplicity, economy, and harmony of the "plan" of nature's operations. The laws, Mach says, were valid, and were afterward restated so as to get rid of the theological implications.[16]

[13] R. Boyle, *Works* (ed. of 1744, in 5 vols.), III, 450ff. This particular essay is entitled "Of the Excellence and Grounds of the Corpuscular or Mechanical Philosophy." Half the titles in the five vols. contain the word "mechanical."

[14] H. Driesch, *History and Theory of Vitalism*, trans. Ogden (1914), pp. 22ff.

[15] E. Mach, *The Science of Mechanics*, trans. McCormack (Chicago, 1893), pp. 463, 464. "The French encyclopedists of the eighteenth century imagined that they were not far from a final explanation of the world by physical and mechanical principles; . . . the world-conception of the encyclopedists appears to us as a mechanical mythology in contrast to the animistic."

[16] E. Mach, pp. 446–465. The great historian of this fundamental natural science here gives what is surely one of the most illuminating discussions to be found anywhere of its early relations with theology.

In the course of the nineteenth century, the notions summed up in the phrase "the Wisdom of Nature" were gradually discredited, and more or less completely eliminated from scientific thought. Eventually the theory of evolution came along, to explain the adaptations or harmonious adjustments found in nature as products of a blind historical process of "natural selection"; and this theory also emphasized the imperfection or incompleteness, at every stage of the probably eternal process, of the resulting "harmony." The conception of natural laws as providential ordinances for maintaining harmony in the universe faded away, and all that was left of the idea was the doctrine of determinism. The beautifully harmonious world-mechanism of the eighteenth century's imagination became the blind, ruthless, purposeless mechanism which oppressed the imaginations of so many nineteenth-century poets and philosophers.[17]

In the last few decades physics itself appears to have been moving away from the rigid doctrine of determinism. A layman can, of course, say nothing with confidence upon this matter, but it seems clear at least that something is happening to the old idea of "inexorable" laws of nature. The view is expressed by high authorities that all scientific laws may be only "statistical laws"; that is, laws of the average behavior of things or entities in "crowds," which leave the behavior of individual entities partly a matter of real "chance," and which may even leave room, in the case of the higher organisms, for "free will." [18] The whole

---

[17] A perfect picture of a mind that had only half completed this transition is afforded by Huxley's famous lecture on "Evolution and Ethics" (*Evolution and Ethics and Other Essays*, N. Y., 1909). Huxley upholds the idea of an Order of Nature, in which parts are made to function harmoniously in the life of the whole. But he finds that in the organic world the harmony is marred by the presence of pain, "a baleful product of the evolutionary process," and by a complicated struggle that is most intense in the soul of man and in society. He goes on to argue that the "ethical process" in society, though it is a product of, is yet in conflict with, the "cosmic process"; an ethical civilization is built up not by "natural" forces (which he takes to mean the forces of man's lower nature), but by unceasing "artificial" resistance to such forces. He therefore damns laissez-faire individualism as heartily as it is damned by Carlyle.

[18] A. S. Eddington, *The Nature of the Physical World* (1928), is my chief authority for this statement.

matter is under lively discussion among physicists. Determinism, if not universally abandoned, at least is under fire. Meanwhile, teleological ideas crop up with renewed strength in some quarters. The general position seems to be that while there undoubtedly are "laws" for science to discover and make confident use of, the implications of this fact, and the nature of these laws, are open to a general reconsideration.

Now it is clearly the mid-nineteenth-century conception of purposeless but inexorable "laws of nature" which has caused most of the trouble in the social sciences. The belief in, and effort to discover, scientific "social laws" was bound to lead to confusion, so long as it was supposed that all scientific laws must be of this type. It is true that there have always been those who could persuade themselves that no violence need be done to our experience of the nature of human thought, emotion, volition, conduct, and social life, by the hypothesis that every mental and social event is mechanically caused and determined by antecedent events, the chain of which leads back into the physical environment, and the physical organisms upon which the environment acts. Some economists may be able to believe that men in business life are automatically impelled into given courses of action by a balance of external stimuli; and some historians to suppose that the course of history is mechanically determined by the action of the material surroundings of men upon their bodies and minds. But such notions clash with the persistent habits of thought developed in practical life, and the usual blending of the two sorts of notions in social theories introduces a sad confusion. In any case, social determinists have not attempted to get down to the level of close studies of the mechanical causation of the actions of individuals and develop sociology from physiology, as their view should lead them to do. They have been content as a rule with vague and sweeping generalizations about social and historical processes, which can hardly pass muster as "scientific laws." Meanwhile, the bias introduced by this whole way of thinking has caused the knowledge of men's motives and purposes which we acquire in practical life to be neglected, because the notions of practical life do not square with the dogma of mechanistic determinism. It may be that the change now in progress in the philosophy of the natural sciences will in time produce a "mental climate" more favorable to the unembarrassed progress of the social sciences.

In the history of the social sciences themselves, during the past three centuries, the belief that there are "natural laws" of human behavior and therefore of the life of society has not always been as closely identified with the doctrine of determinism as belief in such laws has been in natural science. In the seventeenth and eighteenth centuries, numerous writers who tried to develop genetic or explanatory psychological and social sciences were at the same time defenders of the doctrine of "free will." Even the notion of the mind as a "mechanism," and of society as a "mechanism" in which the wills of individuals are the forces that interact, did not always carry with it an acceptance, in the psychological sphere, of the "principle of necessity." Hobbes, who was one of the first to construct what was virtually a system of psychology and sociology on "mechanical" principles,[19] was a rigid determinist. But not all of the later writers who tried to use the same method accepted the doctrine. Descartes and his followers were strict determinists in the sphere of "natural philosophy," but insisted that the human will is "free." Yet they tried to analyze the mechanics or dynamics of the intellectual and emotional life, merely insisting that if the mental mechanism is to work properly, the will must function properly, that is, under the control of "reason"; and that its failures to do so, for which the individual is to blame, are the sole causes of human sin and misfortune.[20] This, incidentally, was precisely the doctrine of Quesnay, who professed himself as in metaphysics a disciple of Malebranche;

[19] See Höffding, *History of Modern Philosophy*, Book III, chap. 4; and best of all, G. Croom Robertson's *Biography of Hobbes*, chap. 4 and *passim*. Robertson, the highest authority on Hobbes, is very explicit on the importance of the mechanical idea, derived from the new physics of the time, as the basis of Hobbes' work; and one need read no more than the first part of *Leviathan*, to see that it was the basis.

[20] See Windelband, pp. 410–420 and *passim*; and H. A. P. Torrey's *The Philosophy of Descartes in Extracts from His Writings* (1892), pp. 15–34 (Prof. Torrey's excellent introduction analysis), and pp. 275–326 (Descartes' writings on Physiology and Psychology).

yet Quesnay conceived society's economic system as a "mechanism." [21]

Of the Scottish school in the eighteenth century, to which Adam Smith belonged, it is more difficult to speak with confidence. They were in the tradition started by Locke; and the sensationalists, associationists, and ideologists of the later eighteenth century, who also professed to build upon Locke, were strict determinists. But Dugald Stewart claimed that they all misunderstood Locke, and that the philosophy of the Scottish school was really the logical development of his ideas; and Stewart, though he believed in psychological and social "laws," believed also in "free will." [22] The greatest of the group, Hume, maintained that the "principle of necessity," or causality, cannot be proved; our reliance upon the "laws of nature" rests only on "custom and habit"; but there is, I think, no indication that in practice he

[21] In Quesnay's time, the philosophies of Descartes and Malebranche had largely gone out of fashion in France, and most of *les philosophes* agreed with Voltaire in professing to take Locke instead of Descartes as their master. Hence the physiocrats, who liked to quote Malebranche, were despised by many as religious and metaphysical dreamers. The anxiety of E. Allix, in the article referred to above on p. 41, n. 8, to clear them of this charge, leads him to go too far, I think, in denying the reality of their debts to Malebranche. See Quesnay's *Works* (ed. Oncken), p. 745, where Oncken in a footnote brings together the chief passages in which Quesnay speaks of, and draws upon, Malebranche. The article on Liberté (same volume, pp. 747ff.) develops a form of the Cartesian doctrine of free will; and I agree with Oncken's estimate of the great importance of this in the physiocratic system. Quesnay finds in the power of "reason" to weigh, analyze, and modify "motives," something that makes human conduct more than a merely mechanical process. The ideas of a mental and of a social mechanism are plainly present in the essay, but he insists that "reason" is free to play, or not to play, its part well in the process of the equilibration of "motives"; and that the course of events is beneficent for human welfare only if it does play its part well. The doctrine of "l'ordre naturel" cannot be understood without a study of this essay.

[22] D. Stewart, *Works* (ed. Hamilton), vol. I, *A Dissertation on the Progress of Metaphysical, Moral, and Political Philosophy, Since the Revival of Letters*, pp. 258–272, 279–280, 295–307, 311–313, 431–449, 489, and *passim*. This work is most valuable to the student of eigheenth-century thought, written as it was just after the close of the century by one who shared all of its most typical ideas, and knew almost the whole of its literature. It was written as a supplement for the first number of the *Encyclopaedia Britannica*, finally published in 1825.

abandoned determinism in psychology or elsewhere.[23] Hutcheson
and Adam Smith are silent on the matter; but in their theories of
the psychological genesis of "moral sentiments," they always
speak as though men were free to act or not to act in accordance
with the "moral sentiments" which their experience generates
through the working of their mental "mechanisms." These examples will perhaps suffice to indicate the frequency with which
belief in psychological and social "laws of nature," or in "mechanically" explainable psychological and social processes, was
divorced in the eighteenth century from any full acceptance of
the doctrine of determinism.[24]

It was in the early nineteenth century that determinism, as
applied to psychology and sociology, became the really prevalent and fully realized concomitant of the application in this
sphere of the idea of "natural laws." Professor Rogers, in his history of English philosophy in the nineteenth century, brings out
the way in which this doctrine seized upon the imaginations of
many in the early decades of the century, and became with some

[23] The doctrine of determinism is sometimes identified with the notion
which Hume *did* demolish and reject, namely, that causation is something
other than empirical sequence or correlation; that we know why a cause
produces its effect, and can prove that it must always do so. But a "faith"
that exact laws of sequence will always hold true, where the same conditions are present, is, I think, determinism; if one is not prepared, in practice, to admit exceptions, his lack of logical ground for his faith makes no
difference. Hume's explanation of this "faith" was psychological; and I
can see little difference between this and the Kantian doctrine that determinism is a "necessity of thought," arising, so to speak, from the way our
minds are made, instead of from the way in which the universe is made.
The very explanation that Hume gives of our belief in the reliability of the
laws of physics involves psychological determinism in the form of a belief
in laws of the "association of ideas."

[24] Even the eighteenth-century writers who were professed determinists,
often distinguished between physical and psychological causation in a way
intended to save what the "free will" advocates were fighting for. See some
of the passages in Stewart's *Dissertation*, cited above, especially pp. 272,
305–307. Perhaps the essential difference between most eighteenth- and most
nineteenth-century conceptions of psychological and social "laws" lies in the
fact that the eighteenth century was building on "introspective" psychology, and was therefore trying to apply the new "mechanical" conceptions
without being untrue to the realities of what the Germans call man's "inner experience."

a kind of gospel.[25] The Benthamites, who utilized in their philosophy the association psychology of Hartley and James Mill, were determinists; and this group, of course, included the Mills and some of the other economists. At the same time, the romanticists of the period, building what systematic philosophy they had largely upon what they knew of the teachings of Kant, Fichte, and Schelling, upheld "free will" and denounced the deterministic and mechanistic philosophy as the work of the hated eighteenth century.[26] In France, after the death of "ideology," some romantic philosophies, and the idealistic philosophy of Cousin, who drew heavily upon the Scottish school, championed "free will"; but there were Comte and many others to uphold the opposite doctrine, or at least to talk of social and historical laws in terms which clearly implied it.[27] Psychological and sociological determinism gained ground rather than lost it as the century advanced. Yet the protest also gained ground, and gained sobriety and philosophical penetration, as trained philosophers began to attack the whole idea of "inexorable" laws of nature. Toward the end of the century, a large part of the educated public lost much of its earlier naïve faith in the theories and "laws" of the psychological and social scientists. What we now need, I believe, is an approach to social science more like that of the eighteenth-century writers, who, despite the fact that natural science in their time was rigidly deterministic, as it is perhaps ceasing to be in our time, were able to conceive of social "laws" in a way that did not commit them to the treatment of men as mere automata.

III

The evolution of the idea of "laws" in economics has closely paralleled its evolution in the natural sciences, except that, as in other social sciences, it did not until the nineteenth century come to carry so strongly the rigidly deterministic connotation.

[25] Rogers, *English and American Philosophy Since 1800*, pp. 128ff.
[26] I am, of course, referring here to the English romanticists — Coleridge, Carlyle, Wordworth, Ruskin, et al.
[27] L. Lévy-Bruhl, *Modern Philosophy in France*, chaps. 11, 12.

The central notion of economic theory of the "orthodox" type has always been the conception of a society's economic system as in some sense a mechanism. Labor, capital, business ability, goods, and the money of consumers, have been pictured as "gravitating" to their best markets, with resultant interactions of supplies, demands, prices, and incomes taking place according to definite "laws." The recent development of mathematical formulations of the general theory has made clearer than ever its formal resemblance to the theory of mechanics. But of course the analogy with mechanics, and the conception of the economic system as a mechanism, do not need to be taken too seriously. I shall argue below that they can be used without at all implying acceptance of a mechanistic metaphysics, or of a deterministic theory of human behavior. But their use in the past has undoubtedly often tended to foster a kind of economic fatalism, which some critics have mistakenly supposed to be a necessary consequence of the orthodox type of theory.

In the eighteenth century, and by many writers in the nineteenth, the economic mechanism was regarded as a wise device of the Creator for causing individuals, while pursuing only their own interests, to promote the prosperity of society, and for causing the right adjustment to one another of supplies, demands, prices, and incomes to take place automatically, in consequence of the free action of all individuals. This doctrine of "economic harmonies" was entirely in accord with the corresponding notions of contemporary natural, as well as moral, scientists. The notion that the mechanical laws which "control" nature's operations, and enable us to explain and predict them, are calculated to insure the harmonious mutual adjustment and proper functioning of things, did some harm in scientific thought, but did not prevent men who held it from making scientific discoveries. Mach's remarks about the eighteenth-century physicists were referred to above. Back in the seventeenth century, Robert Boyle, in a remarkably cautious and critical essay on the philosophy of "final causes," said that Harvey, the physiologist, had told him that he arrived at his discovery of the circulation of the blood by thinking that the valves of the heart must have a "purpose," and then looking for it.[28] And there is little doubt that the minute study of the functions of organs in living organisms, which was prompted by the desire of Paley and his predecessors to bolster up the "design" argument for a Deity, did much to promote the progress of biology. So the doctrine of economic harmonies, while definitely misleading in some of its implications and childish in its extreme forms, was not necessarily a hindrance in the early stages of the search for regularities or laws, and natural processes of adjustment, in society's economic life.

Ricardo and his immediate followers did not particularly emphasize the notion of economic harmonies. In fact the pessimistic tendency of their reasonings about population growth, diminishing returns, and wages and profits have caused them to be contrasted with the optimists, not without justice. It is true that they still supposed that self-interest, or the search for profits, would generally lead individuals to turn their efforts and investments into the channels in which they would do most to increase national wealth; and also that the "natural" prices, wage-rates, and rates of profit, resulting in the long run from the free play of demand and supply, would all reflect and promote a better use of the nation's resources in meeting its wants than would be likely to be produced by legislative "interference" with the flow of things to their best markets. But their picture of the natural working of the economic machine, and of its outcome, was hardly rosy enough to lead them to think that it suggested the presence behind the scenes of a benevolent, divine guiding hand. In fact the Romantic poet and essayist, Robert Southey, attacked Malthus precisely because he had denied this hypothesis and had propounded a theory savoring of the late eighteenth-century French doctrines of "brute mechanism, blind necessity, and blank

[28] Boyle's *Works*, IV, 517ff. This truly remarkable essay was written at the request of the Secretary of the Royal Society, whose members (including Boyle, Newton, and others) had discussed the problem of whether natural scientists should take any stock in the idea that Nature works to certain discoverable, divinely appointed, ends; and wanted Boyle to write out his views (see preface of essay). Boyle supports the idea cautiously, as Newton did also (see last few pages of the *Principia*). Boyle founded a lectureship in "natural theology" which functioned through most of the eighteenth century.

atheism." [29] The classical economists, in fact, shifted the emphasis from the beneficence to the inexorability of economic laws. The tone of their teaching was deterministic. The economic machine was in effect represented as grinding out definite amounts of wages, profits, and rent for the three social classes, almost with the precision and inevitablity of a literal physical machine.

Modern theorists, however orthodox in their general tendency, are aware that economic laws do not have this precision and inexorability. We are ready, I think, for the view that the general laws at which theory arrives, though it arrives at them in the first instance without the help of statistical studies, are of the nature of "statistical laws"; that is, they are laws of the average behavior of men in the mass in response to economic conditions which their behavior in turn modifies. Or, if this view is preferred, they are laws of the average "behavior" of prices and the like, under the influence of such human behavior.[30] Experience of human motives, of the kind that is gained in practical life, enables us to make rough predictions of the ways in which, on the average, men will react to the changing physical and market conditions which affect their business plans. Since each man's actions affect the data of the calculations of numerous other men, there are causal sequences that link business developments in one region or industry with those that follow it elsewhere; and the theory of these processes can be worked out, with some help from the calculus, on lines somewhat remotely like those of the theory of mechanics. But, of course, the ex-

[29] R. Southey, *Essays Moral and Political* (1832), pp. 77ff.
[30] Of course in saying that the laws of theory are of the nature of statistical laws, I am not denying the important and familiar difference between the "curves" of theory and actual statistical correlation curves. Theory "isolates" its variables as the statistician cannot. But I am arguing that even if the *coeteris paribus* assumption were to hold good in a particular case in "real life," the conformity of the outcome of the forces at work in that situation to any definite "law" that had been derived from a study of similar cases or situations (in which the assumptions also had been realized) would be only approximate; and would be due, not to identical similarities in all human behavior occurring at different times or in different places but under identical (external) conditions, but only to broad similarities in reactions of *masses* of men to identical economic "stimuli."

tremely general laws of pure theory do not specify any actual quantities, nor the actual forms of the functions supposed. The formulation of laws that can be used to make definite predictions requires the coöperation of the theorist and the statistician, and we are just beginning to explore the possibilities and surmount some of the difficulties of this undertaking. It is not possible to suppose that even with the help of the best statistical technique, we shall ever be able to make any very exact, or any very long range, economic predictions. All this is familiar. The point to be emphasized here is that it involves, not an abandonment of the method of "orthodox" theory, but a very definite abandonment of the notion of "inexorable" economic laws, since that notion implies that the choices of individuals are so strictly determined by external events (e.g., price-changes) as to be exactly predictable.

Some economists might maintain that the laws of theory are "of the nature of statistical laws," without admitting the reason which I have assigned — that the behavior of particular individuals is not strictly "determined" by their economic situations, that they have not only "non-economic motives" which modify their reactions but also something like "free wills." The economist who, as a philosopher, feels that the doctrine of determinism is a "necessity of thought" may say that *our* laws are only laws of average tendencies, merely because our knowledge of the characters of individuals and of their economic situations is imperfect, but that "in reality" all actions of men in the economic world, and therefore all economic events, are strictly determined by the action of economic situations upon human minds. Personally, I cannot accept such a statement about a "reality" admittedly unknown to us, nor distinguish this doctrine from a hopeless economic fatalism. But at all events, this question does not affect the character of the actual "laws" of economic theory. These are only laws of average tendencies, resulting from the average behavior of men in the mass; and are therefore not "inexorable laws."

There are some other connotations of the notion of economic laws as inexorable laws of nature which have little or nothing to do with the matter of psychological determinism. Business men sometimes speak of these laws as if they were impersonal but active and irresistible forces, which control all prices, rates of wages and the like, in the economic system, quite independently of all human wills, desires, and ideals. They may say, for instance, that they cannot, if they wish to, pay their employees higher wages, because the market rate of wages, which they have to accept, is controlled by economic laws. Modern economists should perhaps be doing more than they are doing to dispel this notion, which has no doubt been encouraged by the too exclusive preoccupation of theorists in the past with the world of "pure competition." If the actual economic world were the world of pure competition, there would be some excuse for the attitude of the business men referred to.[31] In that world, no employer could have a wage-policy, or a price-policy. He could not, out of benevolence or a sense of justice, pay higher wages than his competitors were paying, nor, out of a more than average hardness and greed, pay lower wages. But in the actual economic world, every business man, and every trade union or similar group, is in a situation which gives him or it what may be called, by a useful refinement of theory, some degree of monopoly power. Economic friction, to use the older term, leaves everyone free within limits to have a "policy" in regard to his price, and to try to exact for himself, in his dealings with others, a little more than the gains that would accrue to him under "pure competition," or, on the contrary, to treat others a little more generously than he would or could in that regime. This, of course, is a familiar qualification of the idea of rigid economic laws, to which even the classical economists were not entirely blind; but they did not attach enough importance to it.

A still more serious and more absurd error than the one just mentioned, which economists of the past have unwittingly encouraged in the minds of laymen and opponents, is the notion that economic laws are supposed to describe an inevitable course of events which neither the state nor any other human agency can prevent or alter. Of course the laws are only supposed to

---

[31] Not, of course, for the notion of laws as external constraining agencies, but for the idea that the individual employer in a labor market cannot in the least degree deviate from, nor influence, the market rate of wages.

describe what will happen under given conditions, the absence of "interference" by the state being assumed as one of the conditions. But the impression that orthodox theory has always tended to discourage such "interference" as likely to be futile, or powerless to change the course of events, is not altogether baseless. It has always tended to lead its votaries to a belief that there are rather narrow limits upon the power of society to alter the direction and outcome of the "natural" economic tendencies at work within it. The foundations of this belief can only be touched upon here, but I shall have more to say about them in a future article.

In the seventeenth century, Dudley North anticipated what was nearly the outlook of the classical economists of the nineteenth century, in asserting that "no laws can set prices in trade, the rates of which must and will make themselves." [32] Of course he was thinking of efforts simply to decree that certain prices should be charged and paid by individuals, the decree being unaccompanied by any public action calculated to redress the balance of supply and demand. Such efforts, as plenty of experience in diverse times and places has proved, are indeed futile in societies in which "mobility" and "competition" are at all highly developed. But all economists, of course, know that it is always possible to fix prices, if the government is willing and able to enter the market as buyer and seller on any scale that may be needed to make the fixed price the "equilibrium price." This is, we may say, one way of manipulating the economic mechanism. And there has never been anything in orthodox theory inconsistent with the idea that this mechanism can be manipulated. It is not, like Newton's celestial mechanism, beyond human control, but, like "natural" mechanisms on the earth, can be controlled by a human skill which will increase precisely as we increase our knowledge of economic laws.

The classical economists, far from denying the possibility of

[32] D. North, *Discourse on Trade*, 1690, Hollander reprint (J. Hopkins Univ. Press, 1905). The preface of this tract has been neglected by historians of economic thought. It suggests that the new "mechanical" philosophy (ascribed to Descartes), which North says has begun to renovate "natural philosophy," must be applied to the theory of "Trade"; and is full of other significant hints.

this kind of control of economic events and conditions by public action, opposed various measures of control that were being used in their day, such as protective tariffs,[33] not on the ground that they were futile or ineffective, but on the ground that their effects were socially bad. As I shall try later to show, their own program of public policy was one designed to provide just the few measures of control which seemed to them to be both feasible and in the public interest. Their belief that the government could do only a few things to increase economic welfare, and that much of its more or less well-intentioned and quite effective activity was mischievous, had two main causes.

In the first place, they retained, as I have said, a limited form of the belief in economic harmonies. Individuals, if free to seek their best markets, would generally do just the things that were best for the nation, because the "operation" of economic laws would insure a coincidence of their own interests with the national interest. Hence governmental activity of the kind that sought to cut off any group of buyers or sellers from their best markets, and force them to resort to inferior markets, injured the nation, as well as this group, and all for the benefit of the favored group that got their business. In other words, this kind of "interference" with "natural" tendencies was opposed on the ground that the latter are, not irresistible or unalterable, but better for the nation than the new tendencies "artificially" created by the interference.

In the second place, such methods as were then available or even conceivable for changing or modifying the action of other "natural" economic tendencies that were freely admitted to be less beneficial to the nation were in many cases regarded by the economists, for one reason or another, as unpromising, unsafe, or undesirable. The "natural" tendency of population growth to force wages to the level of subsistence was not a beneficent tendency. But Malthus saw no good remedy except that of

[33] Taxes, of course, are a much simpler instrument for manipulating the system of prices, currents of trade, and the like, than government buying-and-selling agencies. They are one way of controlling what men will do, by controlling what is profitable. The difficulty of resisting economic tendencies is merely the difficulty of preventing masses of men from doing what you leave it to their advantage to do.

urging laborers to practice moral restraint, and advocated this, though it did not promise to accomplish much. Some of his followers, more boldly, advocated the more promising remedy of birth control. Of course state action was hardly involved here. But in opposing the existing Poor Law, the reformers were, of course, arguing that this bit of state action was accelerating, instead of checking, the harmful natural tendency. Again, to glance at a very different field, the monetary theories and policies of the classical economists emphasized the desirability of adhering to the "automatic" gold standard, which leaves the regulation of the value of money to the working of "natural" tendencies. This was not because they thought that the regulation thus secured was perfect, from the point of view of the general interest of the nation; still less was it because they imagined that effective state interference with the value of money was impossible. Their argument, which is still respected by many economists, was simply that "artificial" control in this case was pretty certain in practice to work even less well than the automatic system.

These familiar illustrations, taken together, may suffice to drive home the point that the classical economists never held that "economic laws" describe a "natural course of things" in the economic world which human efforts cannot alter. They believed in natural tendencies, processes of adjustment or equilibration, which are in some cases socially beneficent and in some cases not, which can be engineered, manipulated, or controlled, given sufficient knowledge and the right methods, but which cannot be abolished or thwarted by simple decree, cannot be ignored in devising sound legislation, and should not be tampered or interfered with in cases where we are not in a position to control them properly and in a way that is really in the common interest.

The further development of the orthodox type of theory, in the last two generations, has brought with it an ever-increasing interest, on the part of economists, in schemes for "manipulating" the "economic mechanism" in socially desirable ways. Control of currency and credit systems is the most conspicuous case. But most of the new forms of governmental activity for the betterment of economic conditions, which many economists have supported from their inception — forms of labor legislation, social insurance, regulation of public utilities — may be said in a sense to fall within this category, as they all involve attempts to alter the direction and effects of natural tendencies, not by passing laws against them, but by creating new conditions under which the play of supply and demand will have new effects. As economic knowledge advances and society's facilities for effective control of its economic system increase, the limits upon its power to redirect economic tendencies are pushed back.

There remains still, however, a difficulty with the conception of an economic "mechanism" which can be "manipulated." The human beings who have to do the manipulating are, so to speak, themselves parts of the mechanism.[34] The conception seems to involve a dualism which leaves the "economic man" a cog in the mechanism, but regards the same man in his capacity as a "political man," a citizen, reformer, legislator, or public administrator, as "free" to act in the light of his knowledge of what is needed to promote the general welfare, instead of having his action even approximately or partially "determined" by the economic or the political and social situation in which he is placed, and by the way in which it affects his economic or his political interests, or his *mores* and prejudices.

Now just this dualism was, in a way, the most marked feature of the outlook of the eighteenth-century reformers, the French *philosophes*, the physiocrats among them, and the English utilitarians and classical economists who carried on this eighteenth-century tradition in the early nineteenth century. They all had the mechanistic idea, and worked out explanatory theories of the forces that determine the actions of individuals and the processes of social life. At the same time, in their programs for political, economic, and social reform, they were naïve "rationalists"; that is, they assumed that a society of enlightened men would be able to use government as a scientific tool for

---

[34] This point is developed in a somewhat different way in an article by the late A. A. Young: "Economics as a Field of Research," *Quarterly Journal of Economics* (November 1927).

carrying out purely rational measures in the common interest. Man the citizen would use a "reason" ungoverned and undistorted in its working, or in the ends in whose service it would work, by the pressure of his particular environment upon his particular interests and desires. But man as the being whose conduct the rational measures of the state were to control would remain something like an automaton, reacting in predictable ways to his environment and to the forces brought to bear upon him by the new social order.

It is true that they all tried to get around the difficulty by applying in political theory, as well as in economic theory, the conception of a harmony of interests. The physiocrats contended that the king's real interest was necessarily identical with that of his subjects taken as a body: "poor peasants, poor kingdom; poor kingdom, poor king." Other reformers, notably the English utilitarians, did not find this harmony working out under existing governments, but proposed to create it by setting up a complete system of democratic control. In both cases, however, the argument presupposed the possibility of the achievement, by rulers and by ruled, of a level of intelligence or rationality at which conduct would be determined, not by the immediate and particular environments and interest of the actors, but by those "real" interests which were held to be identical with the general interest of society. It was the "enlightenment" that was counted upon to make the political mechanism work as harmoniously as the economic mechanism which it was to control (or whose freedom to operate "naturally" it was to maintain). But the mechanistic theory of human behavior, if rigidly adhered to is not really compatible with this belief in the power of men to make their conduct completely rational. The eighteenth-century reformers never really explained or accounted for those irrational prejudices, and narrow and anti-social interests and passions, which they expected to see eliminated in the new "natural" or rational order of things. Men's mental mechanisms were and through the centuries had been reacting to their particular environments in such a way as to produce conduct that was largely irrational; and the hope of changing this really required a belief that man is more than a mechanism, that he can assert his reason and his will and change the nature of his motives. The physiocrats, with their belief in a measure of "free will" and in the power of reason to judge motives and ends from an ideal standpoint, were consistent. But the strict determinists, including the English utilitarians and perhaps the classical economists, were I think unconsciously caught in a circle.

The same dilemma, I think, must be faced by the modern behaviorists in psychology. And it must be faced by economists who conceive the economic system as a mechanism to be manipulated. One can fancy that a man trained in economic theory might transfer his energies to the field of political theory, and attempt to formulate the laws of the natural working of the democratic political mechanism on certain assumptions taken from experience as to the motives and purposes of average voters and average politicians. The result might be interesting. But would it increase our faith in the practical possibility and desirability of governmental manipulation of the economic system? Of course there is only one way out of the difficulty. This is to admit that the mechanistic approach to social theory, while useful within limits, does not reveal the whole nature of social reality. The motives of individuals, which are the ultimate "forces" dealt with in this type of theory, are themselves changeable, and do change, as civilization develops; nor can we afford to admit that this historic evolution is itself rigidly determined and fated to proceed in a given direction. Man has a measure of "freedom" to bring the character of his motives under the control of his "reason." To deny this, I think, is to be a fatalist. The classical economists and their utilitarian allies in reality escaped complete fatalism only because they inconsistently assumed that a democratic legislature could work consistently for the "greatest good of the greatest number," and do all necessary manipulating of the circumstances that determine the paths of conduct of private men, without having its own motives manipulated by irrational political forces. When Carlyle accused them of being fatalists, he was mistaken, but he was not so far wrong when he criticized them for supposing that all society's problems could be solved by tinkering with mechanisms, and insisted that a change in the spirit and ideals of the nation might be far more important.[35]

To return to my original proposition in this whole part of the discussion, we have to conclude, I think, that in more ways than one the "laws" of economic theory are far from being "inexorable." The classical economists strongly tended to regard them as inexorable, but only in the sense that under given conditions, which society certainly could alter in some cases, certain adjustments in the economic system would inevitably work themselves out, and prices, wages, and profits, in all industries, would seek certain levels. The more modern view is that the laws describing these processes of adjustment are only rough descriptions of tendencies, or are of the nature of "statistical laws," and in no sense rigid "laws of nature" in the nineteenth-century meaning of that phrase.

But while the notion that economic laws are inexorable has been decaying in recent decades, the notion that they are in some measure beneficent, or that they guarantee a certain measure of "harmony" in the working of the whole economic system, has hardly shown the same signs of disappearing completely. Accepted by the classical economists only in a limited form, it enjoyed, in the second half of the nineteenth century, a certain renaissance and further development. Bastiat and his followers, a little earlier in the century, carried it out to absurd lengths. The marginal utility and marginal productivity schools, when they came along, developed a terminology which almost inevitably suggests it, and some of them went far in accepting it outright. More "optimistic" views about population growth, the continual "postponement" of the stage of "diminishing returns," the "natural" factors making for "increasing returns" in many or even in all industries with the growth of population and of capital, and the action of the forces that determine wages, came to prevail. To look at a different aspect of the matter, opposition to socialism was undoubtedly a factor in causing various economists to argue that in our present economic system the play of "natural"

---

[35] For the charge of fatalism, see *Past and Present*, Books I and III *passim*; and for the other charge, *Signs of the Times*, in Illustrated Library ed. of Carlyle's Works, I, 465ff.

forces brings about a large or maximum social product, and a fairly equitable division or distribution of it among individuals and among social classes. The great majority of the theorists now writing are more cautious; but the doctrine of "economic harmonies" — understood not as meaning that we live in the best of all possible economic worlds, but as meaning merely that the "natural" or spontaneous tendencies which work themselves out in a more or less freely "competitive" society are very often socially desirable tendencies — this doctrine, or opinion, cannot yet be said to be entirely dead.

It is useful to compare the persistence of this idea in economics with the persistence of the corresponding idea in natural science. In its origins, the idea in both cases was undoubtedly connected with the eighteenth century's theological and teleological philosophy of natural laws. But it does not follow from this that it was bound to be, or should have been, discarded completely, as soon as science became completely separated from theology. For even when we reject the notion that Providence ordained the laws of nature, we do not therefore necessarily reject the belief, which must of course be tested by facts, that the processes described by scientific laws are processes of adjustment of things to changing conditions, which tend to preserve a certain measure of "order" and "harmony," or to insure, under all conditions, the effective functioning of individual entities in the systems of which they are parts. Nor has this idea ever disappeared from scientific thought. Even the theory of evolution by natural selection, which has done more than anything else to undermine the design argument for a Deity, is an alternative explanation, and not a denial, of the "adaptations" on which that argument was based. In other words, it still encourages the view that nature's processes, as seen in the biological world, are processes of adjustment of things to their environments, or of the attainment of an increasing measure of "harmony." There is certainly an analogy between this and the idea that in the economic life of human societies the "natural" working of competition brings about an adjustment or adaptation of the whole economic system to the physiographic environment, and of every individual to the economic system of which he is a part.

The eighteenth century's optimistic philosophy of the harmonious order and wise laws of nature was perhaps not so much a deduction from *a priori* theological postulates, as an inference from facts which were in the main correctly analyzed. But the inference was overstated and turned into an argument for the "design" hypothesis.[36] Of course this tended to happen because the hypothesis was there from the outset, and facts were selected and interpreted and theories stated in such a way as to confirm it. But the effect of this was not wholly bad. The faith that the "plan" of nature's operations would turn out everywhere to be rational and wise probably guided modern science in its beginnings to its most valuable discoveries. It stimulated the search for "order," for uniformities in nature's procedure under similar conditions and for differences of procedure adapted to different conditions, for the simplest and the smallest number of principles to explain complex and apparently diverse phenomena, and for indirect causal connections that would give every event, however isolated and inexplicable it might seem at first sight, its appropriate place in the general "scheme." But the same faith also led to some unwarranted conclusions. Too much meaning was read into the order and harmony which science seemed to be discovering in nature's plan. Being taken as proofs of the wisdom of God, they had to be regarded as completely worthy of that wisdom. The coming of Darwinism, while it did not do away with the idea that nature works toward adjustment and harmony, called attention to the fact that she works toward them, so to speak, by methods which are from the human point of view most often wasteful and cruel, or which involve the perpetual recurrence of a certain amount of maladjustment and disharmony.[37] In a word, what has happened since the eighteenth century, in natural science as in economics, has been a serious modification, but hardly a complete abandonment, of the belief in an harmonious Order of Nature.

[36] Adam Smith, for one, distinctly held that whatever is valid in theology is an inference from, and not a postulate from which to deduce, the harmonious Order of Nature, which is independently revealed by science. See his (much neglected) "philosophical essays," especially the essay on the history of physics.

[37] See the comment above, p. 44, note 17, on Huxley's views.

That a trace of that belief remains implicit, legitimately as I think, in modern orthodox economic theory, it seems impossible to deny.[38] It is true that modern theorists are aware that there is no marvellous perfection in the working of our economic system, that its quasi-automatic adjustments do no insure anything like the absolutely wisest utilization of society's resources in meeting its wants or the largest possible output of useful goods and services, and that distribution of the output among the agents of production in accordance with the "marginal productivity" of each agent is not necessarily synonymous with distributive justice. The adjustments that do work themselves out, in a rather haphazard and wasteful way, are at all times imperfect. It is certainly conceivable that a sufficiently intelligent, well-informed, efficient, and wisely zealous central planning authority, of the type desired by socialists, might eliminate much waste and maladjustment. But many theorists still believe that socialists, and most laymen as well, underrate both the effectiveness of the forces that make for tolerably good adjustments in our present system, and the difficulty of securing even equally good adjustments in a planned economy; and that at all events, so long as we retain our present system, sporadic interferences with the flow of things to their best markets, and with the resulting levels of prices, are very often in danger of doing more harm than good. This much qualified version of the belief in economic harmonies is not, I think, at all out of keeping with the tone of the most "up-to-date" and "scientific" thinking in the natural sciences.

[38] Many modern theorists say that evaluative judgments upon the working of the economic system, and upon public policies, are no part of the business of the economist, *qua* economist or scientist; and repudiate justificatory inferences from theory on this ground. But this seems to me less important than the fact that their scientific theory does lead, naturally if not logically, to a certain measure of "optimism," if one accepts it as valid and then applies his common sense to the evaluative problem. I am convinced that the way to divorce economic theory from dogmatic and doctrinaire philosophies of public policy is not to try to dodge the evaluative problem, but to try hard to solve it as honestly and carefully as we can.

IV

A brief recognition of some possible doubts about this last conclusion, and of the further problems which they raise, will provide the best transition to the second installment of this discussion, which I hope to publish in the near future.

I have argued that modern science still supports the view that in the inorganic and organic worlds nature works in the direction of a certain measure of what is in a certain sense harmony: equilibrium of forces, adjustment of things to their environments, development of organs to perform necessary functions. This is truly analogous to the view that the natural working of competition tends in the economic world to produce a general "equilibrium," adjustment of supplies to demands, of prices to costs, and so on. But there is the difficulty of what is meant by calling the economic process, which is supposed to bring about these adjustments, a "natural" process, and regarding it as *the* process in economic life which corresponds to other "natural" processes, outside of human societies. This difficulty arises from the fact that in our society a particular fabric of "institutions," *mores* and customs, and business methods, in large degree peculiar to our own civilization, constantly changing, and changeable by deliberate, collective effort, condition the working out of the process in its every phase. No doubt if the word "nature" is used in its widest and perhaps its proper sense, mankind and its societies are parts of nature, and everything that goes on in society, including the growth of institutions, is part of a system of natural processes. But this is not the sense in which the adjective is used when and if the quasi-automatic working of the competitive economic system is called natural. A contrast is implied between the "natural" or spontaneous tendencies which are there at work and are described by economic "laws," and the "artificial" or deliberate regulation of economic life by the state or by some other authority. But in fact the working of the economic system is in all times and places, and even in the theorists' imaginary world of pure or perfect competition, regulated in manifold ways by legal institutions and social conventions which are per-

haps as artificial as the interfering methods of control deplored
by old-fashioned liberals. Why draw the line at this particular
point between the "natural" tendencies in the economic life of
society, and other tendencies, represented in the activities of labor
unions, of governments, of socialist agitators, and the like, which
perhaps are also a part of the general system of tendencies toward
better adjustment to environment on the part of society and of
its members?

The same objection may be stated in another way. The adjustments which work themselves out in the inorganic and organic
worlds cannot properly be judged or evaluated by human standards and called "good." To say that nature works in the direction
of an equilibrium of forces, and of adaptation of things to their
environments, is not to say that she works toward results that
accord with human ideals. Biological "adaptation" insures only
"survival"; and while some thinkers have tried to get an ethic
out of Darwinism, and connect all valid human ideals with the
struggle of human beings and of groups and races to survive by
achieving biological or economic adaptation to environment, this
ethic does not seem to many, nor I confess to me, at all adequate.
Whatever of good, or social welfare, is achieved by human communities is achieved not by any purely automatic and in that
sense natural process, but by deliberate efforts guided by human
ideals. If the whole of social life is called a natural process, then
nature in this case is working toward humanly valuable ends, but
only because we have enlarged nature to include man and his
ideals and his conscious efforts to attain them. Now the natural
economic process of orthodox economic theory is of course not
wholly an automatic or blind process. It is the result of the interplay of the conscious efforts of all individuals to achieve their
more or less private and self-centered ambitions, by achieving
economic "adaptation." Society, moreover, has evolved a division
of labor which makes men interdependent, a system of institutional restraints to limit what we stigmatize as robbery and exploitation, and a regime of "competition" of a particular kind of
which one aspect is "competition in service." As a result there
is a partial coincidence of individual and social interests, and the
indirect and unforeseen results of private actions directed only

to a private and therefore partial good are often contributory to a larger social good. But precisely in so far as it is blind or automatic, and in that sense natural, in so far, in other words, as it is not guided by human foresight employed in the service of completely ethical ideals, in just so far does the economic process described by economic laws fall short of being the kind of social process that can result in the complete "harmony" that would really "maximize welfare." What is good in the process and its outcome is the result of what is good in the purposes of individuals, and in the *mores* and the institutions by which their purposes are partly socialized, or by which, at least, their actual conduct is partly socialized, the element of social purpose being embodied in these very institutions and *mores*. There can be no warrant, then, for the belief that a more complete socialization of economic life and activity, a more complete control of it by human intelligence engaged directly in the service of social welfare, would not increase the amount of economic harmony achieved. The securing of this harmony cannot be left to an automatic natural process. The process to which it is entrusted at present is defective just in so far as it is in this sense natural; and to make it a less automatic and more socially purposeful process ought to be our aim.[39]

Of course the social purpose behind institutions and *mores* is not at present a fully *conscious* purpose. They have been built up by compromises among more limited purposes, by a kind of automatic "natural selection" of elements in the institutional fabric which further "group survival," and by periodic reform movements that have tried to bring a fully conscious social purpose to bear upon them. The automatic or "natural" part of the process of the growth of institutions may do better work in the long run than deliberate effort guided by insufficient knowledge

[39] It should hardly be necessary for me to say that by "socializing" economic activity, and making it "socially purposeful," I do not mean, necessarily, what socialists and other critics of "the profit-motive" mean by such terms. The desire, and the freedom, of individuals to choose and carry on the lines of activity in which they can make, legitimately, the largest gains for themselves, by supplying services that others want, is not incompatible with a will on the part of all to make the general good, and not any private good that conflicts with it, the supreme end.

and foresight can do, but it can never do as good work as a conscious social purpose can do, when fully armed by social science. It can fit societies to prosper materially and morally to the extent needed for "survival," but not to the extent needed for full achievement of the "good life."

These objections to the notion that the automatic operation of "natural" economic laws can be trusted to take care of all needed adjustments in a community's economic system, and to make it work for the general welfare, have been for a century the chief burden of the arguments of most rebels against orthodox economics. As against that notion, stated in just that form, I think they are undoubtedly valid. The processes described by economic laws are real processes, and they are processes of adjustment comparable in a sense to other natural processes. They make in a measure and in many cases for economic harmony and social welfare, but only because and in so far as the human purpose to promote these ends is, in a sense, active in them, in the wills of the individuals who carry on economic life, and in the institutions and *mores* that help to control their activities. To make this human purpose as strong and effective as possible, and to modify our institutions to this end in so far as that may be necessary, must be our aim. If I believed that this conclusion was really contrary to the spirit and purport of the traditional type of economics, I should be among the "rebels."

But I believe there is another, neglected, aspect of the philosophies of the eighteenth-century pioneers who gave this type of economics its direction. The present article has considered only those aspects of the notion of natural economic laws, as accepted in the past, which have strict parallels in the history of the idea of such laws in natural science. But the reader will recall that the physiocrats, and Adam Smith, believed not only that there are *causal* "laws of nature" which control the course of events in the universe at large and in society, but also that there is a *moral* "Law of Nature," consisting of the rules which, as Adam Smith said, "ought to run through and be the foundation of the [civil] laws of all nations." [40] This notion pervaded their philosophies

[40] *Theory of Moral Sentiments,* Part VII, Section IV; in 6th ed., II, 395–399.

of what the institutions of a rationally ordered society ought to be. It was, in the case especially of the physiocrats, confusingly blended with their notion of causal or explanatory economic laws, by a twist characteristic of eighteenth-century thought but not readily intelligible or comprehensible to modern minds. A clearer interpretation than has ever been given of this whole side of their teachings would, I believe, throw new light upon their conceptions of economic laws, their ideals as to *laissez faire* or natural liberty, and the foundations of such faith as they had in economic harmonies; and would give us a new point of departure for a study of the historical relations of orthodox economic theory to social ideals, reform movements, and ethical and legal philosophies. To make this clear will be the purpose of the second part of this discussion.

3

ECONOMICS AND THE IDEA OF

"JUS NATURALE"

❧

I

In a former article in this journal,[1] I discussed certain notions about "natural laws" which have been common in the past to economics and the natural sciences, and the effects which those notions have had, in economics, in producing mistaken ideas about the nature of the laws at which our science has arrived. The present paper is intended to be a logical sequel to that article, but it deals with a different topic. It is concerned with those ideas about "natural law" in the ethical and juristic sense of the phrase (*jus naturale* or *droit naturel* — the rules of natural right or justice), and about a "natural" social order or scheme of institutions, which were so prominent in eighteenth-century thought; which the physiocrats developed with great vigor and in a somewhat unique way, in intimate combination with their pioneer work in economic science; and which also appear, in a very different form and philosophical setting, in the works of Adam Smith. In a future article I hope to deal with the relation between these eighteenth-century notions and the ideas of the English utilitarians and the classical economists of the early nine-

---

[1] The present article first appeared in the February 1930 issue of the *Quarterly Journal of Economics*. "Economics and the Idea of Natural Laws" is the former article referred to.

teenth century. The present discussion is limited to a consideration of their role in the economic philosophies of Quesnay and
his disciples, and of Adam Smith.[2]

The two problems which I have thus endeavored to separate
are, indeed, not independent of each other. Eighteenth-century
ways of thinking about social problems were produced by a
certain blending of ideas inspired by natural science with ideas
developed out of the traditions of religious, ethical, juristic, and
political philosophy. Efforts to discover the "natural laws" of
the mental and social life of mankind were commonly combined
in more or less confused ways with efforts to discover or to
formulate the supposed precepts of Nature for the proper regulation of conduct and of social arrangements. Political economy
as it emerged from this century was, perhaps even in a peculiar
degree, a product of this interweaving and blending of scientific
and ethical ideas. To unravel this web of thought, and find out
how the warp, which was a theory of the natural laws of the
economic process, was interwoven with the woof, which was a
theory of the legal regime ordained by Nature as the one under
which the economic process would best promote the general
welfare, is no easy task.

The failure to unravel it, or analyze it into its two elements
and distinguish the role played by each, has hitherto misled most
of the numerous critics who have attacked "the old political
economy" as a body of doctrines inspired by a "metaphysical"
eighteenth-century notion of "natural laws." A century ago
Auguste Comte confused the two in his strictures on political
economy as a surviving product of eighteenth-century "metaphysics."[3] T. E. Cliffe Leslie confused them in just about the
same way in his essay on "Adam Smith's Political Economy."[4]

[2] Some of the better discussions bearing on this problem are to be found
in Bonar, *Philosophy and Political Economy;* Hasbach, *Die philosophischen
Grundlagen der von F. Quesnay und A. Smith begründeten Politischen
Ökonomie;* and various articles in the *Journal de l'histoire des doctrines
économiques,* by A. Dubois, E. Félix, B. Raynaud, and others.

[3] *Cours de Philosophie Positive,* IV (5th ed., Paris, 1893), iv, 210–223;
especially (for interpretation of the economists' ideas of natural laws), pp.
213–214.

[4] T. E. Cliffe Leslie, *Essays on Political Economy.* See also J. K. Ingram's
History of Political Economy, pp. 54–55, 89–91, etc.

In recent times, Thorstein Veblen has disseminated in this country an interpretation of the old doctrines which is based in part upon the same mistake.[5] But it is indeed a "natural" mistake, and many others besides those mentioned have made it.

The eighteenth-century economists had a conception of the natural laws of the economic process which was a conception of beneficent laws, like that of the physical scientists of the time. The faith in their beneficence was due to a "metaphysical" or, more properly, a theological influence; but as I pointed out in my former article, this influence did not prevent either physical scientists or economists from making progress in the discovery of actual scientific laws. In the case of the economists, however, the notion of beneficent laws which control the "natural course of things" was combined with, and complicated by, the conception of precepts of Nature, which men ought to recognize or discover and carry out. The result was a belief that things could take their beneficent "natural course" only in the rationally organized society which men were to create in obedience to Nature's precepts.

The content of this theory of an ideal social order, ordained or intended by Nature, was such as to make it the first form of the philosophy of what we now look back upon as old-fashioned economic "liberalism." As I shall try to show, the character of this liberalism has generally been misunderstood. It was not a doctrine that selfish interests should be given absolute free play while the state and society remained passive. It was a particular theory of an ideal legal order, imposing equal restraints upon all in order to give equal and maximum liberty to all, so that a "natural" interplay and adjustment of interests might ensure the welfare of all. But though the ideal behind the liberal program for the regulation of economic life was admirable, the program itself was inadequate for its purpose, even in the epoch of its origin. The simplicity of the program and the dogmatic confidence of its advocates reflected the quality of the eighteenth century's faith in "Nature's simple plan" for a harmonious social order. And the close partnership of economic theory, in the

[5] T. Veblen, *The Place of Science in Modern Civilisation and Other Essays*, especially pp. 86–89, 109, 112, 114–116, etc.

period from 1750 to 1850, with liberal philosophy and the liberal movement, and the close contact, in the first half of this period, between its conception of "natural" economic laws and the ethical and juristic notion of "natural law," though they did not prevent the economists from laying the foundations of a real science of economic life, did give this science, in its infancy, an unfortunate bias in favor of the dogmatically held ideals of this simple liberalism. The desire to understand the sources and nature of this bias is the motive of the present discussion.

II

It will be impossible, in the space here available, to discuss the history of the ethical and juristic doctrine of natural law.[6] A few remarks about the meaning which it had for its seventeenth- and eighteenth-century champions, and about the one body of literature in which economic theory had come into close contact with it before the time of the physiocrats, will serve to introduce a closer study of its meaning and role in their system of thought, and in that of Adam Smith.

In a very general way, the doctrine is of course familiar enough. It held that there is a set of rules of right or justice, and perhaps even of morality in general, which are, or may be, known by all men by the help either of "reason" or of a moral sense, and which possess an authority superior to that of such commands of human sovereigns, and such customary legal and moral regulations, as may contravene them. In other words, natural law meant a body of ideal or perfect "law," possessing in itself the full authority of actual law, but having its source, not in the will or command of any human authority, or in "custom," or in any supernatural revelation of Divine will, but in the knowledge or perception, somehow possible for all men, of what is in itself right or just.

[6] The well-known essays of Bryce and Pollock give summary treatments of its history, which are perhaps as good for the purpose as anything readily available in English. J. Bryce, "The Law of Nature," in *Studies in History and Jurisprudence* (Oxford, 1901); and F. Pollock, "The History of the Law of Nature," in *Essays in the Law* (London, 1922). Pollock's is, I think, the better of the two essays. See also his *Essays in Jurisprudence and Ethics*, chap. 2.

It is probably fair to say that by most of its expounders this body of "law" was called "natural" *mainly* because it was supposed to express the ethical ideals "natural" to mankind, or characteristic in a general way of *human* nature. The normal faculties of human nature, if exercised in the right way, would lead men to recognize its rules and acknowledge their authority. It is well known that Grotius connected natural law with a social instinct, supposedly possessed by all men as an intrinsic part of their natures.[7] Pufendorf defined natural law as those commands of God which are known, not from revelation or scripture, but as the result of reasoning from experience.[8] The supposition that the law was ordained by God was really unimportant for the theory, as Grotius explicitly said; the law as recognized by the morally reasonable man bore its own evidence of rightness and supreme authority.[9] For Hutcheson, the teacher of Adam Smith, it expressed the rules of conduct approved by an innate "moral sense."[10] For Adam Smith himself, it expressed the "sentiments" of justice evolved in men's minds by the play of "sympathy" in their contacts with one another in social life.[11] For the physiocrats, it was a code of exact rules to be discovered by the use of "reason"; but of reason as applied to the facts of experience about men and their social relations.[12] The essential point in all theories was that, through the use of some faculty or faculties belonging to human nature, men could discover the rules of this law.

However, in the eighteenth century especially, there was often a reference also to cosmic "Nature" as the lawgiver. The idea of "Nature" as a power that works toward ends was embodied in commonplace phrases which occur with special frequency in

[7] The social instinct makes men desire a peaceful and well-ordered society. Their reason or intelligence shows them how to attain it, i.e., reveals to them the rules of natural law. Grotius, *De Jure Belli ac Pacis, Proleg.*, secs. 6–11 (Scott's ed., 1925), trans. Kelsey, II, 11–13.

[8] Pufendorf, *Law of Nature and Nations*, bk. II, chap. 3, sec. 20 (Eng. ed. of 1703), pp. 113–116.

[9] Grotius, *Proleg.*, sec. 11, p. 13.

[10] F. Hutcheson, *A Short Introduction to Moral Philosophy* (5th ed., Philadelphia, 1788), pp. 20–22, 91–94.

[11] See below, section IV of present article.

[12] See below, section III of present article.

eighteenth-century literature. Physical science appeared to have revealed a harmonious order in the physical universe, which "Nature" was supposed to maintain or ensure by imposing the laws of physics upon all bodies. And there was a belief that "Nature" would produce a similar harmonious order in the system of human activities constituting the life of society, if men, rightly using the faculties which Nature had given them for this purpose, would recognize and obey her moral laws or precepts for the proper regulation of these activities. This notion involved a certain blending or confusion of the idea of Nature's precepts to individuals with the idea of scientific social laws.

In the main body of economic literature produced during the seventeenth and the first half of the eighteenth century, the ethical conception of natural law as a body of Nature's precepts rarely appears, and in any case plays no important role. The so-called "mercantilist" writers were not concerned with the wider ethical, juristic, and social problems which the physiocrats and Adam Smith brought within the scope of political economy. They were interested only in the narrower problem of finding out how a nation could best foster the important branches of its industry and commerce and so increase its wealth, mainly by suitable regulation of its foreign trade. Mun's doctrine that the general "balance of trade" over fairly long periods was the thing to watch became the accepted one. The idea was to use taxes, bounties, and the like to divert the expenditures and investments of the people into the desired channels. This involved something like a conception of the economic system as a mechanism which could be manipulated; and the best of these writers — Mun, Child, and others — made much progress in analysis of the interconnections between economic phenomena.[13]

These seventeenth-century English writers on "Trade" seldom referred to economic "laws," but the idea was always present in

[13] The latent notion of manipulating the economic mechanism, and the effort to trace causal sequences among economic events in order to decide upon policies, may be seen not only in their discussions of the balance of trade, but also in their writings on money, interest, and other topics. An excellent illustration is Child's discussion of the ways in which a low rate of interest would affect the economic system. Sir Josiah Child, *A New Discourse of Trade* (4th ed., London, n.d.), chap. 1; esp. pp. 46–86.

their writings. Petty, whose work was of a somewhat different order, did refer at times to "laws of nature," and apparently tended to confuse the idea of causal laws with the ethical and juristic notion of natural law, as when he spoke of "the vanity and fruitlessness of making civil, positive laws against the laws of Nature." [14] Yet Petty's economic theories were entirely scientific in spirit.[15] Locke, in his essay on money and the rate of interest, referred casually to "laws of value," using the expression, as the context shows, entirely in the modern, scientific sense.[16] When North wrote that "no laws can set prices in Trade, the rates of which must and will make themselves," and suggested that the theory of Trade, like natural philosophy, must become "mechanical," he was giving explicit statement to notions which had been implicit in the best work of his predecessors.[17]

North's analysis of commercial life led him to discard the balance of trade doctrine and adopt the position of later laissez-faire liberals. But he made no suggestion that a liberal regime was decreed by any moral Law of Nature, or that any "natural rights" or "natural liberties" of men were involved. His contention was simply that analysis of the facts of commerce would prove this to be the policy best calculated to increase national wealth.

The eighteenth-century "mercantilists" were inferior on the whole to their seventeenth-century predecessors. But Cantillon, Hume, and a few other writers carried forward to new achievements that analysis of the interrelations of trades, and of prices, incomes, and movements of goods and of money in commerce, which had been started in the preceding century. There was thus a long period of progress in economic theory of an essentially scientific type, in which it did not come under the influence of the ethical conception of natural law.

But in another body of literature produced in the same period

[14] *Economic Writings of Sir W. Petty*, ed. C. H. Hull, I, 48. But see separate references to the two ideas on page 9 of this same work of Petty's.
[15] See Hull's admirable discussion of Petty's scientific background, aims, and method. Introd., pp. lx–lxxiv.
[16] "Considerations of the Lowering of Interest and Raising the Value of Money"; in Locke's *Works* (London, 1823), V, 36.
[17] Sir D. North, *Discourses Upon Trade* (1691; reprint, 1907), pp. 11, 12.

a certain amount of economic theory was worked out, from a very different starting point, in close connection with the juristic doctrine of natural law. The works of Grotius, Pufendorf, and other writers on the Law of Nature, contain chapters or sections on money, value and prices, interest or usury, monopolies, and other economic topics.[18] Hutcheson's work in economics, which probably suggested some of Adam Smith's cardinal ideas, was parallel and similar to that of Pufendorf.[19] This early modern school of natural law jurists and moralists had given up the idea of the medieval lawyers and schoolmen that equity in business transactions must be ensured by imposition upon the parties, in every case, of the jurists' idea of a "just price." They reasoned that in a free market, where every buyer and seller had alternatives made available by the prevalence of competition, the market price which would establish itself would always be a fair price, corresponding to the seller's costs and a fair reward for his own services, and also to the value of the article to the buyer. They developed some economic theory in order to prove this, and gave the rest of their attention to the legal regulations necessary to ensure free markets.

It remained for the physiocrats and Adam Smith to combine the theory of how to promote national prosperity, and the theory of the interrelations between economic phenomena upon which that was based, with the theory of the legal system which would protect everyone in his "natural rights." They argued that the two aims must coincide; for "Nature" had so arranged things that the just legal system which she prescribed or "recommended" would also prove to be the best and indeed the only effective means of promoting national opulence. In their schemes of doctrine, political economy became a development of the eighteenth-century notion of a harmonious, "natural" social order. "Nat-

---

[18] Grotius, bk. II, chap. 12 (on Contracts), secs. 14–26, deals with (just) prices, monopolies, money, rentals, interest or usury, and partnerships. Pufendorf, bk. V, chaps. 1–8, gives a much fuller treatment of the same topics.
[19] Hutcheson, *A Short Introduction to Moral Philosophy*, bk. II, chap. 12. Cf. Cannan's introduction to A. Smith's *Lectures on Justice, Police, Revenue, and Arms*, pp. xxv–xxvi, for a fair account of Hutcheson's relation to Pufendorf, and to Adam Smith.

ural" institutions, prescribed by Nature but to be achieved by human effort, would facilitate a beneficent "natural" economic process. Their very different developments of this doctrine must now be examined.

III

The physiocrats are important for our purpose only because they did in a bold, rigorous, and doctrinaire way what Adam Smith did in a much more cautious way, and in the spirit of a very different philosophy. Their influence upon Smith, especially in respect of such ideas as I am here concerned with, was probably almost nil; and their general influence upon the development of economic thought was not very great.[20] But they gave explicit and clear-cut development to the fundamental ideas of the political economy of liberalism, ideas which in the writings of other and more influential architects of that system remained latent or half-expressed. Their expositions are therefore an excellent guide, if cautiously used, to the interpretation of the teachings of the English economists, who were not always so sure of, or so apt to express in rigid formulae, their general philosophies.

A student's attitude toward the physiocrats will always depend upon his temperament. Like many other "philosophers" of the epoch in France they were not broadly and thoroughly equipped scholars, or careful students of facts, but facile builders of somewhat airy intellectual structures. But they intended, and pretended, to base their work on observation of facts; and they did observe many important facts about agriculture as then carried on in France, and analyzed them in an acute way. They had a clear conception of society's economic life as a single, continuous

[20] Cannan, in his introduction to the report of Smith's Lectures has made it clear that, with the exception of his theory of "distribution," Smith's debts for his economic ideas were to British writers, not to the physiocrats. That the philosophical ideas with which we are concerned here also came, in Smith's case, from British and especially Scottish philosophy, and were of a different color from the analogous ideas of the physiocrats, is brought out by Hasbach. See also D. Stewart, *Dissertation*, pp. 336–337, 380–381, and 474–478.

process, and excellent insights into many of its features. Their effort to combine economic theory with legal philosophy was one which badly needs to be renewed in our time, though of course in an infinitely more careful way and in a very different spirit.

There is some confusion of ideas in the physiocratic conceptions of *lois naturelles, droit naturel,* and *l'ordre naturel,* but not so much confusion, I think, or so much mystery, as has often been supposed. Political economy, in their conception of it, included the whole of social science; or rather, their conception of this science was limited to include only political economy.[21] It was to discover "les lois naturelles morales," which they held to be as exact as "les lois naturelles physiques." [22] Dupont cites the achievements of physical science in his time, and declares that only men's prejudices make them unwilling to believe that these achievements can be paralleled in social science.[23] The partly religious or theological orientation of thought which was still fairly common at that time, even among natural scientists, led the physiocrats to describe both the physical and the social laws of Nature as laws which are "as advantageous as possible to the human species." [24] But there are plenty of passages in their writings which show well enough what they meant by this.

Quesnay's argument to prove the beneficence of "les lois naturelles physiques" has two parts. In the first place, he argues that those conditions and events in the physical environment of a society which come about, not as results of any human actions, but as results of the operation of such forces of Nature as are beyond human control, are generally productive, on balance, of

[21] Cf. Dupont de Nemours, *De l'origine et des progrès d'une science nouvelle,* ed. Dubois (Paris, 1910), p. 6.
[22] Dupont, *De l'origine,* pp. 6, 8; and Quesnay, "Droit Naturel," in *Works,* ed. Oncken, pp. 374-375. The reader will recall that what we now call the "social sciences" were until recently, in most places, called the "moral sciences," and their "laws" would be called "moral laws." Of course this terminology itself tends to carry with it confusion of scientific laws with precepts.
[23] *De l'origine,* p. 6, to be read in context of pp. 5-7.
[24] Quesnay, "Droit Naturel," p. 375. A natural law of either variety is always the law "le plus avantageux au genre humain." Natural laws are "immuables et irréfragables et les meilleures lois possibles."

more good than harm to human welfare; and further, that such harm as they may do is always an inevitable result of the same "properties" of these conditions and events which make them useful or beneficial to mankind. The storm which inconveniences the traveler waters the farms. This illustration is supposed to be typical of natural phenomena in general as they affect human welfare. The conclusion is that of the theodicy of Leibniz. God has left none but logically inevitable evils in the world; its laws are as conducive as possible to human welfare; to make them any more so would require an omnipotence which could make rain both wet and dry, or could make two plus two equal to five. It is an argument to be smiled at; but it shows that Quesnay was thinking of the actual laws of physical science, and affords no foundation whatever for Veblen's charge that he was thinking of "animistic," constraining laws which mould, not the actual course of events, but an ideal course of events, which is truly "real" and somehow latent in the actual, into harmony with human desires.[25]

The second part of Quesnay's argument is more interesting. It is that men, being endowed with "reason" and "free wills," can adjust themselves to their environment so as to secure its benefits and avoid the incidental evils. The Creator gave them reason and free wills for this purpose. This completes the proof of his benevolence. He has made a world which, on balance, is more friendly than hostile to its human inhabitants, a world to which they can so adjust themselves as to be prosperous, comfortable, and happy; and has given them the faculties which enable them to make the adjustment. This leads to the Cartesian argument that human ills are really due to man's "abuse" of his freedom of will, i.e., to his failure to keep his will under the control of his "reason," and act always and only after acquiring full knowledge of, and giving rational consideration to, all of the effects of his actions. Quesnay's "optimism" was really that of the rationalistic "enlightenment," which believed that the prog-

---

[25] Quesnay, "Droit Naturel," p. 368, whole of paragraph in middle of page. For Veblen's interpretation see *The Place of Science in Modern Civilisation and Other Essays*, pp. 87–89.

ress of science was going to result in a completely rational ordering of human life.[26]

The interpretation of "les lois naturelles morales les plus avantageux au genre humain" is another story. Here we encounter that blending of the idea of scientific social laws with the idea of moral rules of conduct which has puzzled so many readers of the writings of the physiocrats. These laws were regarded as the laws of the ideal social process, or procession of interconnected but severally "free" and rational human actions, which will take place as men come to understand and obey the moral precepts of Nature. Nature *prescribes* to men as members of society certain courses of action or conduct, by making these courses *necessary*, in the situations in which she has placed them, for the attainment of a maximum of both individual and social wealth and welfare. It is for them to discover, by the use of their "reason," what these best courses of action are, and pursue them. Then they will set up, and carry on their economic life in, the ideal order which Nature prescribes.[27]

This notion of normative social laws really includes three ideas, which are not as clearly separated as they should be. It includes the rules of *droit naturel*, which, as embodied in legislation and in the moral consciousness of citizens in the new social order, will regulate their behavior in accordance with their natural rights and duties. It may also be said to include the rules of rational economic behavior, which will guide individuals in pursuing their economic interests within the limits fixed by the rules of justice. Both of these sets of rules are precepts or injunctions of Nature, which men must discover and obey. But the general conception also includes the laws of economics in the

[26] What I have distinguished as the "second part" of Quesnay's argument will be found on pp. 368–371 of the *Works*, beginning with the last sentence of the paragraph cited for the "first part" and running through to the end of chap. 3. "Abuse" of the power of free will, or irrational action, is called a "violation" of natural laws — of natural *moral* laws (see below) and of the beneficent intent of physical laws, which are intended to ensure the effects that will result if men make the proper use of reason and free will.

[27] Dupont, *De l'origine*, p. 7.

proper sense of that expression, i.e., the laws of the causal interconnections among the actions of separate individuals which
make up economic life. Each individual behaves "freely," and in
the ideal order rationally, in the economic situation which confronts him at a given time; but that situation is partly determined
for him by the previous actions of other men, and he in turn
helps to create situations which affect the rational choices of
others. The laws according to which the separate actions and
situations are thus linked together are the explanatory laws of
the general economic process. It was the view of the physiocrats
that this process would ensure the working out of all desirable
adjustments in the economic system, when all individuals should
have become rational or prudent men, living in a rational or just
society with its "natural" scheme of institutions. But they united
the three conceptions, of rules of prudence, rules of justice, and
economic laws of the process formed by the linking together of
individual actions, in a single conception of Nature's wise laws
for the regulation of the social economy.

In spite of their confusion on this point, however, their work
in explanatory economic theory forms a part of their writings
which can be separated readily enough from their work in ethical
and legal philosophy.[28] When they are describing and analyzing
the general process of economic life, they are plainly working
simply to discover causal or explanatory economic laws. On the
other hand, when they are describing and eulogizing the institutions of *l'ordre naturel*, and the rules of *droit naturel*, they are
as plainly advocating an ideal to be realized by human efforts.
The effect of this inclusion of their theory of the economic
process in a wider social philosophy was to make it a theory

[28] To a large extent the two things were even given separate places in
the arrangement of their expositions. Thus in Mercier de la Rivière's
L'Ordre Naturel, the first 35 chapters are devoted to ethical, political, and
legal philosophy, with only incidental bits of economic theory. The remaining nine chapters are concentrated economic theory — analysis of
"commerce." On the other hand, Baudeau's *Première introduction à la
philosophie économique* — one of the most readable and attractive works
of the school — is descriptive and analytical throughout, a picture of the
structure and operation of the nation's economic system, with attention
everywhere to the institutions and rules of conduct required to make it
work for the general welfare.

of the process as it would go on in the ideal social order. But this did not make it a thing wholly detached from observation of the existing society. It was possible to see what *tended* to happen, wherever men were free and able to take the courses of action indicated by their circumstances as most conducive to the simultaneous advancement of their own and of the nation's wealth; and to reason out what would happen in a better society, free of existing hindrances to the achievement of ideal adjustments. The physiocratic *ordre naturel* was a utopia, but a utopia less unlike the existing state of affairs than many others that were being projected at the time. It was to be a social order adjusted to the facts with which Nature confronted mankind, the order which Nature required them to achieve in order to fulfill her purpose, and their need, for the best possible adjustment to one another and to their common physical environment. Some approximation to it had already been achieved everywhere, being indispensable to the continuing existence of society.[29] Hence the economic process in the existing society would be an approximation, somewhat remote, to the process as described in their economic theory, i.e., the process which would go on in the "natural" social order and would result in the best possible adjustments in the economic system, from the point of view of the wealth and welfare of the nation.

The main interest of the physiocrats was in showing what the institutions of the natural order must be. Their science was to discover the exact scheme of institutions which Nature had made necessary for attaining the greatest good of the nation as a whole. Dupont criticizes Montesquieu for teaching that no general and exact science of what institutions ought to be is possible, because those of every nation are and must be adjusted, not only to its peculiar conditions of topography, soil, climate, etc., but also to the tempers, habits, and inclinations of its people. This doctrine would lead to fatalistic acquiescence in local tradition and prejudice. The ideal end of all political societies, says Dupont, is the same, namely, to make all of their

[29] Dupont, *De l'origine*, p. 7: "un ordre qu'on ne pourrait abandonner entièrement sans opérer la dissolution de la société et bientôt la destruction absolue de l'espèce humaine."

members as prosperous and happy as possible. There must be a science of the best means of attaining this end, under the conditions which Nature imposes. The "laws" of this science must be exact, and independent of all traditional opinions of what ought to be done, because "there can be nothing arbitrary in physical acts directed to a definite end. One can arrive at a given point only by taking the route that leads to it." [30]

The institutions of *l'ordre naturel* were to conform to the principles of *droit naturel*. In his article on Droit Naturel, Quesnay begins by saying that previous writers on this subject had arrived only at vague and confused ideas, because they had not built upon observation of definite facts about human beings, their physical and mental characteristics, and their various relations to one another in specific social situations.[31] A study of these facts would show what Nature intends men to recognize as their respective rights and duties, in order that they may coöperate with one another in the most effective way. Thus Nature has obviously made it the duty of parents to do certain things for their children, and has given children a corresponding right to these parental services. The facts of the situation in which parents and children are placed are enough to show this.[32] All rights and duties among human beings are to be determined in the same way — by the facts and requirements of the situations in which they stand in relation to one another.

The general character of the institutional regime which the physiocrats arrived at as their ideal is familiar enough. All men were to be free to dispose of their own persons and of their labor to the best advantage, to acquire and control property in land and movable goods, and to have access at all times to the best markets at home and abroad. There was to be a government, headed by a monarch with the sole power to promulgate laws and control their administration. But the monarch or "despot" could not "make" laws; he could only promulgate as statutes of the realm the rules of "natural law" (*droit naturel*); and he was to be checked by an independent judiciary, trained in natural

[30] *De l'origine*, p. 7.
[31] Quesnay, *Works*, pp. 360–363.
[32] *Works*, p. 365.

law, and possessing a judicial veto. An important function of the
state was to educate all citizens, especially in the principles of
natural law. The land-owning aristocracy would be trustees for
the nation of the *produit net*, the net income of their lands, which
was the nation's only net income above the costs of keeping production going and supporting the producers and the "sterile"
urban population. A part of the *produit net* would go to the
state, as the only tax; and the landowners would use part of what
was left in improving lands, so that production would not merely
be kept going, but would be increased. Though a net income,
the *produit net* was the landowner's reward for those original
"advances," made by himself or by his ancestors, which had
prepared the land for cultivation. It provided him with both
the means and the incentive to make new advances of the same
kind. The larger the *produit net* the greater the incentive would
be to improve land and thus make economic progress cumulative.
With free markets, rents no greater than the *produit net*, and
no taxes, the peasant cultivators would be able to stock their
farms with adequate equipment, make adequate "annual advances" for cultivation, and bring their fields to the highest
efficiency in production. The useful, though "unproductive,"
industry and commerce of the towns would be similarly freed
from its handicaps and enabled to function "naturally" in the
new regime. With universal free exchange and competition,
prices and incomes would be kept at their "natural" levels, supplies in all markets would adjust themselves to demands, and the
economic system would become the efficient and harmonious
mechanism which Nature intended it to be.

It should be clear from what I have said that the laissez-faire
maxim, as used by the physiocrats, was not a counsel of inaction.
Their "legal despotism" was to be a vigorous and active government, but active only along the wise lines pointed out by
Nature. The immediate program of action which they had in
mind, of course, was one of destruction of old abuses. But the
permanent task of enforcing the rules of *droit naturel* meant the
carrying out of a definite though simple program of "social
control" of economic life. To protect every man in his natural
rights was to restrain every man from encroaching upon the

natural rights of his fellows. To give every man the same liberty and opportunity to pursue his own interests, was to prevent individuals, groups, classes, and localities from claiming and exercising privileges of a monopolistic character, or asserting their own interests beyond the limits of justice or to the detriment of the legitimate interests of others. The particular forms of public and social action to which they objected were such as really impeded and crippled the normal activities of some groups and classes, for the sake of protecting the vested interests of others.[33]

The utilitarian character of the whole philosophy of the "sect" is also evident from what I have said. Nature's purpose is to maximize the wealth and happiness of mankind. Her injunctions to men are the indications she gives, by the situations in which she has placed them, of the things they must do to play their parts in attaining this end. Ascertaining the precepts of Nature thus means ascertaining what is necessary to the greatest general good. But the utilitarianism of the physiocrats lacks that fully and truly empirical and experimental character which is the mark of the most genuine utilitarianism. The distinctive meaning of the doctrine that whatever is most useful is "right" is that absolute and a priori ideas of what is "right" are to be thrown away, and men are to set themselves in all openness of mind to learn by experience what really is most useful. In spite of their intention to arrive at the principles of *droit naturel* by observation of facts, the physiocrats did not escape from the arbitrary dogmatism which that conception has always been too apt to carry with it. They assumed that "Nature's" indications of what is right in every social situation are always obvious upon a merely abstract consideration of its general features. Their doctrine of "évidence" is here in point. In the spirit of Descartes, they reasoned from "clear ideas" about the facts of social life, which seemed to them "evident" as soon as stated.[34] These ideas were generally "evident" enough, if taken as the abstractions

----

[33] My contention here is sufficiently supported by the fact that the physiocrats *always* coupled individual rights with correlative duties. See for instance Dupont, *De l'origine*, p. 11.

[34] See Quesnay's article "Evidence," *Works*, pp. 764ff.; and Mercier de la Rivière, *L'Ordre Naturel*, chap. 9.

which they really were; but the physiocrats reasoned as if they were complete descriptions of concrete social facts, in which capacity they really could figure at best only as half-truths. The system was a kind of abstract social geometry, useful as such, but needing an almost infinite amount of modification and filling out by detailed studies to make it an adequate map of the most useful social order.

IV

Adam Smith's philosophy of the natural order of things in social life was very different, evolved by a mind and temper very different from that of Quesnay, and built upon a much broader basis of scholarship and of careful empirical studies. Smith belonged to the school which trusted not so much the natural human faculty of reason as the natural instincts or propensities and the natural feelings or sentiments of mankind to achieve the natural order. Reason also had its part to play, in his view, but it was a minor part. Things would turn out best if men attempted a rational or deliberate management only of their personal affairs and of such public affairs as could be brought within the range of their limited powers of foresight and control. If every man would attend to the little part of the social system that was under his immediate charge, and for the rest would let his natural instincts and feelings be his guide, the system as a whole and the general welfare would take care of themselves. Ambitious efforts of rationalistic reformers and statesmen to make men work together in accordance with their logical plans would always come up against the fact that human beings could not be moved about like pieces on a chessboard. The wise statesman would therefore learn to coöperate with Nature; i.e., to let natural tendencies, resulting from the natural propensities and sentiments of men, work themselves out in social life, with only a certain minimum of regulation by institutions which should themselves express or harmonize with the feelings, habits, and even to some extent the prejudices of the great mass of the population.[35]

[35] *Theory of Moral Sentiments*, Part VI, sec. 2, esp. chap. 2. See also Part VII, sec. 2, chap. 3.

This view that a "natural" social order, including "natural" institutions, is to be achieved by the normal operation of the instincts and feelings of men, supplemented by their intelligence as that may work in the spheres in which it is effective, puts Smith in the class of such thinkers as Bacon, Montesquieu, and Burke, who were more apt to appeal to traditions that had grown up in this way and become adapted to local conditions than to urge abstract theories and schemes of sudden reform. Bacon's conception of the *leges legum* was less like other conceptions of juristic natural law than it was like a conception of social or even historical laws, which ensure a gradual adjustment of systems of law and policy to the tempers, habits, and requirements of the population.[36] Montesquieu indulged in some abstract doctrines, but his main idea was that institutions should be adjusted, and will in the end adjust themselves, to conditions, and to habits and impulses of the people, which are beyond the lawmaker's control.[37] Burke opposed the abstract "natural right" theories of the French *philosophes,* but had his own theory of the way in which "Nature" instructs mankind in the evolution of sound institutions — chiefly through instincts and sentiments which, through a long historical process, find expression in institutions that work and become objects of loyalty.[38] Adam Smith was closer to the camp of Montesquieu and Burke than to that of Quesnay or Bentham.[39] He differed from the later historical jurists in his ability to combine with this largely anti-rationalist philosophy an acute and minute analysis of the social "mechanisms" which, with some help from human intelligence, produce that adjustment to one another of all individual interests which is social "order." [40]

[36] Cf. D. Stewart, *Dissertations*, pp. 71–74.

[37] *Dissertations*, pp. 189–193.

[38] Burke, *Reflections on the French Revolution.*

[39] Bentham, of course, was not an adherent of any form of the doctrine of juristic "natural law," but his own legal philosophy relied entirely on abstract logic to construct an ideal system of law.

[40] As bearing on this conception of social "order," see J. Dickinson, "Social Order and Political Authority," *Am. Pol. Sci. Rev.* (May, 1929).

Smith's neglected "Essays on Philosophical Subjects"[41] throw much light, I think, upon the philosophy which pervades both the *Theory of Moral Sentiments* and the *Wealth of Nations*. The task of the natural sciences, according to Smith, is to find "connecting links" between events or phenomena which at first appear unrelated. In this way it reduces the apparent chaos of phenomena to an ordered system, and in the end gives us the inspiring conception of the universe as a single, vast "machine," whose parts work together as if according to a plan.[42] When the philosophers of antiquity first arrived at this conception, they could not help inferring that the unity and coördination of parts in the cosmos implied a unity in the "cause" of the whole, and an intelligent design; and thus "science gave birth to the first theism," i.e., monotheism as distinguished from the earlier polytheism, which had pictured the gods as interfering in the natural course of things, instead of as planning that course.[43]

It is not too much to say that in the *Theory of Moral Sentiments* and in the *Wealth of Nations* Smith was trying to do in social science what he described natural science as doing in its field, i.e., to discover "connecting links" among the minds and among the actions of separate individuals in social life, and thus arrive at the conception of a systematic order among social phenomena. He did not sharply distinguish "order," in the sense of a system of uniform causal relations among social events, from "order" in the sense of a set of harmonious adjustments among individual interests, resulting in a well-ordered society. But in the social processes which he described as maintaining order and equilibrium among individual interests, human intelli-

[41] The history of these essays, and their connection with Adam Smith's teaching, are touched upon in Francis Hirst's biography of Smith. Auguste Comte praised them, and, largely on the basis of the indication they give of Smith's acquaintance with natural science, made an exception in favor of their author in making his general charge against the "metaphysical" economists. *Cours de Philosophie Positive*, 5th ed., IV, 212–213.

[42] "The Principles Which Lead and Direct Philosophical Inquiries, Illustrated by the History of Astronomy," Section II. In *The Whole Works of A. Smith* (London, 1822), V, 10–18.

[43] "The Principles Which Lead, etc., Illustrated by the History of the Ancient Physics," pp. 89–90.

gence and planning, human moral feelings, efforts of men as responsible beings to achieve social order, and human legal institutions, all had parts to play. The natural propensities and feelings of men, however, rather than their powers of rational foresight, were represented as the main agencies at work. And in the fact that these propensities and feelings, which were due to the original endowments of human nature, tended to produce a harmonious order in social life, he found warrant for an inference that "Nature" or the "Author of Nature" was working through human propensities and feelings to realize a beneficent purpose that transcended human purposes.

The character of this optimistic teleology is perhaps best brought out in his argument against Hume's explanation of the sense of justice, which prompts us to approve the punishment by the state of every individual who commits what we regard as an unjust act against another. Hume had explained this feeling of indignation as due to a perception of the social utility of compelling every man to respect the rights of his fellows, and to "sympathy" with the general happiness thus protected. Smith does not deny that this social utility *is* the good which is accomplished by enforcing justice; but he denies that perception or foresight of the social benefit is the cause of the feeling in question. To make it the cause, he says, is to forget to apply in social science the principle of natural science that a scientific explanation must run in terms of "efficient causes," not of ends or "final causes"! The wheels of a watch make it give the correct time, not because they intend this result, but because they are controlled by a spring. The intention was in the mind of the watchmaker who designed the mechanism, but the task of explaining the movements of the hands is one of explaining the working of this mechanism. In the same way, Smith thinks, the moral feeling that makes us approve what is in fact socially useful is produced, not by our conscious intention to promote society's welfare and our knowledge of how to promote it, but by the springs with which Nature has equipped our mental and emotional machinery. He admits that conscious purposes and rational foresight play *some* part in the operation of human minds; but many of the socially useful results that flow from individual feelings and actions are planned, not by men, but by the Author of their natures. Much that is imputed to the wisdom of men is due to the wisdom of God. Psychological and social science has to explain the operation of the mechanisms by which the Divine purpose is achieved. This argument makes it clear that Smith's references to the purposes of Nature, the "guiding hand," etc., were not substitutes for scientific explanations of social phenomena but an appendage to them. They were set up in opposition to the *human* teleology that attributes everything which comes to pass in social life to deliberate and far-seeing human purposes.[44]

As we should expect, in view of these characteristics of his thinking, Smith's theory of the natural economic order differed from that of the physiocrats in being less a theory of an ideal order to be achieved by a rational plan of reform than a theory of an existing order among economic events.[45] The *Wealth of Nations* is a descriptive and explanatory treatise. The natural propensity of men to truck and barter, rather than rational foresight of an advantage to be gained, has led to the development of a system of division of labor, which makes men interdependent, and increases their economic efficiency.[46] The natural desire of every man to better his own condition, rather than rational plans of statesmen, ensures the continuous progress of national wealth.[47] The gravitation of men, money, and goods to their best markets keeps all prices and incomes near their "natural" levels, and carries men, without foresight on their part of the socially good result, into the fields of activity in which they can do most to increase the wealth of the nation, as well as their

[44] *Moral Sentiments*, Part II, sec. 2, chap. 2 (6th ed.) I, 216–229. I do not mean to deny that Smith's belief that Divine wisdom had designed the mental and social mechanisms had a tendency to bias his "scientific" account of their working, in the direction of "optimism." But a belief that individual behavior often promotes social welfare, without a conscious intention to promote it being in the mind of the individual, does not necessarily depend on theology. See in this connection the praise of Smith's *Moral Sentiments* in T. H. Huxley, *Evolution and Ethics* (New York, 1899), pp. 28, 30.

[45] Cf. Viner, "A. Smith and Laissez-Faire," *Journ. of Pol. Econ.* (April 1927), p. 198.

[46] *Wealth of Nations*, ed. McCullock, 4th ed. (1850), bk. I, chap. 2.

[47] Bk. IV, chap. 9, p. 304.

own wealth.[48] All this comes about *almost* regardless of the wisdom or folly of governments. Smith criticizes the physiocrats for regarding their precise "regimen of laws" as absolutely essential to the health of the economic organism. His own view was that, though misdirected public policies could do some harm, the persistent pressures toward adjustment and progress kept in play by individual interests would always act as the *vis medicatrix* to maintain a tolerable degree of health and soundness in the organism.[49]

Yet Adam Smith also had his ideal of an institutional order, a little different from the system existing in his day in Great Britain. His account of economic tendencies was intended to be close to the facts of contemporary society, but still closer to the facts as they would be if existing impediments to "natural" economic adjustments were removed. The inquiry was in the main quite objective and scientific in spirit, but it is true that it was directed to the end of making out a case for the program of public policy which he believed to be "recommended by Nature." This program he described, in negative terms, as an abolition of "all systems either of preference or of restraint," which would enable "the simple and obvious system of natural liberty" to "establish itself of its own accord." [50] This language has obscured for his readers the fact that the "system of natural liberty" was Smith's ideal legal system, corresponding in its own way to that of the physiocrats.

The evidence of this, and of the character of his ideal, is to be obtained from a comparative study of the *Wealth of Nations* and the *Theory of Moral Sentiments*.[51] The relation of these two treatises has never, I think, been rightly understood. The view that the central doctrine of one is inconsistent with that of the other is without foundation.[52] The "sympathy" of the *Theory*

---

[48] Bk. I, chap. 7, and bk. IV, chap. 2, pp. 198–200.

[49] Bk. IV, chap. 9, p. 304.

[50] Bk. IV, chap. 9, p. 311.

[51] Some additional evidence is also provided by the report of Smith's lectures on jurisprudence, published by Cannan. See page 29, note 20.

[52] G. R. Morrow, *The Ethical and Economic Theories of Adam Smith*, and Hasbach, *Untersuchungen über A. Smith*, are fairly good on the relation of the two.

is not benevolence or altruism, and the "self-interest" of the *Inquiry* is not selfishness. A German historian of philosophy says truly that in the former work Smith found "in the mechanism of sympathetic transfers of feeling an adjustment of individual interests similar to that which he . . . found in the mechanism of the exchange of external goods." [53] A more precise statement of the matter can be given. In one work we have a theory of the way in which "sympathetic transfers of feeling" set limits to the assertion of individual interests and promote social harmony: partly by creating moral sentiments in the minds of individuals which directly modify their conduct, and partly by causing society to evolve a legal system which expresses the moral sentiments common to the mass of mankind, and imposes restraints which not every individual would always impose upon himself. In the other work we have a theory of the way in which the individual interests, thus limited, themselves promote economic adjustment and harmony. The two treatises therefore give us complementary halves of Smith's social philosophy.

The *Theory of Moral Sentiments* is a study of the sociological and psychological *genesis* of moral feelings. I cannot wholly agree with Professor Viner's opinion that it embodies a more extreme and repellent form of its author's optimistic teleology than is to be found in the *Wealth of Nations*.[54] There is a difference of degree of this sort, but it does not seem to me to be very marked. It is to be remembered that the *Theory* is dealing, not with the actual behavior of men, but with the genesis of the moral feelings which tell them how they ought to behave. That the feelings are not always developed strongly enough to be effective in controlling conduct, is frequently admitted.[55] The ethical element in the treatise lies just in the idea of the individual's responsibility for making the effort to develop and strengthen in his mind, and to act in accordance with, the feelings and the rules of conduct suggested to him by the social

[53] Windelband, *History of Philosophy*, trans. Tufts (2d ed., 1914), p. 518.
[54] J. Viner, "Adam Smith and Laissez Faire," *Journ. of Pol. Econ.* (April 1917), pp. 200–201.
[55] E.g., Part 1, sec. 3, chap. 3; Part 3, chap. 3, pp. 379–388 (6th ed., vol. I); Part 3, chap. 4; Part 5, chap. 2, pp. 19–20 (vol. II); Part 6, sec. 3, pp. 120ff.

experience which comes through his faculty of sympathy. The "connecting links" between the minds of men in the social mechanism that is being described stop short at the thresholds of the free volitions of individual minds. If the volitions play their proper parts, the mechanism works harmoniously. But the admission that they frequently fail to play their parts properly makes the *Theory* an account, not strictly of what social life *is*, but of what it can be.

The complex account of the operation of sympathy can only be summarized here. Individuals tend to be led, by their sympathies and desires for sympathy, to restrain their selfish desires, ambitions, and impulses, and keep them within certain limits. Immediate feelings not always sufficing to define and enforce these limits, they build up rules of conduct from their experience of what their feelings normally are. These rules, he says, are the celebrated moral laws of Nature.[56] The limits which they impose upon the assertion of private interests are at a mean between those which, in the absence of sympathy, other interested parties would impose upon the individual to prevent him from encroaching upon *their* interests, and those which, in the absence of sympathy, he would allow himself to reach in giving rein to his expansive desires.

A vigorous pursuit of one's own interests, within the limits thus imposed, is treated in the *Moral Sentiments* as the virtue of prudence. Desire for the sympathy and approval of his fellows tends to make a man practice this virtue, just as it tends to make him stop in the pursuit of his interests at the limits beyond which he would be doing injustice to others. Mankind in general applauds every man who gets ahead in the race for wealth and social position, so long as he does not trample on the rights of his competitors. The truly prudent man is therefore also the just man. The chief thing that perverts the sense of justice and turns prudence into grasping selfishness is the bias that develops if one lives in a group of his allies and is in sympathetic contact with the minds of partial, not of impartial, spectators of his actions. The prudent man retains his sense of justice by keeping

[56] Part VI, chaps. 4 and 5.

a little aloof from his group and mixing as a friend in all kinds of company.[57]

It is unfortunate that Smith never wrote his promised treatise on "the rules of natural justice which ought to underlie and be the foundation of the laws of all nations." [58] But the *Theory of Moral Sentiments*, supplemented to some extent by the copy of a student's notes of his lectures on natural jurisprudence, which Professor Cannan discovered, enables us to learn what his views were as to the general spirit of these rules.[59] They would simply protect every man's right to pursue his own interests within the limits imposed by the necessity of giving similar protection to every other man. Now I think it is clear that the legal system embodying the rules of natural justice is the system of natural liberty of the *Wealth of Nations*. When the systems of preference and restraint are abolished, it will "establish itself of its own accord," i.e., not without human effort, but as an expression of the moral sentiments "natural" to mankind.[60]

The other systems violated those sentiments, in Smith's opinion. They were not only detrimental to national wealth, but they were also unjust; they involved "preference" or partiality as well as "restraint." They had been established, not in obedience to the sentiment of justice, but in pursuance of excessively clever — and mistaken — ideas of "policy." Men had supposed that, in order to get ahead of other nations in commercial rivalry, it was necessary to disregard moral scruples and sacrifice the interests, not only of foreigners, but of large classes in the home population to the interests of those engaged in the favored industries and trades. Within the nation a similar belief in every locality had led to local ordinances which invaded rights or

[57] *Moral Sentiments*, Part VI, sec. 1 (of Prudence); Part II, sec. 2, chap. 2, esp. p. 207 (vol. I, 6th ed.); Part III, chap. 3, pp. 382-386.

[58] *Moral Sentiments*, Part VII, sec. 4, vol. II, 395-399; and introd. to this 6th ed., vol. I, vi-vii.

[59] The lectures add only a little to our knowledge of his views on jurisprudence. See Cannan's editorial introduction.

[60] In the paragraph in which this system is referred to — the next to the last paragraph of Book IV, chap. 9 — he explicitly says that under it the state or sovereign still has the duty of "protecting . . . every member of the society against the injustice or oppression of every other member of it."

legitimate interests of numerous individuals, and interfered with that free movement of all things to their best markets so necessary to the proper working of the economic system. The *Wealth of Nations* aimed to prove that justice, or equal liberty for all, was the best economic policy for nations and communities.[61]

In harmony with this is the further fact that the individual self-interest approved in the *Wealth of Nations* as a socially beneficent force is the prudence of the *Theory of Moral Sentiments*, i.e., a self-interest working within limits fixed by rules and sentiments of justice. This is shown, in a negative way, by the many vigorous criticisms of the selfishness of manufacturers and merchants, who band together to exclude new rivals from their trades and exploit the public.[62] Hasbach and others have commented on the contrast between the ideal prudent man of the *Moral Sentiments* and the business men portrayed in the *Wealth of Nations*. Adam Smith was no admirer of business men as a class, and no spokesman or mouthpiece of a "rising bourgeoisie." The pursuit of private economic gain or advantage ceased to be regarded by him as a worthy and socially beneficent activity whenever it took the form of efforts to secure or to protect monopolistic advantages.

Universal free and fair competition was his ideal. But his attacks upon the greed of those who sought to escape from or to limit competition show that he recognized that the kind of competition which he had in mind could exist only if all the competitors were like the ideal prudent man — men anxious to get ahead in all fair ways, but unwilling to do injustice to others. The failure of so many business men to live up to this ideal he explained, in both of his treatises, as a failure due to the warping of their sense of justice by constant association with those who were more their allies than their rivals.[63] The resulting exaggeration of legitimate self-interest into anti-social selfishness was precisely the cause of those systems of public policy against which the *Wealth of Nations* was directed. The system of

[61] Bk. IV, chaps. 1–8, repeatedly attacks the injustice of the restrictions of the "commercial system." See especially chap. 2, and end of chap. 8.

[62] *Wealth of Nations* (McCulloch ed.), pp. 203, 207, 218–219, 298–299.

[63] *Moral Sentiments*, 6th ed., pp. 382–386; *Wealth of Nations* (McCulloch ed.), p. 203.

natural liberty, by guaranteeing to all men the same liberty to compete on equal terms in every market and every field of employment or investment, would thereby deny to all men the right to assert and protect their vested interests at the expense of others and of society.

Competition, in Smith's economic theory, played the role of a restraining force, which would limit the selfishness of every individual by making it necessary for him to treat all with whom he had dealings just as well as his competitors would treat them. There is an analogy between this role of competition in his economic theory and the role of sympathy in the *Theory of Moral Sentiments.* But my present argument is that there is more than this analogy between the two. There is also a dependence of one of these restraining agencies upon the other. Competition could work as Adam Smith thought it should work only in a society whose legal system, and whose current and effective standards of business morality, were products of the effective working of the force of sympathy. It was the moral sentiments engendered by sympathy which dictated the system of natural liberty as the just legal system. And the business man whose sympathies were working normally would accept this regime, seek no favors from the state which would be inconsistent with it, and practice competition in the spirit of it. That many business men were in fact unwilling to do this he was quite realist enough to acknowledge. But he directed his argument mainly against legislative policies which aided groups of grasping business men to escape from the restraints of competition. It was perhaps one of his greatest mistakes that he tended to assume that, if the law and public policy did not help any man to escape from the restraints of competition, he could not escape from them and would be compelled by competition to behave very much as if he had normal sympathies, whether he had them or not.

V

The economic and social philosophies of the physiocrats and Adam Smith, though very different in character, thus came to very similar results. Under a "natural" regime of institutions, or of law and policy, a "natural" economic process would ensure the working out of the right adjustments in the economic system and the maximization of national wealth. For the physiocrats the "natural" legal system was the one indicated by Nature, through certain simple and obvious facts of social life, to the "reason" of the reformer, as the system intended and calculated to promote the general welfare. For Adam Smith it was the system which harmonizes with the moral sentiments that Nature engenders in men's minds through the workings of sympathy. The character or content of the ideal system was about the same for both. It would guarantee to all men certain rights or liberties, thereby denying to every man all privileges inconsistent with the rights of others. It was therefore not a system that implied passivity on the part of governments, or an absence of "social control" of individual behavior and the course of economic events. The "natural" economic process was not an uncontrolled process but the process intended by Nature, and capable of complete realization as the actual economic process only if the state should do its part by establishing the laws and policies prescribed by Nature.

It is, of course, true that the functions of the state, in the ideal regime, were very narrowly conceived and limited, and that the need of any general or far-reaching collective or public control of the economic system, beyond that implied in protecting individual rights, was denied. But this feature of these two economic philosophies was not an inevitable result either of the notion of "natural" economic laws, or of that of juristic "natural law," or of the combination of the two. It was a result of the *content* which these eighteenth-century writers happened to put into the latter of these concepts. Protecting the rights of all individuals against encroachment by other individuals may involve a great deal of state activity, if the rights are defined in a certain way. But the simple legal philosophies of Quesnay and Adam Smith defined individual rights in such a way that only a very limited amount of state activity appeared to be necessary.[64]

[64] It is also true that the assumption that the "reason" (in one case) or the "sympathies" (in the other) of the individual himself would generally go far to make him respect the rights of others, played a part here.

Moreover, they failed to see that, in addition to its function of protecting rights, the state has a function of leadership of group activities.[65] As it happened, the efforts of governments of that day to exercise this function of leadership, in relation to industry and commerce, or to assist in the promotion of national wealth, had taken forms which they regarded, with much justification, as involving unfair partialities to special groups and interests, and as inept for their purpose. For this reason they condemned those efforts as contrary to the plan and precepts of Nature. But if other functions of the state besides those which they assigned to it had appeared to them to be functions which it needed to exercise, in order to play its own part most effectively in promoting the general welfare, their philosophies would have permitted and would even have compelled them to regard these other functions also as ordained by Nature.

In saying this, I am neither denying the importance of, nor condoning, the laissez-faire note in these two economic philosophies. The physiocrats and Adam Smith did say that, in guaranteeing to all men impartially those rights or liberties which they regarded as "natural," the state would be doing about all that wise Nature required or permitted it to do, for its part, in promoting the general welfare; and that, in doing much more than this in the way of controlling economic activities, it would be violating the precepts of Nature and interfering with the harmonious "natural" working of the economic system. In thus claiming the sanction of "Nature" for their particular ideals, they gave those ideals a certain dogmatic rigidity. And in interweaving the exposition of their ideals with their expositions of explanatory economic theory, they built a laissez-faire bias into the structure of economic thought.

[65] Cf. Dickinson, "Social Order and Political Authority," *Am. Pol. Sci. Rev.*, May 1929.

4

ECONOMICS VERSUS POLITICS

~

I

The foregoing essays in this pamphlet[1] have dealt with parts
of the New Deal, exclusively or mainly from the standpoint of
the economics of recovery, in each case analyzing important
economic facts conditioning the progress of recovery, and the
probable effects, in the light of these facts, of measures embodied
in the New Deal upon that progress. In other words, the criticisms offered have been based upon the economic realism which
insists that policies aiming to promote recovery will, in fact,
retard recovery if and where they fail to take account correctly
of stubborn facts in the existing economic situation and of the
arithmetic of business as it must be carried on in the economic
system we are trying to revive. The antithesis of this economic
realism is the vaguely hopeful or optimistic idealism in the field
of economic policy as such, which feels that good intentions,
enough cleverness and the right appeal to the emotions of the
people ought to insure good results, in spite of inconvenient
facts. The arguments built upon facts, in the foregoing essays,
are an antidote to "wishful thinking" of this kind.

There is, however, a similar error in the field of *politics*,
which must also be avoided in any *fully* realistic discussion of

---

[1] This article is reprinted, by permission, from *Economics of the Recovery Program*, by Seven Harvard Economists. Copyright, 1934. McGraw-Hill
Book Company, Inc.

the merits of the New Deal. If the valid arguments that start with economic facts only, and lead only to conclusions about the effects of policies upon recovery, are construed, in every case in which these effects are found to be unfortunate, as adequate grounds for immediate, total condemnation of the policies in question, this further inference is unwarranted. For it may be said to involve *political* idealism in the sense of the bland assumption that policies *ideally* adjusted to *economic* realities *must be possible*, in spite of all of the inconvenient *political* realities to which, in fact, intelligent policies must also in some measure be adjusted in our complex world. Political appeasement is a necessary part, although it is not the whole, of the effort to promote recovery; and only wishful thinking, or no thinking, about political possibilities could lead us, the authors of this pamphlet, to take the leap beyond our findings which have to do only with economic results of measures now in force, to final judgments unrestrained by any serious attempt to face the question whether, in view of the political situation created by the depression, the less fortunate measures in some cases may not be, in large part, the practical alternatives to *worse*, not better measures.

My colleagues, however, in their contributions to this pamphlet have not taken this leap, from judgment or appraisal of one set of results in the light of one set of data, to any absolute or final judgment; and in undertaking, as my contribution, to say something about political and other non-economic considerations which a final judgment must take into account, I am *not* undertaking or proceeding *either* to criticize any legitimate interpretation of their views *or* to interpret away anything of the very definite, real and substantial force of what is adverse to the New Deal in their findings about its economic results. As it is one thing to say that a policy is hindering, not helping, recovery, and another to condemn it without asking whether, through political appeasement, it is not preventing resort to policies even *more* detrimental to recovery, and in this very different sense *relatively* aiding recovery, or doing as much to aid it as can be done in the circumstances; so also, it is one thing, even if we reach this latter conclusion in a given case, to justify the policy on grounds of political necessity, and another to gloss over or deny or minimize the fact or the importance of its still unfortunate economic results.

For if we assume that political necessity makes economic error less erroneous, wholly excuses it, or makes it useless or inadvisable to point out the error and insist upon it, we assume that political necessity is absolute; that the wishes of the people cannot be changed in the least by education in economics, or by the economic lessons of political experience, so that the government is bound simply to cater to those wishes as they are and can have no degree of freedom in its choice of means in the effort to retain its prestige by serving their real interests. It is really this attitude of political fatalism, and not the sound political realism of which it is the unsound exaggeration, that so often leads high-minded men in office, and students of politics or political science, into the illusions of the over-sanguine economic idealism that refuses to admit the limitations imposed by economic necessities upon the possibility of giving all groups of citizens their hearts' desires through governmental action. It is human nature to believe that what is strictly inevitable must be beautiful and good; and the statesman who feels that for him the voice of the people as he understands it is the voice of Fate is likely also to feel that it is the voice of God, correctly and certainly, in spite of mere economic laws, revealing the way to better times and a better order of things.

The converse error, against which economists, that is, those who *are* economists, not politicians, and who know their science well enough to know that there *are* economic laws, need to be on their guard, is exaggeration of their economic realism into the kind of economic fatalism that, in practice, carries with it an illusion properly described as political idealism. Economic necessities are real, but they are not absolute; that is to say, the hard facts of the economic situation upon which the government tries to act, and the laws or the logic inherent simply in those facts, do in very definite and decisive ways confine within rather narrow limits the range of real possibilities and the greatest possible measure of accomplishment in the way of successful governmental action to improve the lot of all the people, or of any very large body of the people; but they do not limit the government to *one only* possible or economically defensible program in respect of any or all items of policy. And the one they indicate as *ideal* in the sense of being *ideally* adapted to the economic situation and the end of maximizing the sum of economic benefits to all, attainable in that situation, is practically certain *not* to be in the range of *politically* possible programs.

In other words, the right attitude for both economists and political experts is one in which the special "realism" of each group restrains or limits or makes realistic the "idealism" of the other. Complete or perfect adaptation of policy to economic facts alone is never possible, because the conflict of human interests, ideals and wills, which is politics, forever makes this impossible; and just as definitely, the unsurpassable limits of economic possibility must forever preclude any complete fulfillment of the popular will.

II

The political forces that interfere with or prevent any full attainment of economic rationality in national policies are always in evidence to some extent, even in "normal" times, and are always greatly intensified in the political situations that develop in the course of severe depressions. These forces are political pressures brought to bear upon the government, by the numerous overlapping groups and classes of great "interests," sections, industries, etc., of which the nation is composed, in favor of measures that benefit the groups which manage to "put them over," in each case at the expense of some or all of the other groups. But it is political idealism, disillusioned, that is, embittered or otherwise, not in any case true realism, to blame *merely* the reprehensible group selfishness or cupidity of all these national estates or "interests," and the selfishness, stupidity and low cunning of politicians who serve them, for these political battles and resulting measures of national policy which interfere with the restoration of equilibrium in the national economic system.

The greatest names in the history of real political science or political realism are the names of Machiavelli and Hobbes; and

we still can learn from them the basic general fact of all politics
— that the measure in which any man or body of men *can
afford* to refrain from trying to use political and other available
forms of power to gain advantage over others in the same society
is only the measure in which a like reciprocal restraint is practiced by or imposed upon all others in that society. In the great
society of nations, this hard fact accounts for the extreme difficulty of the problems of disarmament and international peace.
The common interest of all in ending the costly and dangerous
struggle for power, and accepting modestly defined rights and
some impartial, peaceful method of adjusting claims is entirely
clear; yet no one nation, whatever may be the illusions of its
pacifists or international political idealists, can afford not to use
its strength to get more strength, wherever possible at the cost
of others, so long as *the others* are doing the same thing. And
within each nation, in spite of the large extent to which effective
government may restrain and civilize the struggle, the entire
political process is essentially a struggle of economic groups and
classes, sections, industries, etc., catered to by struggling parties,
to gain and use political power and get the greatest relative
advantage by a suitable reshaping of all available and serviceable
economic policies of the state.

In this political warfare, no politician or political party or
faction can afford to sacrifice or gravely endanger his or its
political life, by obeying a much higher or more scrupulous code
than that on the average maintained for all, by such traditions
of honor and fairness and devotion to the service of the nation,
not of partial or special interests, as the nation in question may
have managed to evolve. It is folly to blame any man or body of
men in public life for doing in office — or in getting and holding office — the things that have to be done in order to survive
in politics because in that game everybody does them against
everybody else — because they are the existing rules of the
game. The only hope lies in slow improvement of the rules; and
any nation is fortunate if the unwritten rules of its political life
are good enough to save it from flagrant general corruption in
times of peace and plenty, and from inevitable resort to real

dictatorship or civil war in times of defeat or lowered status in the international struggle, or of economic depression at home.

Moreover, even more important than full recognition by their critics of the hard realities than men in high and low public office in the nation have to face, in the shape of the moves on the part of their political rivals which have to be met or anticipated in kind, is an equally full recognition of the corresponding fact about the positions of the great economic groups or interests in the nation, whose support these men in office require No one great group of this kind — the farmers, labor, the business class, the bankers, Wall Street, tariff beneficiaries, creditors, debtors, tax payers, tax eaters or any other group with a common interest in one side of any possible political issue — *can afford not* to exercise upon the government, through its votes and its lobbies and all the weapons it can use, enough political pressure and unscrupulous cunning to bend the policies of the government in its favor if it can, to an extent at least sufficient to make up for its losses in this game to other groups at other times in the past and future, and on other issues in respect of which it may be losing at the current time. The penalty of failure or inability to exert enough pressure to offset, on the average over the long run, the opposing pressures of other groups gaining governmental favors partly at the expense of the given group is slow or rapid decline into poverty under the influence of governmental policies insidiously operating to alter the distribution of wealth in favor of successful groups. And any group that does not utilize the opportunities afforded by the existing rules of the national political game, or within these rules do as much of what it can do as it must do in order to hold its own in the struggle, is not virtuous but foolish, so long as the rules and the conduct of the other groups are what they are.

Yet while political realism must insist upon these facts, economic realism must, no less, insist upon the no less evident facts, that this political struggle among economic groups is a thing at all times detrimental to the economic progress of the nation; that in times of depression, when the struggle becomes more intense, it hinders national recovery; and that every group has an interest in cessation of the struggle, or in such restriction or mitigation of its scope and methods as is possible, which is as clear as its interest in at least holding its own in the struggle, as long as the latter confronts it as an inescapable fact. Direct and indirect costs or losses incurred by every group in waging the struggle are deductions from any relative advantage it may be able to gain; the national income and wealth are less than they would otherwise be, because the struggle and its shifting fortunes cause continual dislocation of the economic system and reduce its efficiency, and in gaining a relative advantage over others any group can gain only an increased fraction of a lessened total; and the constant threat to its security is a gambling risk, against which it can have no adequate insurance, in the average winnings it may stand to gain over any long run of time.

The real economic interest of every group or segment of the people must lie in an all-around renunciation or very stringent limitation of "class legislation" and of the underlying struggle for power and relative advantage, *unless* some one group or class can really hope to carry through a social revolution on the Marxian model, abolish, that is, absorb all other groups, and create entirely in its own interest the wholly new economic and social structure of the "classless" society. There are only these two conceivable ways of escape from the costs and hazards of a struggle, the existence of which is detrimental to all, in spite of the fact that, while it exists or continues, some groups may, for a time, gain more, or lose less, than others. If any one group could continue indefinitely to gain by the struggle, at the cost of the others, that group *would* in time be able to reshape the social order entirely to its own maximum advantage. The problem in this respect is similar to the problem of international peace. If any one nation in the modern world could grow strong enough to conquer and annex all the others, it might establish a "Roman peace," like that in the ancient Roman empire, and in the end confer an economic benefit upon all peoples. But as this solution is clearly impossible among nations in the modern world, the nations are being forced, by economic realism as well as by ethical ideals, to face the desperately hard task of reaching a general binding agreement giving every nation the security without which it cannot afford to disarm and give up all the procedures of "power politics" in the conduct of its foreign affairs.

As the Roman solution of the international problem is impossible, so also, at least in this country, the Marxian or any similar solution of the other problem is, I think, clearly impossible, in any visible future. We have never had in this country, and there is no prospect that we ever shall have, a straight or simple "class struggle" involving only two important classes and conforming, in its evolution, to the Marxist pattern. Our "capitalist" class is internally divided into groups with rival interests as important as their common interest in resisting the demands of labor. American labor is likewise not homogenous; the "aristocracy of skilled labor" is not proletarian, and even our real proletariat seems likely, in view of the character and effects of recent technological advance, to continue only as a decreasing, not increasing, fraction of our population; for if such advance in a measure threatens the position of skilled labor of the old types, it now calls rather for increased numbers of technicians of many kinds than for great masses of unskilled labor. The farmers are a large bloc by themselves, with some interests on the side of industrial and financial capital as against labor, other interests the other way in that conflict, and its own most important unique interests opposed alike to those of urban labor and of urban capital. Above all, our large and important and by no means disappearing or declining "middle class," of people in all the professions, petty businesses, "white collar" occupations and the like is likely to continue to hold the balance of power among all classes and make it impossible for any group to work its will completely upon all others.

The interest, then, of every American group still lies in some agreed limitation of the special claims of every group by those of all the others. Our essential difficulties lie in the weakness of restraints effectively imposed by our system of law and government upon particular or special interests and their efforts to exploit one another — a weakness which lessens the security of every group and leads, in times of depression, to just such desperate struggles of rival groups for contradictory forms of "class legislation" as are manifested in the New Deal. The rivalry of industrial and financial "capitalist" groups, in times of prosperity, in division of the spoils of exploitation of labor, the farmers, consumers and small investors, intensifies the ensuing depressions and evokes in depressions the bitterness of the formerly exploited groups which leads them, in the access of political power which they gain in the time of general distress, to become in their turn exploiters of the "capitalist" groups and of one another, employing as weapons forms of legislation tending not to renew prosperity for all, but to redress the balance of advantage in the complex intergroup struggle.

There is thus a genuine problem of reform in our social order, indissolubly bound up with the more immediate problem of recovery from this depression. In the circumstances, some concessions to the spirit of revenge or sense of justice on the part of groups formerly exploited in "prosperity" are inevitable; and although in the absolute sense they hinder recovery, they may, if skillfully made, contribute, through political appeasement, a relative assistance to recovery in the way of prevention of alternative measures still more detrimental to it. But the fundamental problem of reform is not that of appeasing present demands for redistribution of wealth and retribution upon capitalist groups; it is the problem of imposing new and more effective all-around limitations upon the future power of every group to exploit the others, and securing now as much limitation of the intergroup struggle for relative advantage in legislation as is compatible with immediate political necessities, in order that the handicap imposed by this struggle upon general recovery may be made as small as possible. The effort to solve — as well as they can be solved together — the economic and the political problem facing the administration involves an effort to solve the ethical problems of reform; and the latter must be approached in terms of a general view of the evolution of our American social order.

III

The laissez-faire ideal of government, which on the whole has been the dominant American ideal until the New Deal came along, was in its origins precisely the ideal of an all-around renunciation of and binding guarantee against all special interest legislation, and all forms of the struggle for power and advantage over others, in economic and political life. If we roughly translate *laissez faire* as "let alone," it never meant that the government should in all matters let business alone, or let the people as individuals or as groups and classes alone, in their business dealings and relations with one another. It meant, rather, that the government should compel all classes and individuals to let one another alone, or keep their hands off of wealth belonging to others, and should itself let alone the pursuit and the fruits of honest labor, investment, enterprise and commerce, or refuse to let itself be used as the agent of any group seeking to gain at the expense of any other. The ideal was ethically as well as economically tenable; the weakness was not in the ideal as such but in the program of measures for its attainment, and was due to an underestimate on the part of the "liberal" idealists, who framed this program, of the strength of forces opposed to the realization of their ideal — the forces of particular as opposed to common interests, and of the unscrupulous greed and cunning manifested in evasions of constitutional and civil law, in the struggle for power and relative advantage in the fields of business and of politics.

The cornerstone of the "liberal" program was the law and ethics of property and contract, which in spirit or intention are the law and ethics of common honesty in all business relations, and in the relations between government and business. Honest business is not pursuit of power and advantage over others; it is production and exchange of goods and services on terms of *mutual* advantage to both parties in every transaction. The liberal theory relied upon universal freedom of contract, respect for the property rights of others, and the general prevalence of competition among many sellers and among many buyers in free markets, to guarantee the mutuality of advantage in every transaction in such markets, by giving each party alternative opportunities to use in bargaining, or opportunities to seek the bargain most to his advantage. The possession by *all* of such opportunities carries with it as consequence a lack of power on the part of *any* citizen or group to gain a one-sided advantage, exploit others, or compel them to accept bargains not in like measure advantageous to themselves.

Discouragement of monopoly, and strict regulation by the state of any and all actually emerging monopolies, always have been integral parts of the actual program of *laissez faire* or economic liberalism, and of the corresponding legal theory of private property. The property rights of every citizen are his rights to what he can lawfully and honestly obtain for his services or products in open, free or competitive markets, and, if he has a monopoly, to what he *could* obtain for the same investment of labor and/or capital, in producing other things to sell in free markets. If he gains more than this, he is confiscating the property of others; and the regulation of all complete or partial monopolies by this criterion is only one implication of the basic ideal behind the law of property and the program of *laissez faire* for enforcing honesty in all business relations. This one implication logically covers not only things traditionally recognized as monopolies, but equally the much more widespread forms of partial monopoly only recently discovered or apprehended in their full significance by economic theory; although in this case, as in much of the liberal program, reliance must in practice be placed much more in the development of effective, high, informal standards of "business ethics" than in the strong arm of the law. Besides abuse of monopoly powers, all violations of trust or confidence, of fiduciary obligations, all forms of misrepresentation and fraud in advertising and in selling goods or securities, the use of opportunities to exploit labor (in most if not in all cases arising from partial monopolies, in this case of readily available jobs, on the side of the employer) and other things of these kinds are, of course, ruled out by the ideal.

The failure in the past to achieve a more adequate realization of the ideal of economic liberalism has been due to persistent misunderstandings which grew out of the fact that its early advocates saw only one side of the practical task before them in anything like realistic terms. The forms of interference of unscrupulous group interests with equal liberty and opportunity for all individuals, against which the early battles of liberalism were directed, were those directly involving the use of the powers of government, law and custom to close markets to members of rival groups; and the "negative" character which liberalism assumed as a protest merely against "restrictions" of one sort became a dogma which blinded later adherents to the development of other evils requiring new measures of regulation, logically demanded in view of those evils by their own ideal. And this failure to develop the positive implications of the ideal has caused it to fall into increasing discredit, so that opposition to these modern evils has unfortunately tended to become the monopoly of new radicals who are not *economic* realists.

The lack of realism in the views of the older liberals was not at all in their views within the true field of economics, but in other views in what is properly the extensive field of political science — the science of "politics," as a class of activities appearing in the field of business or of private pursuits, as well as in the field of government. True realism requires us to build upon observable facts, but it also requires us to make and consistently adhere to the logical distinctions without which we are bound to confuse different problems and different aspects of the facts that we observe. Economic science is the science of situations and activities involved in the effort of society and its members to achieve economy, or efficiency, in the use of material resources and of labor to increase wealth, or the supply of means of satisfying wants; and all that has to do not with this quest for efficiency, but with the struggle for power and advantage over others in the distribution of its fruits, is of the nature of political activities, realistically conceived as such by Machiavelli and Hobbes, and belongs in the domain of political science.

Such things, for example, as the rivalry of groups of great capitalists or financiers for control of industrial empires, and the rivalry of different trade unions for control of employment in certain trades, are not forms of economic competition at all, but political campaigns, of the same nature as the rivalry of political parties or factions and underlying supporting groups in the electorate for control of the government. Most actual business competition is a mixture, in some proportion or other, of true economic competition, that is, rivalry in efficiency of service to

the public and competitive bidding for the unforced patronage
of the public, with the Machiavellian rivalry for power to ma-
nipulate markets, deprive the public of alternatives, or mislead it
in its judgment of alternatives, and obtain the rewards not of
superior efficiency but of superior strategic power and position.
This second type of business rivalry frequently entails the use
of pressure upon the government for removal of legal impediments that stand in the way of the designs of one business faction,
or creation of new legal obstacles to block the designs of the
opposing faction; but whether it entails this or not, in particular
cases, the end sought — the spoils of victory in a struggle for
power — and the means employed — manipulation of opinion,
maneuvers putting opponents and often sectors of the public in
positions permitting only a choice of evils, surprise tactics and
the like — in all cases make this kind of activity describable only
as the politics of business, not economic competition.

The economic realism of the early advocates of *laissez faire*
appeared in their recognition of the fact that the common interest of all citizens in the efficient regular functioning of the
total system of economic activities requires suppression of the
interference with this system, of political activities growing out
of the mutual warfare and insecurity of special interests, and
carrying with them rationalizations of those special interests,
or fallacious views of the common interest, really originating in
them. But a lack of political realism led those reformers to suppose that severe limitation of the power of the government to
interfere at the behest of special interests would be sufficient,
for all time, to remove the evil. They assumed that repeal of the
old forms of governmental interference would result in the
emergence and endurance of pure or perfect economic competition as the only form of actual business competition; and it
logically followed that it would result in a perfect harmony,
under these new conditions, of all private or particular interests
with the economic interest of the public as a whole. The error
lay in failure to foresee the development, within the business
world itself, of large-scale units and groupings, corporate, capital
structures and the like, inevitably leading to new forms of direct
political warfare among these entities, supplemental endeavors

to control and misuse the machinery of government, exploitation of labor, agriculture and consumers, and retaliation by the latter groups through pressure on the government for undiscriminating, punitive and restrictive measures aimed against "big business."

The task of suppressing the interference of all forms of "politics" with honest business and with the economic system as such has thus grown to be, in our time, a task more urgent than ever, extremely difficult, and requiring of those who undertake to show the way a combination of economic and political realism that is usually absent among conservatives and radicals alike. Political realism must recognize that the prior condition of any abatement of the efforts of the radical political leaders of the discontented classes, labor and the farmers, to exploit and oppress honest and dishonest business alike, for the benefit of those classes, is reform of dishonest business and elimination or control of practices involved in the power strategy of business interests. Men must have security against the intervention of governmental and other superior forms of power against them in their markets, if they are not to take all the revenge that they can when they, in turn, have the power. And, on the other side, economic realism must recognize that, in our present situation, the common interest of all in a general recovery of honest business, agriculture and employment is most endangered by the power strategy and economic illusions of the discontented classes; by the passion for reform that indiscriminately attacks, along with real abuses, the normal practices and gains of honest economic competition; and by the fallacious economic theories or fallacious views of the way to recovery for all, which are rationalizations of the rival demands of different groups in distress.

The ethical reform and regulation of industrial competition and finance, in the effort to make a higher standard of honesty possible for each unit in the business and financial worlds, by enforcing a higher standard upon all, is an aim which must have the ungrudging support of all true "liberals" in the older sense of the word, and of all intelligent conservatives. It is dangerous to attempt too much just now in the way of such reform, because the uncertainties attending its progress add to the difficulties even of honest business and impede recovery. But it is more dangerous to hold back too much and not push needed reforms now, because the millions who want reform as' well as recovery know that they will not get reform if they wait until recovery is complete; and if they are not assured that real reform is under way, they will support increasingly radical, undiscriminating, destructive measures. Perfection is not attainable in this world, in the average honesty of business men, of politicians or of any class; but the penalty of failure to make progress in these matters may be retrogression and collapse.

Yet no real friend of progress in the creation and enforcement of higher standards of business ethics will refuse to heed words of caution. The spirit of resentment and retaliation is not disinterested idealism or the truly ethical spirit, but it often wears the mask of the latter; and even the most genuine idealism in this sense of the word is not enough. The task is not one for emotional thinking; it is a technical task of great complexity, difficulty and delicacy. To attack conspicuous individual financiers for doing in the boom years things that were within the rules of the game of high finance as all their allies and rivals played it in those years, or things they more or less had to do in self-defense, the rules being what they were, is both pointless and unjust. Attention should be focused only on the rules of the game. And in the effort to improve the rules, care must be taken to frame them in full view of the real necessities of honest business, in order not to interfere with the indispensable services to the public of institutions and groups which do render such services, even when they are accompanied by indefensible and harmful practices, which must be sheared away while leaving their ability to render their real services intact. The recklessness of ignorant emotional efforts at reform must be held in check, in order to minimize the risks that discourage honest business, while reforms are in the making. And above all, the new codes and regulations must not be allowed to take on forms that will be likely to make them, in the future, new weapons in the power strategy and rivalry of business and other political groups, instead of dampers on that game.

Besides doing all that can be done with safety now, in the way of this kind of reform, the government also is bound, of course, while depression lasts, to give generous aid in various ways to the millions who are in severe distress. But, here again, it is folly to think that only ungenerous or unsympathetic critics will urge realization of the limitations imposed upon the amount of honest, effective and safe generosity possible, by the necessary conditions of the business recovery without which as a concomitant there can be no recovery of agriculture and employment. The wealth of the wealthy cannot all be transferred to the poor, by governmental measures in aid of the latter, and still be available for use within business itself, as capital or the wherewithal to carry on a business recovery; for this recovery cannot be financed in its first stages by an increase of consumer buying — there has to be an increase of investment, that is, investment in new production, long *before* the new products result in products that reach consumer markets. But a still more important point in this whole field of discussion is this: We must get rid of the illusion that, if any two groups, say labor and the farmers, will aid each other to recover by submitting cheerfully to governmental measures that seek to aid each group partly at the cost of the other, they will then be able to enrich each other in a cumulative fashion by exchanging their newly acquired amounts of "purchasing power." As far as each group bears the costs of aid extended to the other, the sum of their net amounts of purchasing power is unchanged. But the crooked theories bred of rationalizations of rival interests or political demands always point to gains in "purchasing power" and juggle the costs or offsetting losses out of sight.

There is also a danger that the effort to balance rival claims upon the government against each other, not by the economically sound method of limiting each by the other or not conceding too much to either, but by the economically unsound method of giving each as much as seems politically expedient, at the cost of the others, will become a precedent and make this policy of mutually canceling subsidies more than ever a lasting tendency in our future scheme of things. The tariff benefits industrial producers competing with imports in the home markets, partly at the cost of the farmers; the farmers have learned to counter this with good political weapons of farm relief; but the damage done to the common interest of all is not lessened, but redoubled, when we simultaneously give both groups what they want. The reward of all labor in goods, or the standard of living of the whole nation, is lowered by increasing the cost to all consumers of both industrial and farm products. Economic realism requires us to see political justice to all groups in terms not of equally generous concessions to all, but of equal resistance to all such demands.

The real economist's utopia is now and forever laissez faire, in the sense not at all of inactive government, but of a scheme of policy eliminating all interference of all "politics," or the power strategy and rivalry of special interests in the fields of business and of government, with the orderly, efficient functioning, in the common interest of all, of the system of purely economic activities. Like all utopias really worth our allegiance, this one is, in its full perfection, unattainable. In contrast with it, what may be called the politician's utopia is a social order in which political forces have free play, in a government equally generous to all politically influential, special interests. It is a fortunate fact for the common welfare of all that this utopia, also, is unattainable in its full perfection, unless mankind should lose the faculty of reason. Our New Order must be a realistic compromise between two unattainable ideals. In the measure in which we are able to suppress "politics" within the business world, we may be able to have government in the common interest of all, not government controlled by "politics." But in the measure in which the power strategy of business interests, in business and in the dealings of the government with business, continues to result in exploitation by those interests of the larger mass of the people, we must expect and allow the great segments of that larger mass to organize their own, offsetting power strategy, and become exploiters in their turn, when they have the chance.

5

ECONOMIC THEORY, AND CERTAIN

NON-ECONOMIC ELEMENTS

IN SOCIAL LIFE[1]

୶

Economic theory of the traditional type is "abstract" in the sense, among others, that its own special subject matter or what it describes is not any concrete, empirical *part* of all that exists and goes on in human societies, but is only one abstract, *i.e.*, one logically discernible or distinguishable *element in* all human action and social life — the element known as economizing, or "economic, rational action." The actual members of actual societies do, with various amounts of intelligence, knowledge, care, and skill, "economize" or practice rational "economy" in the acquisition and use of available, scarce means to satisfy their wants, in various degrees approaching the limit of ideal perfection in this art, or tending to make the economic choices which, in their circumstances, would maximize their incomes and their total amounts of realized want-satisfaction. But economic theory, as the "pure" theory of ideal "economizing," departs in *two* respects from any literal, complete, and exact description of any

[1] This article is reprinted, by permission, from *Explorations in Economics*, F. W. Taussig Memorial Volume. Copyright 1936. McGraw-Hill Book Company, Inc.

concrete, empirical actions and events. For one thing, instead of describing the, in various degrees, imperfect "economizing" actually practiced (in capitalistic societies) by actual businessmen, investors, wage earners, and consumers, it describes the ideal or perfect "economizing" which is only the *limit* approached by this one element or tendency in actual, human behavior. And the other departure from concrete, empirical reality is logically prior to this; that is, the element or tendency in human actions which is thus described in terms of what it would be in its full perfection is first of all conceptually isolated or abstracted out of the whole complex of aims or motives, arts and tendencies which *together* produce and, along with the relevant objective situations or conditions, determine all concrete actions and events.

Now from all this it follows that economic theory of this type can be a usefully close approximation *to* description of concrete realities, *only in or as applied to* societies in which the characters of all the non-economic elements of action having any important effects upon events within the concrete sphere of social life that we loosely call "economic" — the sphere of industry and trade — in fact fulfill two conditions. In the first place, to make economic theory in this sense usefully applicable to a society, the non-economic elements of its social life must be such as to give and allow a *predominant* role or effect, within the concrete "economic" sphere, to pure "economizing" as such, *i.e.*, to "economic, rational action" in a well-developed, nearly perfect form. And in the second place, the characters of these other elements must be *stable* enough, over the whole area and epoch studied, to make it possible to take them for granted as merely forming the constant milieu within which "economizing" goes on. In the measure in which there is departure from fulfillment of these two conditions, in any society or epoch, pure economic theory as applied to it loses concrete relevance or explanatory value; and in any case, a full awareness of the interrelations of the economic element and the major non-economic elements of social life is essential for economists who wish to make the most effective use of economic theory in concrete studies of any kind.

The object of the present brief essay is only to outline a view

of three of the (in this connection) most important, non-economic elements of social life, in their main relations to the economic element; and of characteristics they must have to *minimize*
the amount of divergence of the actual pattern of events in the
concrete "economic" world, from the pattern to be expected in
the case according to economic theory, *i.e.*, from that which
would result from pure and perfect "economizing" on the part
of all the members of the actual society, in their actual *objective*
situations. The three non-economic elements to be considered
are (1) technology; (2) the *power* element, *i.e.*, the pursuit and
use by members of society of coercive power to control the
actions of other members and (as one use of power) exploit
others for their own gain; and (3) the element of prevailing
ethical attitudes. Of these elements the two last named are, in
their mutual interaction, the chief immediate determinants of
the institutional structure of society, social policies, and the
amount of encouragement and free play or the reverse given and
allowed to pure "economic" tendencies. But the character of a
society's technology, as this affects and is affected by all other
elements of its social life, is the element which, in immediate
interplay with the purely objective situations in which men act,
determines *from that side* so to speak, as the element of ethical
attitudes determines *from the other side* (of motives), the degrees
and forms of the manifestations and the interrelations of the
"economic element" and the "power element" in the concrete
structure and processes of social life.

The extent to which any form or kind of society meets the
requirements, in respect of the characters of the non-economic
elements of its culture and structure and the actions of its members, for approximation of the pattern of its *industrial* life to
that predicted for this by the theory of pure and perfect, rational
"economizing" in all production and consumption, is of course
a matter of degree. Thus even primitive societies meet these requirements to some extent, and there is in them some (remote)
approximation to this pattern, as even primitive men "economize" although, on account of the characters of other elements
in their way of life, their "economizing" is not sufficiently systematic, rational, accurate, and un- or little-interfered with by

their other aims and necessities, to make any pure theory of ideal economizing, applied to their concrete economic activities, describe the latter with *a close enough* approximation to reality to be highly useful. Of the types of societies thus far known to history, modern capitalism undoubtedly meets all the requirements here in question in fuller measure than any other; but they *might* be met still more completely in a future socialist or communist society, if that is ever achieved. The requirement controlling all others is a high development, and strong predominance in one (the industrial) sphere of action, of economic rationality; and as this is a phase of rationality in general, it presupposes the existence of a well-developed, widely prevalent, and relatively highly effective, rational culture, in related ways affecting all elements of action or of social life. But we may now turn, bearing this general requirement in mind, to the special requirements, all at least partly implied in it, in regard to the characters of a highly "economic" society's technology, of the "power element" in its structure and functioning, and of the ethical attitudes prevailing in it.

Economy and Technology

Technology, considered as a pure element of action, in conception wholly divorced from the economic element, concretely always in some measure bound up with it, consists only of applications of (more or less) scientific knowledge to the task of using available materials and human and other natural energies, *no matter at what cost available,* to turn out products having desired or specified qualities. In other words, "pure" technology consists only of adaptations of particular, physical means or causes to the end of attaining or producing particular, physical results, and in itself involves no consideration of costs in any sense. Concretely, however, or in practice, a scientific (fully rational) technology includes also a part but not the whole of what is in "pure" terms the "economic" element of rational action; because one part of the economic problem in practice falls so directly into the sphere of interest of technological experts that they always regard it as a part of their own problem

— and are all too likely, at the same time, to mistake it for the whole of the economic problem itself. *Concrete* technology, that is to say, aims not only to produce products, but to produce them in ways or by processes having maximum degress of *technological efficiency or economy*, which means minimizing all *purely physical-quantitative components of* production costs, or quantities of materials, man-hours, and physical energy units consumed per unit quantity of product produced.

Now this calculation of maximum technological or physical efficiency or economy, while appropriate as a part of the practical activity of engineers, does not of itself provide all the knowledge required for the practice of "economy" in the complete sense of the word; for it fails to consider, on the one hand, the *degree of utility* of each product (marginal utility per unit) in relation to consumers' wants, and on the other hand, the "scarcity values" of the means used up in production, which derive from and reflect degrees of utility of alternative products producible with the same means. Thus a process of production which is more "efficient" or "economical" than another, if both are judged by the limited, technological-economic standard, will be *less* "economical" in the complete sense whenever its superiority in respect of purely physical "economy" is more than counterbalanced by higher degrees of marginal utility, in competing uses, of the means required, *relatively* to the marginal utility of the product produced. For "economy" in the complete sense means not production of maximum physical outputs with minimum physical amounts of means, but instead, production of maximum amounts of utility or want satisfaction, with minimum sacrifice of alternative, possible satisfactions (of other wants) obtainable with other combinations of the same means.

From these definitions, two points follow in regard to the relation of the character of a society's technology to the role of "economizing" in its industrial life. On the one hand, existence of a fully rational or scientific technology or general state of all industrial arts, with the accurate knowledge this involves of all the qualities and quantities of all productive means required, and of those of all products obtainable from them, in different processes of production, is one prerequisite for the practice of rational "economizing" by producers, in any highly systematic, accurate, well-developed form. But on the other hand this one condition alone, while a necessary, is not a sufficient condition for this result. Development of the part or side of "economizing" which is only pursuit of technological efficiency is indeed so closely involved with that of science and the scientific technology that it always occurs along with, as in practice a part of, the latter. But the other part or side of "economizing" — entailing as it does comparative measurement or weighing against one another of one's own experienced, and of other men's expressed or indicated, subjective wants, satisfactions, and deprivations, and "economizing" in terms of these subjective quantities — requires for its full development as a pronounced feature of the mental and practical habits of the members of a society, the realization or fulfillment in that society of other, cultural, and institutional conditions, additional to and at least partly independent of development of the physical sciences and their industrial applications. One such further requisite is general prevalence among individuals of the "economic, rational" *attitude toward* their wants and satisfactions, or the *disposition* to practice systematic, rational pursuit of the fullest possible, all-around satisfaction of expansive and multiplying wants for worldly goods. And still another requisite is existence either of a system of markets, money, prices, and business enterprises, or of some equivalent for this purpose (facilitation of objective measurement and hence of maximum satisfaction of economic wants) of this whole set of institutions.

It would take us to far afield here to consider the forms in which these essentials of any highly "economic" society might exist, in possible societies otherwise wholly unlike modern capitalism. In the latter, we have, in addition to the scientific technology, wide prevalence of the "economic, rational" attitude to wants and satisfactions, as a main, distinctive feature of the bourgeois attitude to life; and the price system and all the market machinery of capitalism, as a mechanism which (however imperfectly) affords some measures of the relative magnitudes of different wants and marginal increments of satisfactions, and some guidance of production toward maximization of the social aggregate of satisfactions. In the capitalistic society, however, there is often some conflict between the ideas about or for the planning and conduct of production of the engineers, who tend to think too narrowly in terms of the technological-economic, incompletely economic standard of "efficiency," and those of the businessmen, on whom capitalism mainly depends for achievement of "efficiency" or "economy" in the complete sense of the words. For the businessmen, in their positions necessarily concerned not only with technological efficiency but also with their money costs and selling prices, often cannot adopt what the engineers regard as the most "rational" (efficient) plans and methods of production. Hence the engineers often tend to become economic radicals, severely reproaching the businessmen, the price system, and the profit motive, for alleged, gross inefficiency or waste in production. But the value of their criticisms is in general at best uncertain, because their standard of "efficiency" is not the complete or true economic standard, which requires *some* measures — either those afforded by the price system, or if not, some others — of the relative magnitudes of different wants and satisfactions.

Yet of course it cannot be said, either, that *social* "economy," in the complete or true, or any, sense is ideally well served by the businessmen, and other members of our society, who act upon the indications of demand afforded by market prices in the effort to maximize their *private* gains. For the ideal structure of relative prices for different products and means of production — that is, the price structure required to make it pay each and every member of society best to do just that, in his economic activities, whereby he would also make his largest possible contribution to the social aggregate of satisfactions — this ideal price structure is never at all completely realized in fact. That it is not is due to the fact that numerous individuals and groups within society possess and exercise, in various forms and amounts, *coercive power* over others, which can be used as power to increase their own gains not by increase of service to those others, but, instead, by so controlling and limiting the opportunities of the others as to gain at their expense. Through acts involving exploitation of others, on the part of those possessing coercive power in various forms, and through distortions of the price structure incidental to such acts, production in general is made responsive, not impartially or in due proportion to the wants of all but in disproportionate measure to the wants of the individuals and groups wielding the most power. Thus we are brought to consideration of the second in our list of three non-economic elements in social life — the "power element" — and the conditions in respect of this element, upon the measure of a society's realization of which depends the measure in which "economizing" by its members, in their own interests, tends to good "economy" in the use of means of production, from the standpoint of the whole society as such.

Economy and Coercion

Before considering forms of coercive power, possession of which by members of society enables them to exploit other members, we may consider the "pure" relation of economic exchange between human beings, *i.e.*, the exchange relation free of any such power on either side. In this relation, each party confronts the other as *only* a bidder for the other's money or good or service, *and only one of many* rival bidders for it; and can obtain it (if the other acts "rationally" in his own interest) only by offering in exchange something (*a*) of more value *to* the other, or power to satisfy the other's wants, than what he parts with, and (*b*) of more value to him also, in the same sense, than anything offered by any other bidder. Thus in every exchange made under these conditions, *both* parties gain increase of power to satisfy their wants, and as *each* chooses, out of all the exchanges open to him, the one giving him the largest gain, each party maximizes his own gains only by doing more than anyone else would to increase the gains of the other also. There is thus, between the two who exchange, a perfect harmony of interests in the given conditions; and it follows that in a pure exchange economy, or commercial society in which no members or groups had any power over any others, every member in maximizing his private gains would be making, at the same time, his largest possible contribution to the common wealth.

Of the forms of power in the hands of some to exploit others which destroy this harmony of interests, we may consider first some forms of *private* power directly used in purely private transactions, without the aid of any intervention of the public, state, or governmental power; and then the problem, of chief interest to us here, presented by the latter. The most obvious form of private power is the one most sharply illustrated by the power to inflict physical injury, possessed by the armed robber or holdup man. With this power, the robber confines his victim to a choice of evils — "your money or your life"; in other words, so controls his situation or the alternatives open to him that to give up what the robber wants is his relatively best, least disadvantageous, possible choice. In this case, as in that of free exchange, each party makes the best choice for himself that he can make in the given conditions; but the conditions are so controlled by the power of one party that his gain is the other's loss, and there is no net gain for the two combined. The robber, instead of having to outdo rival bidders for the other's money in the way of *rewarding* him, for parting with it, with a greater addition to his wealth, is able to deprive him for the time of all opportunity to make any such gainful exchange or even to keep all he has, and extract his money by a threat, backed up with power, to inflict a *penalty* for *not* giving it up, even worse for him than doing so. Reflection will suggest many variants of this first general case of private power to obtain desired goods or acts from others by depriving them of better alternatives than simply giving in without compensation, and leaving them, if any, only the worse alternative of paying instead whatever penalty, even more onerous for them, can be extracted.

Another form of power to exploit others is that exerted in the practice of deception or fraud of any kind. Deception is coercion, because, by falsifying the victim's apparent knowledge of some or all of the alternatives or opportunities among which he must choose, it deprives him of the power to choose rationally in his own interest, and creates a cause, external to his will, impelling or causing him to choose according to the interest and will of his deceiver. By deceiving others in exchange transactions with them, anyone who is able and chooses to do this and is not prevented can increase his gains at their expense, by giving them less for what they give him than they could obtain elsewhere, if they only had correct knowledge of their opportunities. Thus the two primary forms of power to exploit others are the powers of intimidation and deception. One other form of such power, however, although not *independent* but requiring the *support* of either (private) intimidation or deception or the public power, is what may be called *non-economic monopoly;* and a word about this will be in order, before we turn to the topic of state power.

Any individual or group having a monopoly of the whole supply of goods or services of any one kind, or several kinds, available to another set of persons, has the power to confine these others to the choice, in respect of the thing or things monopolized, of giving what the monopolist demands for them, or going without them and, at best, substituting things of other kinds obtainable elsewhere. Thus any monopoly confers upon the monopolist the power to increase his own gain by reducing that of his victims to an infinitesimal amount more than they would gain by exchanging for the next best (in value to them), inferior substitute for what is monopolized. Two general kinds of monopoly, however, should be distinguished. Where the monopolist is one, *i.e.,* has no competitors, only because, with the same opportunities, no would-be rivals can produce anything of the same kind or kinds with as great a degree of efficiency or economy as he achieves, the monopoly is, in its basis, purely economic; but in this case, while the monopolist need not give his customers the full benefit of his efficiency, or make their gains from dealing with him as great as he *could* make them, he must, to retain their business and his own gains, give them greater gains than any potential rival could give them; thus he can deprive them of nothing they could obtain elsewhere, and in this sense, cannot exploit or rob them. It is only where a non-economic, power element enters in the *basis* of the monopoly, *i.e.,* where competition is *prevented* by intimidation or deception, or by some use of the public power on behalf of the monopolist, that the latter can gain because others are deprived of opportunities and not because he excels in contributions to the common wealth.

Thus intimidation, deception, and non-economic monopoly (only privately supported, by intimidation or deception, as in cases of "racketeering") are at least the principal forms of uses of private power to exploit others, which can flourish without any assistance of the state power and are always likely to flourish unless they are suppressed by it. Now it always has been a principal function of bourgeois states, as organizations of the collective power (of intimidation in the last analysis) of their populations, to prevent, as far as possible, the exploitation of some by others within their borders by any such uses of private power; in other words, to create and maintain as nearly as possible the ideally pure or free exchange economy, or system of exchange relations free of (private) coercive power on either side — a state of things in which, if it could exist in full perfection, all private interests and the public interest, economically speaking, would coincide. The insuperable difficulty, however, in the way of any complete realization of this ideal is that of preventing individuals and especially groups, or sections of society, from gaining control of the state power itself and using this as another and superior instrument or weapon for exploiting others with less *political* power. In fact, in the measure in which a government succeeds in preventing its subjects from exploiting one another directly, in private transactions, or gaining and using any form of purely private power to do this, the struggle to gain and use power for this purpose is not abolished but transferred to the domain of *politics*, as the struggle to gain and hold control of the use of public power. Thus in states which are effectively governed, the greater part of all exploitation, by coercion, of some by others, is carried on in this way; the exploiters bring about, by deception of (other) voters or intrigue with officeholders, governmental measures purporting to be for the common good but really operating to increase the commercial gains of the exploiters, at the cost of other groups and of the common wealth.

It is needless here to describe or enumerate in detail ways in which this process is carried on. With the limited, traditional powers and functions of (non-socialistic) modern governments, manipulations of tariffs, taxes, monetary policies, government expenditures for public works and the like, bounties and loans to favored industries, grants of power to business corporations, encouragement of monopoly (often non-economic) in various forms or emasculation of measures supposed to prevent or regulate monopolies, and innumerable kinds of "special-interest" legislation, have been the weapons of the pressure groups. With the current tendency in most states to add to the functions and powers of governments, exploitation in some directions, by private power and old misuses of the public power, are being checked or diminished, but new misuses of the public power for exploitation of some groups by others also appear, and the balance of gain or loss in this matter is often extremely hard to appraise. The essential point to be made here is only that this whole process, of the acquisition of private wealth by individuals and groups *through* acquisition and use of forms of power to coerce and exploit others, is always in some degree inevitable as one real element in the life of any society, the dimensions or extent of which, however, must be kept as small as possible, if the pattern of the society's concrete economic life is to conform, as nearly as possible, to that described by economic theory as the "pure" theory of "economizing" unmixed with any such uses of coercive power.

Economy and Ethical Attitudes

The extent to which the members of a society are in fact restrained from seeking and using any form of power to exploit their fellows in turn obviously depends in the last resort upon the character and strength of the ethical attitudes prevailing in it. Thus we may conclude this essay with a few words about these attitudes, as the one element of social life already mentioned but not yet discussed. Restraint of the tendencies of men to coerce their fellows for their own ends is in fact *one* of the *two* functions of the special climate of ethical feelings necessary to the constitution of any highly "economic" society, that is, necessary to enable "pure economizing" to be the main, immediate determinant of what happens in industrial life. For this purpose — restraint of coercion — general prevalence of strong and strict feelings in favor of impartial justice, of liberty for all and special privilege for none, of the nearest possible approach to maintenance of full equality of opportunity, of perfect honesty in all private and governmental transactions, and the like, are essential.

It is *only within* a strong framework, so to speak, of socially enforced rules limiting the "rational" pursuit of private interests to modes of action involving no coercive exploitation of others that such activity can go on in the ways and with the results which economic theory describes. And the other function of the moral climate of an "economic" society is to foster, within the limits already referred to, the rational pursuit of private wealth, by making socially respected virtues of the qualities of men and actions which success in this requires.

6

LIBERAL EDUCATION AND LIBERALISM [1]

By successive additions of new to old usages in the course of its long history, the good phrase "a liberal education" has by now acquired, as I will try to show in this paper, three overlapping but largely diverse and in some respects conflicting meanings, which now tend, respectively, to be uppermost in different minds as vehicles of their differing special ideals for education. And because these meanings of a single phrase much used by all parties, and the special clusters of ideals they stand for, are seldom clearly distinguished and understood in their complex mutual relations, current discussions of educational aims are full of confusions which block convergence toward agreement. To make some clarifying suggestions, by sketching the history of education against the relevant background of social and intellectual history, and the origins, contents, and relations of successively developed views of what "a liberal education" means, is the aim of this paper.

Stated as briefly as possible, the three meanings that I speak of are: (1) a general, broad, rounded, or reasonably complete education, in contrast with a merely vocational or otherwise narrow, specialized education; (2) a self-chosen in contrast with a prescribed or uniform education — the free elective system — what I shall call "liberalism in education"; and (3) "education in liberalism" — education designed to form the students into good

[1] Reprinted, by permission, from *Ethics* (April 1945).

"liberals" or loyal and properly equipped participants in and supporters of a "liberal," or free, society and civilization. But these brief statements fail to bring out the manifold of historically formed presuppositions and connotations, common elements, links or bridges, and points of conflict, in this "triad" of conceptions. The starting point for developing fuller understanding lies in recalling the origin and significance of the ancient use of the word "liberal" for (simply) "general" education; and the connections and contrasts between the sense which this word acquired in that application and the modern senses which derive from the modern climate of "liberal" opinions in philosophy, morals, politics, etc. Hence I must now plunge into my sketch of the history of "liberal" education and historic changes in the meaning of the word.

Liberal (Rounded) Education and Modern Democracy

General education was called *liberal* originally because it was the kind of education given to free men and citizens in ancient slave-owning societies. Most of the routine, specialized occupations were carried on by slaves, who had no other functions, and were trained in their single, useful, or vocational arts, but as a rule received no other, broader education. But the free men and citizens formed a ruling class which also was to some extent a leisure class; and the best ancient thinkers held that education for the free men should be education in "the liberal arts" — not the narrowly specialized and crassly utilitarian arts appropriate for slaves, but those applied in mastering life as a whole and public affairs; in a free or independent, reflective, rational pursuit of "the good life," and pursuit in joint deliberation and collaboration with other free citizens, of "the good society." In other words, the free man was held to need a range of knowledge or understanding as ample as the sphere of all his interests and responsibilities; understanding of the cosmos, nature, man, society, beauty, and the principles of moral and political wisdom. The slave needed to understand only the special tasks, the tiny fraction of reality, alone committed to his charge; but the free man needed to make his reason comprehend the whole of reality, that it might with reference to that direct his whole life and give wise counsel in the common effort to direct the whole life of the city.

Now until very modern or recent times, the later development (after antiquity) of education in the Western world also went on in aristocratic societies, in which the popular majorities, while they were not slaves, still were given little or no opportunity or responsibility to be anything more than workers at their jobs or trades. Effective freedom to seek "the good life" *reflectively*, to share all culture, and to share in managing community affairs, was restricted everywhere to the members of ruling, leisured, upper classes. Hence general education remained only upper-class education, and the many as a rule were taught only, through apprenticeships, the practical skills by which they would humbly serve and earn their livings. General education as developed under those conditions was "liberal" — stood in a relation to liberty or freedom — in that it was, not education for life in a free society, but education for the few who were really free in a largely unfree society. Those "liberally" educated were the "gentlemen" who, having assured incomes and social positions, were free from "slavery" to breadwinning jobs and who required education not in special, breadwinning arts but in the general art of rationally ordering their lives and societies in the light of knowledge of the all-embracing order of the universe.

The idea, however, that free men, entirely responsible for their own lives and sharing responsibility for all community life, need an ample, rounded education to fit them for their large, inclusive responsibilities is clearly as valid in a modern democracy where *all* are in this position as it ever was in the pre-democratic societies were only the favored few were in this sense free. The great educational taks in the modern democratic age is to keep "liberal education," in the ancient, eternal, and basic sense fully alive; adapt its means or contents and methods to attainment of the same ends under modern conditions; and extend it to all, up to the utmost limits of their individual capacities. The best aristocracies in history, in their best periods, have consisted largely of truly, broadly, roundly educated or cultivated men, equipped and trained to govern, order, or form their own lives and their societies with much real wisdom. No modern democracy can afford to aim at anything less than lifting all or a large majority of its people up to as good a level of all-around culture and wisdom as was every typical of the best aristocracy. But, to attain such a goal, there is much to do!

Liberal Education for all — and Certain Obstacles

Democracy requires extension to the many of "liberal education" in the old sense, but it has not eliminated, and in some ways has aggravated, a basic obstacle to this achievement. The many are still obliged by economic needs to give first place in their thoughts to earning their livings, and thus are under much pressure to seek chiefly education of a kind directly useful in that connection. "Liberal" education is hard to "sell" to them; and the tendency, moreover, of democracy to foster ambitions to "rise in the world" makes for predominance of the merely "practical" attitude to education, even where elemental needs do not enforce it. Even our "plutocrats," in many cases, or their sons remain so ambitious for still greater economic success as to care little for studies unrelated to that aim. One must take care not to miss the good side of this in condemning the bad side. Economic ambition in all classes has been the mainspring of the economic progress which has raised the living standards of the majority and the surplus wealth of the nation far enough to make adequate education for all begin to look financially feasible. So we must not condemn economic ambition as such, even in the rich. Only where this one desire in life becomes so intense as to submerge other interests is it harmful. But undoubtedly this sort of narrowness of outlook has been widely prevalent in the modern democratic world; rather inevitably so among the economically hard-pressed millions, and far too commonly so in more comfortable strata. Hence prevalent, strong, and persistent demands have forced inclusion in the educational offerings of our schools and colleges of countless courses having only vocational, and no general, educational values. This has been *one* important factor in the modern dilution and disintegration of rounded, liberal education.

But we need to look at other sides of this problem. The change of conditions from the pre-democratic into the democratic age has confronted education as a whole with a threefold task: (1) meeting the needs of all in a democracy for "liberal" education; (2) meeting their needs for modern types of vocational training; (3) working out a rational adjustment and combination of the two parts of everyone's whole education — for reflective living and citizenship and for usefulness in a definite occupation. For in contrast with the old, aristocratic societies, democratic society not only turns all men into free men and citizens but also rejects the idea of a leisure class and demands that all shall make themselves useful in specific jobs. Thus the two kinds of education, once given separately to different classes, must be given together to all alike. And the apprenticeship method of acquiring vocational training has become unavailable or inadequate for countless modern occupations and the greater part of the population. Farming and handicraft skills may still be learned by actual job work under supervision; but, where this group of occupations once employed up to 90 per cent of all the people, it now employs less than half of them; and today even farmers and various sorts of skilled industrial workers need substantial amounts of formal, technical education or schooling to attain the highest levels of expertness in their occupations. Another part of the industrial wage-earning population needs very little vocational training of any kind, and none not easily acquired from industry itself, if its members are content to remain all their lives in the simple lines of work concerned; but the capable and ambitious sons of members of this class do and should, in both their own interests and those of society, seek opportunities to prepare for and enter other occupations in which their services can be of much greater value. And there have grown up a host of new occupational specialties, many of them requiring much elaborate education in modern sciences and applied sciences or technical arts; a host of new "professions," often "narrower" in their ranges of contact with life as a whole, the ranges of mental and personal powers and qualities they exercise, and the ranges of breadths of mental cultivation they require, than the older and long-respected "liberal" professions. Legitimate demands upon all parts of our whole educational system for instruction in vocationally useful arts of many kinds have multiplied enormously; and we need a system able to meet fully all these demands while *also* giving to all students, whatever occupations they may be preparing for, a genuine, liberal, or rounded education, along with and emphatically not as a secondary "side line" to their specialized, vocational educations.

I believe this matter has more importance than is commonly recognized. Boys who go through engineering or other vocational schools in the "college" years and out into life do not receive the rounded education that free men and citizens require, despite the admirable but inevitably inadequate efforts of the best institutions of this type to provide it via a few incidental "humanities" courses. And too many boys who go through "liberal arts" colleges and out into life shamefully go out unequipped to begin useful, working, and earning lives in callings able to use and needing their abilities. "Liberal" or general education in a democracy cannot remain segregated, available in full measure only to the sons and daughters of the well-to-do and to poorer youths who, to get it, sacrifice the chance to become as useful as they should be in skilled occupations — it cannot remain in this position without sinking in the general esteem of the people to the status of an expensive luxury or "frill" or else getting crowded out of its own supposed centers by intrusion into them of increasing numbers of specialized studies really serving mainly vocational ends but doing neither job well because inserted in a haphazard way into a potpourri which ceases to be either rationally organized general, or rationally organized vocational, education. What is needed is an educational system in which, at all levels and in all institutions, every pupil will be given both a group of studies having no vocational but full of "liberal" or cultural significance, and another, smaller and subordinate but adequate, group of strictly "practical" studies definitely oriented to a range of occupational skills adapted to the pupil's aptitudes and prospects. The present situation represents a badly retarded, unfinished, indeed hardly well-started readjustment of education as a whole to the main requirement of modern democracy: that every citizen shall be an expert both in some definite, useful art or occupation and in the general art of the cultivated free man and citizen — reflective, rational

pursuit of the good life and participation in the common, democratic task of building, preserving, improving, and governing a
good society.

Not only do we need to develop, for all future citizens, educations of both kinds, distinguished and rationally combined as parts
of everyone's whole education; but the two parts need in every
case to be integrated into a whole or made to draw upon and
contribute to each other. The democratic citizen in his dual role,
as master of his job and of his life, including his share in the conduct of community life, not only needs to have both understanding of his vocational art and all-around wisdom — understanding of the world, nature, mankind, human history, national and
world problems, himself and his neighbors, aesthetic and moral
values. He also needs a bridge in his mind between his general
and his specialized knowledge — awareness of all the mutual relevance there is, and the ability to see and habit of seeing his occupational specialty in the context of its place in society and in
life as a whole, its relations to other specialties, and its background and place in the whole of all knowledge and wisdom, on
which it draws and in which it has its special niche. Professional
education for the few old, long-esteemed professions has become
in the best cases fairly well integrated with liberal or general education. The student of law, divinity, or medicine finds much that
he learned in college relevant to his professional studies, uses or
applies it and finds new meanings in it, and finds that his professional learning makes incidental but not unimportant contributions to his general education. It is harder to integrate engineering or accounting with a liberal education — the amount of
mutual relevance is less, and harder to bring out — but something
can be done here and should be. And even down in the schools,
home economics or manual training need not be utterly without
contributions from and to the liberal studies of languages, geog-
raphy, history, civics, and the like. The vocational studies may
be the chief gainers from association with the liberal studies, but
there can be a gain in the other direction also. Liberal education
can stand enrichment — if we make it that instead of dilution, by
a rational organization and combination of the two groups of
studies in the place of haphazard mixtures — much enrichment,

and accretion of reality and vitality, from intimate contacts with the "down-to-earth" quality in good vocational courses of whatever sorts particular students take. The old upper-class liberal education, for all its great virtues, suffered somewhat from a tendency to produce envisagement of life, society, and all reality in an overabstract and overliterary way, congenial and satisfying to leisure-class persons having few "earthy" contacts with the maze of petty, stubborn actualities continually wrestled with by working people in their jobs and daily lives. And all aristocratic governments in history have shown tendencies to err in their policies in a way reflecting the lack of complete, genuine realism as well as the lack of full, universal humanity or humaneness to all human beings, engendered by the lacks in the educations and leisure-class lives of the ruling personnel. The lack of realism has typically appeared in tendencies to cling stubbornly to policies dictated by love of glamorous traditions and orthodoxies and pursued with too little understanding or awareness of their actual consequences, the latter being shaped by actual conditions not known or understood in detail. Democratic citizens should be so educated that they will fruitfully combine the wisdom dependent on knowledge of high, general principles with the flair for empirical and practical realism emphasized in their vocational specialties and transferable in a measure to all their judgments, if their educations have shown them how to make such a transfer.

One other source of difficulty in the task of extending liberal education to all in a democracy must be noticed briefly. Democratic ideals imperatively require that this be done to the fullest possible extent, but the fact must be faced that all men do not have equal mental capacities. Not all can ascend all the way to the top of the educational ladder; millions cannot, with profit to themselves or to others, go beyond the elementary-school level; other millions can do no more than finish secondary-school educations; the colleges can benefit only a fraction of the total population. Yet any idea of restricting the privilege of receiving a liberal education to a select minority is rightly to be condemned as antidemocratic. One part of the answer to this must lie in making the main (not vocational) part of the education given in the

Economics and Liberalism

lower school true liberal education as far as it goes: education implanting in the children not merely assortments of temporarily memorized information, unrelated rudiments of 'sundry intellectual techniques, and vague, unreal impressions of all sorts, but a lasting comprehension of sound generalizations about the world, nature, human nature, society, and history in their own and other countries, international relations, the rights and duties of citizens, neighbors, parents and children, etc. And the rest of the answer must lie in making continuance on up the educational ladder depend solely on individual abilities and not at all on financial resources.

But I have so far been touching only on the fringes of the great problem of realizing liberal education, in the old and basic sense, in a modern democracy. Extending it to all and combining it with vocational educations for all are important, but the most essential and most difficult part of the problem is to preserve it in being at all — some would say to restore it after a long absence — for anybody. Of course, the means or particular contents — subjects of study, etc. — must differ a good deal from what they were in the upper-class liberal education which became standardized in the later predemocratic centuries. The aesthetic good taste and moral and political wisdom in the Greek and Latin classics; the knowledge of science and nature supplied by a simple corpus of mathematics and "natural philosophy" (inclusive natural science, mainly physics, in an early stage of development); and the knowledge of "first principles" and the unity of the whole realm of reason, supplied by general philosophy or philosophy proper as long as there was a generally accepted synthesis; those were the essential elements in the truly admirable and effective, rounded education, received by the whole upper class or governing class in every civilized occidental country down to about two centuries ago. But the modern free man and citizen needs education in modern languages, literatures, and fine arts, world history and that of his own country, various natural and social sciences which are now much subdivided and immensely complicated, and various, rival views in philosophy. And here emerges the really crucial problem: preserving (or restoring) liberal education in our time is made immensely difficult by the vast variety, complexity, and lack of understood unity in the total corpus of modern knowledge.

The Crucial Obstacle: Specialization and the State of Modern Knowledge

It is essential to grasp and face the truly overwhelming nature of this obstacle to real renewal in the modern world of the sort of education which former ages deemed necessary for all free men and citizens: a rounded, catholic, complete, or universal education in all fundamental, general principles or truths about the universe, nature, man, society, and values, leading to all the wisdom required for entirely rational, individual, and social living. Modern science and scholarship have made immense progress into more precise, detailed, and reliable knowledge of masses of facts and the "middle principles" immediately exemplified in them, in countless special or limited domains. But the sum of all knowledge of this kind is already infinite, and only minute, arbitrarily selected fractions of it can be assimilated by single minds, even of men who specialize throughout their lives on intensive study. And the unifying, higher, and broader or more general principles involved in the "middle principles" of diverse specialties are today hardly glimpsed or sought after or even believed to exist except by a few philosophers, and even they cannot agree at all as to what they are. Efforts toward a universal synthesis, proceeding, as of course they must, upon a far higher level of abstraction than any to which modern scholar-specialties are accustomed, and without benefit of much understanding of more than a very few branches of modern knowledge, are scorned by "sound" investigators in all fields of learning as visionary efforts, futile speculation, "superficial" surveys, or attempts to replace free or open inquiries on lower levels of abstraction nearer to the touchstone of "facts" with some new or old metaphysical dogmatism. But as all the disciplines are now organized, no single discipline and no small group of them (assuming that a significant grasp of several could be gained in a four-year college education) can at all supply that inclusive wisdom for the conduct of life as a whole and for citizenship at which liberal education in the old sense aimed. All the modern specialized disciplines individually supply not wisdom, but only specialized, narrow skills or techniques, applicable either in other vocations or in that of research and teaching in the discipline itself. Thus it is not merely the pressure which I mentioned in a previous section, of popular desires for vocationally useful education, which has been tending to transform our colleges into more or less disguised collections of vocational training schools. The character of the structure of modern knowledge itself works, in a wholly different, independent and far more irresistible way, to bring about the same result. Having no commonly accepted body of general knowledge of reality, life, and values to teach, but only a myriad of narrow, intricate specialties, we are perforce, in growing measure, educating students, not to live and function wisely as free men and citizens, but only to serve in special activities and earn their livings, by either using or advancing and teaching the specialties they have studied; while the many who do not learn enough in the field of any specialty to use it in either way merely fill their minds temporarily with fragments of the elements of assorted specialties, which scarcely continue to function in their lives in any way whatever.

Is the situation, then, utterly hopeless, from the standpoint of those of us who believe in the permanent importance of the ancient concept of "a liberal education"? I do not think it is hopeless, but I do think that the indicated task is indeed colossal and not to be accomplished either by minor, marginal reforms or palliatives or by hasty, impatient, radical crusades, not backed by sound and thorough, fundamental thinking, and patient persuasion of the reluctant and suspicious majority of scholar-specialists. I cannot here develop my own views on this problem, without too greatly enlarging this paper; but I must say a few words, just to indicate the two complementary approaches which I think should be made to it. The ambitious, long-range ideal or fundamental approach must aim at eventual reorganization not only of education but also of the total corpus of all modern knowledge itself — a philosophic synthesis such as Aristotle and Aquinas achieved with the vastly inferior bulk and quality of knowledge in being in their times, but built upon and doing justice to all modern knowledge, and not, like Neo-Thomism, ignor-

ing most of that and making the preposterous and futile attempt
to revive merely the wisdom of our civilization's largely ignorant
childhood as the basis of modern education. I believe, indeed, that
a modern formulation of the total pattern of all the fundamental
concepts and principles involved in all modern knowledge would
turn out to have far more in common with the ancient synthesis
than most "moderns" can conceive that it would have. But there
are bound to be important revisions, deletions, and additions; our
vastly greater and much better knowledge of empirical details
and "middle principles" cannot but hold the potentiality of leading on "up" to a fuller, truer, and surer understanding of the
"highest" principles and affording, through deduction and verification, a much better confirmation of many of them. Pre-modern thought, having but scanty knowledge of actualities, moved
too exclusively in the region near the most abstract end of things
and mentally "saw" what is there — the universal and eternal pattern of all completely general truths — imperfectly, on account
of lack of full knowledge of many special exemplifications. Modern thought, on the other hand, is overweighted and unbalanced
by a plethora of detailed knowledge in diverse, limited, special
fields and dwells habitually too near to parts of the infinitely
spread-out, concrete end of things and finds it extremely difficult
to pursue "induction" or "speculation" (they are the same) all
the way "up" to the highest generalities or true "first principles,"
from which the "middle principles" and facts of all special sciences must be deducible. Study of the ancient philosophies —
Plato, Aristotle, Aquinas — may be very helpful to modern thinkers endeavoring to overcome the modern difficulty. But a modern
philosophy or synthesis of modern knowledge must utilize all the
modern resources, at least as fully as the ancient philosophies
utilized theirs. Also the modern synthesis will certainly have to
be a collaborative, not a purely individual, achievement, since no
individual can begin to compass all these modern resources; but
individuals of genius must lead, suggest the seminal ideas, and
persuade the specialists in many specialties to collaborate. Only
when there is a comprehensive, modern, philosophic synthesis
which can command really widespread assent can we hope to
restore the unity and catholicity of education by making study

of the achieved synthesis of truly general principles and of some of their exemplifications in several areas the principal content of education. But as research and inquiry go on in educational institutions in a manner that is correlated with the organization of teaching, the reorganization of teaching and of inquiry must go hand in hand. Pending real achievement and wide acceptance of the new synthesis, however, the more immediate steps toward giving undergraduates a more "liberal" or rounded education than they now get must be more modest and cautious. This brings me to the other one of the "two approaches" to which I alluded — the less ambitious, more immediately feasible approach.

Here, I think, the first task is to separate, within each modern discipline, those of its contents and elaborations thereof which are important only for the specialists who make its study or use their lifework from those (if any) which have an important place in or contribution to make to the general education to be given to all free men and citizens. When that is done, we can then determine how best to organize the teaching of the latter elements of each discipline or specialty having general educational value — the teaching of them alone or (in more general courses) along with the elements meeting the same requirement out of other, related specialties. And we can then separate the training of future specialists in the different fields from the general education of all students by organizing appropriate courses for the latter purpose, in all departments and/or groups of departments in the same larger areas and requiring all students to take an adequate and balanced program of these general courses, while allowing those qualified and wishing to become specialists in particular fields to take also a limited number (in each case) of the specialized courses reserved for them exclusively. The crucial step in the series I have outlined is the first step — dividing the material now taught in each discipline, correctly, into what should be taught only to specialists, and what can be of fundamental importance in helping all who learn it, throughout their lives and regardless of their occupations, to live and function wisely as free men and citizens. Numerous specialties may be unable to contribute anything to general education sufficiently vital to it to deserve any place in it in competition with other, more important ingredients; but snap decisions to this effect by persons ignorant of the specialties in question must, of course, be avoided. Enthusiastic scholars in every specialty are sure to overrate its importance for general education and, above all, to overrate the importance for that of many of its technicalities, so important in their own specialist's eyes that they cannot see or admit their relative irrelevance to general education. But, equally, those ignorant of each specialty are likely to underrate its potential contributions, and even those of some of its somewhat "technical" elements, to the general education of the modern citizen, who certainly needs many glimpses and a general appreciation of the major intellectual and practical "techniques" through which all modern civilization functions. Sound decisions on what parts of what disciplines to include in the "general education" courses can be reached, I think, only by patient discussion and collaboration between departmental spokesmen and "outsiders," or scholar-specialists jealous of the prestige, integrity, and proper teaching of their specialties, and persons concerned not for those specialties as such but for "liberal education." Once the "general" courses are set up and functioning, those who teach them should be freed from all pressure to do research in the now existing, narrow specialties. But they should become inquiring thinkers on the somewhat higher planes of generality on which they do their teaching; and collaboration among them as thinkers should lead in time toward the new philosophic synthesis of all modern knowledge, which is so much needed.

So far, I have been trying to bring out the full meaning of "liberal education" in the ancient, original, and fundamental sense and the essential features of the task of realizing it under modern conditions. But recent generations of educators have been torn by a confused conflict of the ideals embodied in this ancient meaning of "a liberal education," with discordant elements or tendencies in newer, modern ideals, embodied in other meanings of the word "liberal" and, thereby, of "liberal education." These modern meanings involve the "liberalism" which, as a pervasive "climate of opinion" on all or a very wide range of subjects, has been closely associated with the rise of modern democracy and generally dominant in our Western, now democratic, nations ever since about the middle of the eighteenth century. "Liberalism" has taken and continues to take many forms or to develop variants which often seem, and in some degrees and ways are, mutually contradictory. But there is a common root or core in them all — intense belief in liberty or freedom for all human beings; in a truly universal humanity or humaneness leading all to concede liberty to all and to practice a consistent, mutual respect for one another's liberties or rights, involving mutual, voluntary fulfillment of the "duties" of which "rights" are the other, receiving ends; and in pursuit by all of the common welfare of all through free inquiry, expression, discussion, and agreement on effective means of implementing or assuring, simultaneously, the freedom of each and the welfare of all. Extension to the many of the freedoms, opportunities, and responsibilities once reserved for the few — the democratic ideal — is one important "liberal" aim; the "liberal" and the democratic "ideologies" overlap or coincide to this extent. Freedom for new innovations of all sorts, in all spheres of intellectual, cultural, and practical life, with a view to "progress," and opposition to the worship of old traditions, is another element of "liberalism" — the element properly called "progressivism." But the basic element is the demand that freedom from arbitrary coercion — coercion not sanctioned and regulated by impartial, humane, moral, and procedural rules — be made secure for absolutely all human beings, no matter whether they be members of the popular majority or of unpopular minorities, or what economic, racial, religious, social, political, or other groups they may belong to; the demand that no human power whatever shall be authorized or allowed to trespass on any pretext upon any of the morally valid, sacred liberties or rights of any human being. Different sorts of "liberals" are distinguished chiefly by their different proportions of emphasis upon these different ideals, which, although allied in the main, can run into some degree of mutual conflict. For example, politico-economic "liberals" of the nineteenth century or now old-fashioned type stress private liberties, including property rights and business liberties, in a way involving much restriction of the "right" of the popular, political majority to control public policies with a view to the majority's welfare and also much restraint of "progress" in adapting public policies to new conditions; while "New Deal liberals," on the other hand, are prone to go far in curtailing individual liberties of the kind most valued (as a rule) by the well-to-do, in order to carry out humanitarian reforms intended to benefit the many and to "free" them from the power of the prosperous minority. But as long as both sides acknowledge that both the businessmen and "the masses" have "rights," that the question is one of the best relative adjustment between the two sets of "rights," and that it must be settled by free discussion and democratic decision — this dispute is clearly one within the by nature catholic, "liberal" household, and those on either side who call their opponents "Communists" or "Fascists" are talking ridiculous and dangerous nonsense. "Liberalism" is a many-in-one, and the one remains identifiable through all its varieties, if we look for it with a broad enough concept in mind. But a deeper dilemma than the one just mentioned is the one arising in the sphere, not of politico-economic but of basic, intellectual "liberalism," between stressing "open-mindedness" to the point of extending it as an attitude even to antiliberal isms, and stressing the ultimate convictions definitive or constitutive of "liberalism" itself. There are some truths which none can be free to reject or remain ignorant of, if all are to remain free and have the wisdom through which alone their freedom can bear fruit in good lives and a society good enough to be able to last and preserve their freedom. And that point illuminates one issue in the mutual conflict between the incomplete "liberalism in education" — pure individualism applied to education — which led to such things as "progressive education" and the free elective system, and the present spreading urge for "education in liberalism," or an education designed to give all students the essential convictions, knowledge, and wisdom which they must have to carry on and preserve our "liberal" civilization. But before going on to discuss either of these modern developments, I must insert a transitional discussion of the relations of "liberalism" in general, on the one hand, to democracy and, on the other, to the old, Western culture which formed the content of predemocratic "liberal education."

Liberalism, Democracy, the Classical Philosophy, and Modern Science

Extension of the freedoms formerly reserved for the members of elites or upper classes to the many as well is the meaning of democracy. With this must go extension to all of an education and a culture equipping them to achieve good lives and a good society; what the old upper-class liberal education aimed to do for its recipients modern democratic liberal education must do for all. But the latter must draw its contents from a largely new or greatly changed and now perpetually changing culture; and, along with the changes favorable and vital to democracy and therefore certainly to be upheld in modern education, there have been other changes productive of confusion and skepticism in the sphere of values, hence full of menace to the moral idealism that is basic for democracy and for its success, and confronting modern education with a baffling problem. The old, predemocratic culture betrayed real defects in not supporting or encouraging democracy or freedom for all in the many centuries before that arrived; in supporting or justifying, instead, slavery or serfdom, aristocracy, etc. Nevertheless, that old culture itself was the source of the complex developments of and out of it, in the early modern centuries, which led to the modern, "liberal," and scientific culture that fathered democracy and all other aspects of "liberalism." And along with the real and great improvements that were made, the transformation of the ancient-medieval into the modern liberal-and-scientific culture also included, I think, certain changes for the worse, which have led to serious weaknesses or faults in all varieties of "liberalism" — the prevailing ethos in the modern, democratic world. "Liberalism" as a whole includes (*a*) an attenuated or partial continuation of some ancient, eternally valid, and vitally important insights; (*b*) some equally valid and important, new, modern insights, correcting and replacing ancient errors and ignorance, but themselves requiring the support of the ancient insights which have long been "fading," to give them enduring firmness and full clarity; and (*c*) some serious errors, in conflict with both those ancient and those modern insights. Let me now say a little in explanation of that threefold assertion, beginning with (*a*).

Recognition of the rightful and needful supremacy of reason is one central and permanently valid and vitally important insight, inherited or continued by the modern from the ancient-medieval culture. A society of free men cannot flourish and endure if its culture abandons the exaltation and full use of reason, nowhere more complete than in Plato, Aristotle, and Aquinas, and succumbs to irrational and antirational tendencies of "thought." But the ancient "rationalism" is generally accused by modern "liberals" of involving an illiberal, authoritarian "dogmatism." There is some truth in this, but the nature of the problem at stake is seldom understood. Deductive or demonstrative reason has to proceed, of course, from premises, and the validity of the basic premises or "first principles," whatever ones are chosen, never can be demonstrated. But this does not mean that they must be chosen at random or affirmed arbitrarily and cannot be tested critically at all. "Induction" from experience — ascent from "particulars" directly experienced, to principles exemplified in them — is the proper source of premises to be used in "deductive" arguments. Plato, Aristotle, and Aquinas recognized this and strove to practice it, as fully as any modern thinkers ever have done. "Induction," however, is no simple but a very difficult process; in itself (apart from the deduction which must follow and lead back to the final step of "verification," not to be confused with the initial phase or induction proper) it is not, strictly speaking, a *logical* process at all but is rather imaginative or speculative; experience of particulars "suggests" ideas or hypotheses about the principles they *may* exemplify, and the development of these suggestions of experience into provisionally trusted principles is "speculation." Only when a speculative set of principles has been developed can strictly logical thought begin — analysis of the implications or consequences of that set of principles; and only when this analysis has been carried out to the point where definite expectations about new experience emerge, and the latter are "checked" against the actual new experience, can the confirmation of premises occur (through confirmation of conclusions from them). Now what the ancient-medieval, classical philosophy lacked was adequate techniques for the final step, empirical "verification"; it was an inductive and deductive, or speculative and logical, philosophy, but could not properly test its conclusions and thus its premises by joining theoretical with extensive and intensive, systematic, and accurate factual, or experimental and other observational investigations. Also it was (quite properly) even more concerned with values ("the good" and its elements) than with "facts" (without explicitly separating these concepts and combining them *correctly* — something modern thought has still not achieved) and was led to formulate and rely on premises or first principles whose implications in the sphere of the natural and all purely explanatory-predictive sciences were not suitable to make the latter effective rational-and-empirical sciences.

The defects of the classical (Aristotelian) natural philosophy and the failure to develop adequate techniques for "verification" were interdependent; imperfect theories, not of a nature to be scientifically verified or dis-verified, inhibited development of experimental techniques, and the lack of the latter prevented correction or improvement of the theories. Now the modern sciences (those concerned not with values but solely with actualities considered in abstraction from their values) have corrected those defects of the ancient-medieval, primitive sciences out of which they have developed and become successfully empirical as well as rational sciences. But there has been no similar or parallel achievement in the sphere of the study of values — aesthetics, ethics, jurisprudence, and the ethical sides of political philosophy or science and political economy. In this sphere, efficient techniques for verifying or in that sense testing general "value judgments" by or upon the relevant (emotional) ingredients of particular experience are still lacking, as completely as they ever were. Hence in this sphere there still is only the choice between the firmness of convictions which those with opposing convictions will always call "dogmatism" and the kind of skepticism or permanent indecision which merely invites some more irrational dogmatism to supplant it and meet the inevitable demand for convictions which it fails to meet. Modern "liberals" are often fully as "dogmatic" in their way of holding their own basic convictions as any Thomist ever was; and, when they are not, they are so confused, unstable, and extremely "open-minded" in all directions that they drive many by reaction against them into the arms of the worst modern isms. The basic premises or principles or "dogmas" of the classical philosophy in the sphere of values undoubtedly need revisions if they and conclusions from them are to figure at all in modern education; but I think a revival of them, with revisions, is needed to restore the full rationality or sanity of "liberalism" itself.

For "liberalism" as a civic morality began as just such a revival and revision, during the "enlightenment," of the classical ideas of ethical "natural law" and "natural rights" which had been universally accepted in the Middle Ages but had undergone a widespread, partial eclipse in the intervening epoch of the Renaissance and the Reformation. And the general desertion of those ideas again by more recent "liberals," since the end of the eighteenth century, has meant or entailed a progressive disintegration of the "liberal" outlook and paved the way intellectually for the rise of the present-day antiliberal "ideologies." General acceptance in a society of free men of a definite pattern of principles of ethical "natural law" (principles of objective right or justice in mutual dealings and human relations) is necessary in the long run to the orderly functioning and the preservation of such a society. Freedom for all as individuals, and the preservation of an orderly society which works effectively for the common welfare of all, can be reconciled only in so far as all or most individuals tend to recognize, agree on, and act in harmony with the morally valid rights of all, and the moral obligations everyone has in virtue of the rights of his fellows. And impartial perception of one's own and other people's interrelated rights and duties, in particular cases or situations where action is contemplated, requires (and feeds) conceptual or rational knowledge of the moral laws, of which the particular rights and duties in question in the particular case are instances. The "natural," moral laws define the conditions of realization of good human lives and societies, as aesthetic laws define the conditions of real beauty in works of art, as the laws of logic define the conditions of arriving at truth in rational inquiries, and as physical laws define the conditions of occurrence of the specified types of physical events. All these and other groups of "natural laws" must be internally and mutually consistent subpatterns within one all-embracing pattern of cosmic order; and they must all be discoverable by human reason, by induction from experience (of particulars) leading up to the laws or principles, and deduction from them leading down again to their exemplifications in the same and other particulars (old and new experience). Such were the convictions, implicit or explicit, of Plato, Aristotle, the Stoics, many Church Fathers, the medieval Schoolmen, and plenty of early-modern writers down through the eighteenth century. And it was this belief in a rationally knowable, cosmic order or system of systems of "natural laws," including the moral laws through observance of which men can achieve good lives and societies, which supported the belief that cultivation of and education in "the liberal arts" — philosophy and the fine arts and the natural and moral sciences — would lead to the full-rounded wisdom for living needed by free men, including moral and political wisdom.

Medieval thought was completely permeated by that belief in a rational, cosmic order conceived to include as an integral part of itself the true moral order, or system of ethical natural laws defining the reciprocal rights and duties of all as members of society. And while it is true that the prevalent medieval "version" of the ethical natural laws in their detailed elaboration contained *to some extent* a conservative, aristocratic or undemocratic, and authoritarian bias; it also is true at the same time, as the best authorities on the Middle Ages agree, that important, liberal implications were developed much further and had much more effect than modern "liberals" ignorant of the Middle Ages ever recognize. The prevailing theory of the "contents of the code" of civic-ethical natural laws, sanctioned monarchy, aristocracy, a hierarchy of social classes, serfdom, and the rest. But the kings and lords and all human superiors were universally held to be under and not above the laws, which they could not make but could only "find," declare, and enforce; and the laws were held to confer on the rulers not only rights and powers but also definite duties to their subjects, and to confer on all, even the humblest of the latter, definite rights; and the subjects as rational men could apprehend the only true laws independently and be justified in resisting wicked rulers who tried to impose false human laws in violation of the natural and only true or valid laws. Even serfs had rights, defined in the customary laws of each locality which served as rough expressions of the natural laws applied to local conditions, and protected by definite procedures in the manorial courts. In short, while sanctioning great inequalities of wealth and power and social position and much control of "inferior" by "superior" persons, medieval law (all held to be, if valid, simply formulated natural law) imposed real restraints on sheer human power and arbitrary will and gave real protections to important liberties and rights for all individuals. Political machinery for enforcing respect for the rights of the many or the humble was defective, and the rights assigned to them in theory were too limited, as the prevailing apprehension of the moral laws was biased in favor of the upper classes. But the degree of this bias was not unlimited, and the ideas of the sacredness of all human personalities, their equality before God, and the rights of all in justice to all the freedoms, opportunities, and means required for good human lives were definitely all there in medieval thought as seeds of the modern liberal conception of a democratic society of free, equal, and fraternal citizens.

Over much of the interval, however, between the end of the thirteenth and the second half of the eighteenth century, the philosophic theory of ethical natural law underwent a widespread, partial eclipse; and this statement must be expanded a bit in order to bring out the character of the immediate background of the "liberal" revival and revision of that theory. Disintegrative tendencies in the modern development of Western culture appeared very early and were at a sort of first climax in the epoch of the Renaissance and Reformation. To begin with, the late-medieval triumph of nominalism in philosophy destroyed, for minds thoroughly affected by it, belief in the reality of "natural laws" of any kind; if only particulars are real and all universals (concepts) and patterns of them are invented, convenient, mental fictions, the physical scientist's pattern of order in events and the moralist's pattern of order in real values or elements of the good life and the good society are alike imaginary. But this purely philosophical, disintegrative influence has taken centuries to work out its full effects in the history of philosophy — leading eventually to the kind of "empiricism" which involves subjectivism (even as to particulars), and still later to those recent, diverse developments of subjectivism — romanticism, positivism, and pragmatism. And in the meantime other disintegrative influences in spheres of culture and life other than that of explicit, general philosophy have also been at work. One such influence was widely conspicuous in the Renaissance — the growth of expansive, worldly, economic and political ambitions, both in private men and in the rulers of emerging nation-states, and the associated growth of purely means-to-ends or applied cause-and-effect thinking, and the tendency of ambitious men and groups to throw off moral scruples openly, as hindrances to the most efficient pursuit of their ends. Machiavelli is the perfect illustration of that tendency. The rulers and leading statesmen of the greater nation-states long after Machiavelli's time, in the seventeenth and eighteenth centuries, were full of the same spirit and, while sometimes paying lip service to the old ideas of divine and natural moral laws, claimed powers and a position above the laws binding on their subjects, and "rights" to use unscrupulous means in their incessant "game of power politics," which no medieval mind would have sanctioned.

In a wholly different way, the Protestant reformers, for all their merits, contributed a disintegrative influence of still another kind; in religion and in morals as well, they withdrew much that medieval thought had placed in the domain of "natural reason" into that of the supernatural and extra-rational authority of revelation, and thus discouraged rationalism and the belief in ethical natural law. They diminished the prestige of authority and aided the growth of liberty, of course, by attacking the authoritarian church and proclaiming the right of private judgment (about the meaning of each passage in the Bible). But not only was the new authority (the Bible as interpreted by each believer) conducive to disintegration of the body of Christians and their faith instead of to unity; at the same time, also, the denial that reason working independently of what it found in the Bible could be trusted to discover the true moral law or any part of it was a ban on continuation of the sort of effort to reach rational agreement, which had done at least as much as the authority of the church to produce the substantial unity of medieval thought. Henceforth in orthodox Protestant circles, in the main, moral as well as religious thought emphasized not the attempt of reason to discover the principles of ethical natural law but only rival interpretations of and arguments from Bible texts — supernaturally revealed and authoritative, unquestionable premises. Melanchthon and a few other Lutherans defended the theory of ethical natural law but got no support there from Luther himself; and the latter not only belittled reason but did German culture an immense disservice in another way also, through his doctrine that this world, and especially the political state, is the devil's own domain and cannot be moralized; that Christian morality is purely an affair of "inner" rectitude in the soul of the individual Christian and cannot reform earthly society. Calvinism, on the other hand, did set out strenuously to reform earthly society and make all its practices truly Christian, by Calvinist standards; but orthodox Calvinists looked almost solely to the Bible for all the premises of true morality and were chary of recognizing any capacity in "natural reason" to develop an independent, philosophic ethics, or, in other words, to discover ethical natural laws. Calvinistic ideas of civic morality soon developed in the direction of democratic ideas, and modern democracy owes much to Calvinism; but the liberal philosophy of ethical natural law and the natural rights of all men was developed in the largely Calvinistic countries not by orthodox Calvinists but by dissenters from that body of dissent; Arminians like Grotius, liberal former Calvinists like the Cambridge Platonists and Francis Hutcheson, Proto-Unitarians like the poet Milton, near-deists and deists like Locke and Shaftesbury, etc.

Most Catholic thought after the Reformation and the Counter-Reformation seems likewise to have grown less rationalistic and less liberal or more exclusively supernaturalistic and authoritarian; little was heard of Thomism from Catholics in the eighteenth century, and the purely modern dogma of papal infallibility marked the growth of authoritarianism within the church, while its support of Catholic monarchs and all their claims to power and its tacit complicity in their often unscrupulous policies grew more pronounced. Hence the development of liberal thought in Catholic countries was forced to be strongly anticlerical; and this goes far, I think, to account for the failure of both the church and most modern liberals to recognize the important resemblance or partial agreement, despite the measure of real disagreement, between late eighteenth-century liberal and medieval ideas of ethical natural law and the natural right of all human beings. The liberal ideas were developed, from the Renaissance on but with a culmination in the late eighteenth century, by three sorts of writers: Renaissance "humanists" like Erasmus and many others, representing an outlook entirely different from that of Machiavelli and his kind, building on ancient classical thought more than on Christianity, and standing as disregarded moderates on the fringe of the Reformation controversy; the liberal dissenters from Calvinism already mentioned, in the mainly Calvinistic part of the Protestant world; and anticlerical writers in the Catholic countries (chiefly France). But the continuity with medieval thought is clear in all these writers who made much of ethical natural law; Locke's account of the latter, for example, derives from Hooker (*Ecclesiastical Polity*), who repeated and quoted Thomas Aquinas; and the eighteenth-century French "physiocrats" (the first modern liberal economists) talked of ethical (as well as economic) natural laws in very nearly Thomistic terms. Most political and social thought and practice — all that the liberal reformers protested against — had long been influenced chiefly by other sorts of ideas, involving *no* real recognition of *any* conception of ethical natural law. Amoral doctrines of absolute authority and "reasons of state" excusing unscrupulous policies had long been uppermost; the "old regime" in its decadent old age had developed a wholly different spirit from that predominant in the Middle Ages and became a system not only of aristocracy and privilege but of frankly cynical or amoral statecraft — not too dissimilar, except for its polite elegance, from modern "fascism." The liberal-democratic movement was, of course, supported by insurgent middle-class and popular "interests" as well as by moral ideas; but the latter as developed by liberal intellectuals played a guiding role, and they were in form and content a revival, as well as a revision, of medieval ideas of ethical natural law.

Of course, the revision was important and, in part, a great improvement — replacing the aristocratic bias of the medieval applications with a fully democratic and liberal assertion of the equal moral rights of all human beings, and vision of the moral end as the common welfare of all mankind. But, at the same time, this eighteenth-century liberal theory of the system of ethical natural laws or the moral order included in the cosmic natural order had very serious new weaknesses which led to great errors while the theory remained in vogue and caused its speedy and complete collapse in the nineteenth century. Unlike the medieval theory in the total context of medieval thought, the liberal theory in its total context of eighteenth-century thought had no adequate general, philosophical foundation. Real metaphysical inquiry into first principles concerning the ultimate structure of all reality, had gone out of fashion in the early-modern period. The trend of all thought toward preoccupatioin with the infinitely spread-out and varied, empirical end of things had gone far enough to produce a prevalent aversion to serious pursuit of full understanding of the most fundamental and general truths. Hence the liberals for the most part merely asserted their views of the principles of ethical natural law, with little effort to derive them from more basic premises about the nature of things. There were interesting efforts, by Quesnay (the "Physiocrat"), Adam Smith (in his *Theory of the Moral Sentiments*), and others, to derive them inductively from experience of particular moral values. But these attempts ran counter to another aspect of the prevailing trend of modern thought, into exclusive concern with actualities considered in abstraction from their values, and with only predictive and technical, cause-and-effect or means-to-ends thinking; and so made no widespread, deep, or lasting impression. But, worst of all, the early-modern liberals invariably confused their ideas of the ethical natural laws with their ideas of predictive social scientific laws analogous to the laws of Newtonian physics; and this confused blend of ethics and determinism involved an egregious optimism — a tendency to imply that nature and human nature do actually and necessarily function so as to insure an eventual, perfect, and automatic conformity of all actual deeds and social events with the requirements of ideal justice among all and final maximization of the true welfare of each and all. Men came to be thought of as mechanical units in a social mechanism — human, rational units, to be sure, but "reasoning machines," directed by their circumstances, experience, interests or desires, and merely instrumental reason, to act so as to attain the fullest satisfaction of their wants. And the ethical ideal for conduct was merged with actuality through a tacit assumption that men are by nature good as well as rational — that they want and pursue only ends or satisfactions always in harmony with the greatest welfare of their fellows in general or the whole community. Soon the development of "social science" theory on these lines made a separate notion of ethical natural laws superfluous for it, and the latter was dropped in favor of pure utilitarianism — a theory of universal pursuit of want-satisfactions simply. And in both forms, liberal theory tended in that epoch (1750–1850) to lead to an extreme individualism or failure to emphasize the moral obligations of individuals to the community; to imply that if all were free and simply pursued their private interests rationally, the common welfare of the community would be an automatic by-product which none need worry about.

More recent liberal thought has swung, by now, far away from that individualism to ideas of democratic (popular majority) control, through government, over self-interested private activities, to *make* them conform to the requirements of best service to the common welfare of the whole community. But this newest variety of liberal thought has one thing in common with the old individualism: neither view has any effective vision of a pattern of objective principles of justice, to be not derived from subjective, arbitrary, human desires but apprehended by reason as defining the really valid rights and binding duties of all, or the real structure and requirements of the real common good. The arbitrary, collective will of the political majority is no more certain to coincide with the real requirements of the real welfare of all than is the resultant of the free interaction, in the markets, of the arbitrary, private wills of all individuals. Nor can scientific-technical study of the conditions of maximizing the social aggregate of material welfare alone solve the problem; there remain not only the problem of what distribution of that welfare is just, and the problem of rightly identifying, emphasizing, and obtaining the far more important, nonmaterial constituents of individual and social welfare, but also the problem of making evident to all individuals and groups, and effective through their rational minds upon their emotions and wills, the superior importance of the true common good above their selfish, special interests or desires. The majority, and "pressure groups," and legislators and officials, as well as the governed in their private activities, need a control of their aims not merely by "expediency" in their situations but by moral knowledge — knowledge of the real, objective, moral laws. Most "liberals" of all varieties have long been without any clear acknowledged belief in and definite elaborated vision of the pattern of real moral laws; but, without this, "liberalism" is bound to go on disintegrating and giving way to the antiliberal isms which frankly exalt the sheer power or might and cleverness and arbitrary desires of dominant groups as the architects of "order" in an otherwise chaotic world of lawless "freedom" for the conflicting, arbitrary desires of all. Freedom and order can be reconciled only through prevalence of knowledge and acknowledgment of the moral order not created by human power but discovered by human reason as the right order and actualized by coöperation.

I am now ready, at last, to return to education, and point out briefly, in conclusion, the problems posed by the impacts of confused "liberalism" on ideas of "liberal education." It has seemed necessary to sketch the historic relations of "liberalism" to the older culture and philosophy which supplied the content or pre-democratic, general education for the "free" minority, and to the present-day problem of moral order in societies in which all are "free," in order to bring out the bearings of "liberalism" on the task of organizing general education for all in this modern world to fit our free citizens for their responsibilities. Our thinking about this educational task is affected both by what remains alive among us of the ancient ideal of a rounded, adequate, and coherent patterned education and by modern ideals that derive from a now past, or the current state of circum-ambient "liberal" feeling. Rounded education ("liberal" in the ancient sense) and the requirements it would have to impose on all students to learn all the essentials of a free man's equipment for life and citizenship are opposed by some in the name of "free-dom" for each student to choose his studies according to his "interests." This attitude reflects the surviving influence of the older, extremely individualistic "liberalism" on educational thought and practice. Rounded education, designed among other things to produce moral and political wisdom, and "compulsion" to get this to all students, is in line, however, with the current desires of those more "up-to-date" liberals who stress not in-dividualism but community welfare through democratic control and are concerned to use education to inculcate liberal as opposed to antiliberal sentiments. But *this* redoubles the opposition of the old-style educational "liberals," making them fear not only a return to uniform, prescribed education or "compulsion," but also a conversion of education into "propaganda" for social ideals in conflict with their own. And the new-style "liberals," while ready for some program requiring all to get a rounded educa-tion, fight anything savoring of renewal of the pre-democratic or pre-modern content, the classical philosophy, etc., as "re-actionary." My views on these conflicts have already been im-plied pretty clearly and may now be stated rather briefly.

Liberalism in Education

The old, or nineteenth-century, individualistic liberalism in-spired both progressive education in the lower schools and the tendency at the college level most fully expressed in the free elective system at Harvard under Eliot. Let the spontaneous interests of the child or the young man find free expression and satisfaction in his education; discover and respond to those interests only and don't impose studies to which there is no interested response; let the free individual learn all that he de-velops a desire to learn, and nothing else. Back of this, implicitly, was the optimism of the early-modern liberal philosophy — the

assumption that all are endowed by nature with all the interests
that are best for them and for their best functioning in an automatically harmonious society and that all they need to do, for
their own welfare and that of their fellows, is to follow their
own interests or "natural bents." There was no perception of
the fact that interests reflect opinions about values and that having a valid set of interests depends on having knowledge of the
real order of real values — the pattern of final and instrumental
goods essential for a really good life. One acquires interests by
discovering values; and, while effective education requires that
the interests of the students be aroused, the task is one of making
the values of appropriate studies evident to them and not one
of catering to their already conscious, accidental sets of interests, based only on whatever opinions about values their
backgrounds have given them. This does not mean, of course,
that different individualities do not require, in part, different
educations; the pattern of real values is not uniform in all details
for all, but in some degree unique for each person — although
many values are essentially the same for all. But still it is
essential that educators play the leading role in working out with
different students the proper adjustments of the common program to their special needs and aptitudes. This they cannot do on
any but an arbitrary basis, however, if they themselves have no
rational knowledge of the real order of real values but are
merely pitting their opinions or prejudices and resulting interests
against those of the students; "compulsion" that is arbitrary, not
grounded in a clearly superior wisdom eventually understandable
as such by all rational minds as they mature, is indeed tyranny —
unjustified infringement of individual liberty. This is the real
explanation of the origin of the free elective system, and the
real dilemma in the quest for an adequately good substitute for
it. The old "compulsory" program for all had become a "dead
tradition," ill adjusted to its ends under modern conditions and
carried on with no adequate understanding of its grounds or
raison d'être even on the part of its defenders; and as teachers
could no longer convince themselves, their colleagues, the students, and the public that they knew what all educated men
ought to know and why, the easy solution was to offer every-

thing and let every student take what he pleased. And our basic difficulty now is that we still lack a reasoned philosophy of what the common content of general education for all ought to be and why it ought to be that, on which rational agreement among all or most of those concerned at all with education can be reached. This means that there is indeed some danger now that one or another group with an arbitrary program to impose may succeed in imposing it in this or that institution, by force or maneuver, against substantial opposition which they cannot win over by rational argument because the grounds of their own convictions are not really clear and convincing. And the still greater danger is that of clash and deadlock among rival programs, all lacking adequate, persuasive wisdom. Attainment of and agreement on a rational philosophy of educational values is not easy in the midst of our largely distintegrated culture, which has long lacked anything approaching universal agreement on the real pattern of real values in any sphere. In this situation it is best to proceed slowly, with great patience and moderation, and introduce educational reforms only in steps when wide agreement on each step is reached by patient inquiry and discussion. Chaos is bad, but drastic efforts to achieve order by imposing factional programs while they are still that, and many are unconvinced of their merits, can hardly fail to breed worse chaos. In education, as in liberal society at large, we need to discover the truly rational order or pattern which can win general assent and be made actual by general, free coöperation. And it will make room for proper freedom for students, too, to discover and fill their special needs with the help of their teachers and to question requirements and be shown the values behind them and acquire the interests called for.

Education in Liberalism

But in what way *can* we discover what the common content of a modern, rounded education should be? It is natural to look for a unifying objective, to bring ideas into focus; and the current crisis for free societies makes many intent on the objective of forming students into loyal and effective defenders of all the values that are threatened. But the "fighting faith" of the free societies is a chaotic hodgepodge of quarreling varieties of "liberalism"; and an educational program premised on any one version of the set of "liberal" values, will appear illiberal, anti-liberal, "reactionary," or "socialistic" in implied social aims, to other sorts of "liberals." Moreover, since no group of "liberals" has a complete and thorough rational philosophy of its own scheme of values, there is bound to be an element of "propaganda" in the bad sense — manipulation of minds by dogmatic eloquence or by subtle influence, rather than education leading to rational convictions through examination of all alternatives and real reasoning by students and teachers on all the issues — in any program for making education a bulwark of liberalism as defined by its sponsors. And, finally, the whole idea is too narrow in that it suggests subordinating all education to the one aim of making students believers in some idea or vision of the good society, when that is only a part of what they need. Each free man needs a proper outfit of social ideals, and ideals for his personal life, and knowledge of general conditions of and means to realization of his ideals in both respects, and knowledge of how he reached those ideals and that instrumental knowledge, and how he can, throughout his life, proceed to modify and improve them all by extracting the meaning of all new experience. "Liberals" in their sudden discovery of the need to have, keep, teach, and perpetuate a definite set of civic-ethical ideals or convictions instead of indifferently tolerating all convictions and only questioning them all perpetually, and mainly stressing the nonvalue or factual and scientific technical inquiries, are in danger of swinging to the other extreme — concentrating too much on teaching values or ideals and forgetting the importance of the great part of education where detachment should reign and the stress be on what is provable to all whatever their ideals are. This is especially important in the "social sciences," where much, although by no means all, is independent of all social-moral value judgments. We had better think of the educational task as one of equipping the members of free society to approach its problems and the problems of their lives with informed intelligence, giving them enough knowledge of natural science and social science (not moral but explanatory-predictive) principles and methods to enable them to add to knowledge of this kind through later reading and experience and reflection and become intelligent about the actualities and processes they may have to cope with or help to control, and initiating them into reflective thinking about values — aesthetic, private-moral, and civil-moral — and the achievement of reasoned but eventually settled and firm convictions, by using for this purpose courses in literature and the fine arts, philosophy and ethics, and social philosophies, where teachers combining "breadth" of mind with convictions they express and defend freely, and different such teachers with different sorts of convictions, lecture and argue with each other and the students. Above all, we had better make sure that reforms in education which look in the direction of restoring breadth, generality, catholicity, and unity to every student's whole education, do not at the same time also look or seem to look toward molding students into liberals of some special variety. The scholar-specialists who want to preserve free election of concentrations and distribution courses, and keep things much as they are, will offer enough resistance to any plan for making the student's whole education more liberal in the ancient sense, if that is all they see at stake; but they will be still more disturbed, and rightly, if enabled to suspect an intention also to impose "education in liberalism" as the sponsors of the new plan conceive the latter.

7

FREE ENTERPRISE AND DEMOCRACY

❧

Other parts of this volume[1] are economic studies of various particular problems of national policy. This essay, in contrast, is concerned with general ideas about an over-all problem, and owing to the nature of its theme is a discourse more in the domain of political thought than in that of economics. My hope is that it may throw light on, and help readers to appraise, the current American liberal and conservative attitudes to public authority and private liberties in our economy. My own position on this question places me — along with the other contributors to this volume — in the liberal group. But that in itself cannot become a very informative statement until some clarifying "light" has at least diminished the "dark" confusions today pervading most American thought, as to what we liberals and our conservative opponents, respectively, stand for. To do what I can here to dispel those confusions is my purpose.

History of the Word "Liberal"

As is indicated by the word "liberal" itself, and demonstrated by the entire history of "liberalism," we liberals — apart from extremists who misuse and are not entitled to the name — are friends of liberty and loyal heirs of the main American tradi-

[1] *Saving American Capitalism*, edited by Seymour E. Harris. Copyright 1948 by Alfred A. Knopf, Inc. This chapter is reprinted here by permission of Alfred A. Knopf, Inc.

tion, aiming at the nearest feasible approach to a society of (in the main) voluntarily coöperating, free individuals. But by an accident in the history of American political terminology, the word "liberal" has come into general use here only in the quite recent period, which has been marked by some new enlargements of the sphere of activity of the people's government. And in this period the expansion of our government — while occurring chiefly under the pressure of prevailing conditions and the resulting insistent needs and demands of the popular majority — has been brought about through a movement led precisely by those (the liberals) most anxious to see the full blessings of liberty extended to *all* Americans. Not the group's liberal purpose, however, but merely its support (in seeming conflict with that purpose) of new governmental economic controls has been most clearly evident to the public. Thus it has come about that, ignoring both the literal and the older historic meaning of the word, our national usage means by "liberals" persons advocating a degree and kind of humanitarian "big government"; a thing which the conservative opposition can all too easily represent as, and which if misdirected can degenerate into, a general, dangerous curtailment of traditional and still desirable private liberties.

Birth of the Liberal Creed

Now I think a glance over the long history of liberal and conservative thought and controversy in the democratic-capitalist world as a whole, on the question of governmental controls and private liberties in the business economy, may help us to see in the right perspective, and appraise, the present-day American phase of this controversy. The old gospel of entirely or very "free enterprise" and very limited government is today identified in our politics with conservatism, and even in that quarter is not much more than a wistful memory. But in the epoch of its birth — the late eighteenth and early nineteenth centuries, the epoch of the American and French Revolutions and England's first steps toward democracy — the same gospel (with a subtle difference) was a vital part of the *liberal* creed. Along with the ideal and theory of political democracy, it was then the first philosophy of the liberal-democratic movement to emancipate the common people from oppression by the privileged few. For in that age, this movement was directed against the regimes established in the preceding epoch — regimes of despotic monarchy, oligarchy (actual rule, under the reigning monarchs, by small groups of aristocratic landowners and rich merchants), and "mercantilism," the economic policy of those governments. The character of mercantilism, above all, is the key to the original, liberal meaning of the gospel of free enterprise. Mercantilism was a system of governmental promotion and friendly control of high "capitalist" enterprise and wide control of economic affairs for the benefit of the ruling, privileged, rich minorities and to bolster up the military power of each great imperial nation-state, and not for the sake of improving the economic welfare of the common people. In short, the liberal movement in its earliest phase was a revolt against the alliance of "big government" and what was then "big business."

Liberalism versus Mercantilism

It was in opposition to mercantilism that the first liberal economists — Adam Smith and others — developed the ideal and theory of an economic system of universal free enterprise, free competition, and free trade. Governments were to function only as "impartial umpires." Central in mercantilist policy were lavish grants of legal monopolies to associations of established, wealthy businessmen, and a mass of restrictive regulations of the normal, gain-seeking activities of "little" businessmen and of farmers, working men, and the people as consumers. And so, by opposition, it became the central idea of the liberal economists that a regime of minimal government and maximal economic freedom for all individuals would subject the former monopolies and all businesses to competitive pressures beneficial to the public; distribute opportunities impartially to all the people, and elicit from all the people their best productive efforts and contributions to the common welfare; and in general, harmonize the self-interest of each individual with the collective interest of mankind. With

its strong individualism, that economic-liberal philosophy combined, inseparably, a no less strong internationalism. All individuals everywhere were to have large, equal, and sacred freedoms
to pursue their interests anywhere, across as well as within the
national frontiers; and the national governments were to be made
to stop "interfering" in the economic world in those ways which
had favored the already rich and oppressed the common people,
as well as served the spirit of aggressive nationalism, to the
detriment of international trade, prosperity, and peace.

Economic Liberalism and Political Democracy

Now that ideal and theory of the free world economy attained
a fairly full development and some influence a few decades
before the ideal and theory of political democracy — the other
half of the complete philosophy of nineteenth-century liberalism — became of equal, practical importance. In other words,
the main body of the liberal reformers first tried for a while
only to make the old, pre-democratic kind of government as
little harmful as possible by curtailing its powers and sphere of
activity, before they went on to the further effort to replace it
with a new kind of government, so organized as to be responsive
and responsible to all the people. But then in the second, more
complete, phase of the liberal movement, most leading advocates
of fully democratic, popular government long remained also
advocates of minimal government and the economic system of
free, unregulated, individual enterprise, competition, and trade.
The utmost freedom for all individuals at all consistent with
their common welfare was still the first concern. Fear of "big
government" as likely to be oppressive misgovernment, perverted
to the ends of a rich, powerful, and selfish few, was still the
dominant fear. Generations of experience of the old type of
government had produced in the people a deep distrust of government in general, which could die out only with the gradual,
full development of, and new generations of experience under,
political democracy. Political democracy at first was usually
thought of, not as enabling the popular majority to control and
use a widely active, strong government to attain their ends by

positive action, but rather as enabling the people to protect themselves from too much government, by using the vote as a veto on ambitious governmental plans.

Moreover, the theory of the ideal "free market" economy still impressed most democratic leaders as a "democratic" conception in its own sphere and the logical counterpart of political democracy. Free competition of all enterprises for the patronage of the people would oblige them to serve all the people as amply, well, and cheaply as possible, just as political "free competition" of parties, candidates, ideas, and programs for the votes of the people would force *them* into line with prevailing, popular desires. Thus, through the early decades of the nineteenth century, free enterprise and democracy were as a rule supported together in pro-popular, progressive, liberal, and democratic quarters, and opposed together in well-to-do and conservative quarters. For example, in this country then it was the Jeffersonian and, later, the Jacksonian Democrats who preached free enterprise and limited government along with full political democracy. The Hamiltonian Federalists and, later, the Whigs — representatives of the northern, larger business interests and forerunners of the present-day Republican Party — were not supporters either of free enterprise or of full democracy. Instead, those early parties of the "well born," well-to-do, and conservative families in our land still more or less openly favored a regime of oligarchy or rule, in effect, by themselves; a strong and active federal government, responsive mainly to their interests and ideas; and an economic policy on the part of that government akin to the traditions of European mercantilism.

The English Experience

Not only here but in every country of what was to be the democratic-capitalist world, conversion of business leaders to the creed of free enterprise and democracy was a more or less late development. But this development occurred earliest — in the early-to-middle decades of the nineteenth century — and most completely, in England, the first country to go through the Industrial Revolution or enter the industrial machine age. For the rise of the new industrialism, in England then and later elsewhere, transferred the controlling voice in the business community to a new set of men with new attitudes. In the place of the former class of "merchant princes," whose hopes of large profits lay in monopolistic or/and state-aided control of markets, there arose the new class of manufacturing capitalists, whose hopes lay at first in a wholly free competition of ever-improving methods of production. Having as their best route to profits free exertion of their own individual enterprise and ingenuity, the new industrialists in general tended to be more independent, "rugged individualists," asking the state only to give them a wide, free, unobstructed field for their endeavors. Moreover, in the special case of the early British industrialists, their whole situation — never fully, in all aspects, repeated elsewhere — gave them inducements to become especially complete supporters of democracy and humane reforms as well as of free enterprise, and of free trade abroad as well as free enterprise at home. As it bears on other points yet to come in my narrative and argument, let me now spell out this last point briefly.

In Britain's old-world social hierarchy of a century and more ago, not her businessmen but her landowning aristocrats and "gentlemen" were and had been the ruling class. No matter how rich they were the businessmen in general ranked only as members of the middle class, and had much tendency to be, in feeling, a part of the common people. And this now became more significantly true than it had been earlier; the earlier "merchant princes" had been accepted into the governing-class circles and could feel identified with the old, traditional, social and political system of the country. But the new industrialists in most cases rose from humbler social origins and long retained "democratic" feelings. And those feelings were often accentuated by the tendency of their social superiors — the aristocrats and "gentlemen" — to dislike their "pushing" ways and so to snub them. Again, being the chief "backers" of and first gainers from the technological progress in industry which was transforming society, the industrialists tended to aspire to be leaders of social progress in general — leading supporters of new, progressive ideas in all fields, including politics. Also, industrialism required a mass market, enlargement of the market for all commodities to include all the people, or progressive elevation of mass living standards. This requirement aligned the interests of the businessmen with democratic progress. They could well support political democracy, for it enlarged their own political influence as well as that of the working people, and as yet any fears that the latter would use the new political system against them were lulled by the fact that the gospel of free enterprise was still a part of the democratic creed. In the higher, non-business circles of the aristocracy and gentry, or patrician landlords, there was in that half-century just after the French Revolution much reactionary fear of democracy, of the new cult of liberty or individualism, and of all progressivism. There was a vigorous growth of a new conservative or Tory philosophy of authoritarian, "paternal" government over all the people and the economy by the ancient, limited, hereditary ruling class. But in the main the British industrial capitalists opposed that reaction and joined the liberal, democratic, progressive movement. And finally, the resulting political alignment of labor and capital together against the "Tory Landlords" became crystallized around the special issue of the corn laws, or agricultural protectionism, versus the complete freedom of foreign trade which the British industrialists, in their special situation in that epoch, desired as in both their own and the national interest. They saw free trade as the way to cheapen food and thus lower money wages without injuring labor, and as a means of facilitating expansion of industrial exports in exchange for imported food and raw material.

Self-Interest and the Common Welfare

Such were the backgrounds of the first and fullest adoption, by any national business community, of the entire philosophy of the now old, obsolescent, early, special form of "liberalism" which included the gospel of very free enterprise and very limited government. Nor did its adoption by business at once transform the old liberalism into the new conservatism it has since become; that transformation was to be another, still later, development, and is yet to be explained here. The mid-nine-

teenth-century British liberal businessmen had, I think — in a
measure not often excelled by normal, not saintly, human beings
— the true liberal, generous, humane, idealistic, democratic, and
progressive spirit. At the same time it is true, as I have indicated,
that a shrewd perception of where their own interests lay in
the special circumstances they confronted in their time and
country had very much to do with making them adherents of
the liberal outlook. They should not on that account be singled
out for special censure. The tendency to be much influenced
by self-interest in arriving at political opinions — which even
so are usually honest and sometimes valid beliefs as to what
public policies are morally right and best for the welfare of
the entire community — is a tendency not at all peculiar to
businessmen or to any class, in any epoch or society. It is an
all but universal human weakness; and I do not share either
attitude of those among my fellow American liberals of today
who apparently, on the one hand, see only nobility in the devotion, say, of union labor to any cause of its own, and yet on
the other hand, see only immoral selfishness and hypocrisy in the
exactly similar devotion of business to ideals in harmony with
business interests. The point is, there was a time, especially in
England, when conditions were such that a genuine liberalism, in
the form then current, harmonized with the interests and so had
the support of business, together with the common people.

The American Experience

There was never at any time in this country, however, or
indeed elsewhere outside of England, any complete parallel to
that situation in mid-nineteenth-century England. American business, for example, never as a whole accepted the old economic-
liberal views on the question of the tariff, or on that of the
trusts — free trade abroad, or free competition at home. Conditions here, during and after our industrial revolution, which
came later by a few decades than England's, did not so generally
align the interests of our industrialists with those policies. We
have had, in great numbers, our own ruggedly individualistic
captains of industry; but by and large our business leaders in

the past have sought and won much active governmental help — interference for their benefit in the economy — and governmental tolerance of their own collusive endeavors to build up monopolies and to handicap their competitors. Since we never had a European-model aristocracy, the top layer of the American business community has always constituted our topmost social class, wielding from the outset a very great influence over all American life. Through all generations and changes in our country, and despite steady growth of the reality and vigor of our political democracy, this group has continued to seek to retain its early control over government, and insure a mixed set of policies: protection of the business freedoms desired by big interests, and active furtherance of their designs entailing restrictions of the free enterprise of other people. Until very recently, American progressivism had to concentrate its efforts mainly on the task of ending business control and misuse of government, or in other words perfecting our real political democracy. And despite some appearances to the contrary at times, I think it is true that until very recently American individualism — the ideal of great freedom for all individuals and very limited government — remained more a popular than a business ideal. Precisely that fact is what now gives our business defenders of free enterprise, the opponents of present-day liberal, democratic, governmental controls over business, an unfair advantage in political debate.

Expansion of Democracy and the Rift with Business

Meanwhile, there began long ago in the democratic-capitalist world as a whole and even in mid-nineteenth-century England, a rift in the early harmony — which was never complete even there — of business, democracy, and free enterprise. Democracy began to go beyond removal of the pre-democratic, governmental controls over individual enterprise which had suited the "big business" of an earlier day, and impose new and different controls of its own on the new industrialists. For while the Industrial Revolution and its consequence, the new industrial capitalism, brought great benefits to all the people, they also brought new evils into being; and as governments became more democratic and responsive to popular needs, they were obliged even while professing the free-enterprise creed in general to begin to take on new functions and evolve new organs in the effort to alleviate the new evils. Thus, for example, the English Factory Acts came into being in the very heyday of the country's devotion to extreme individualistic liberalism. And a steady, gradual expansion of government and social legislation of many kinds followed, there and elsewhere, right on down to the present.

Also, in the meantime, in a minority quarter far to the left of and unconnected with that main trend but adding still more to the distress of business, socialist movements got under way. The grain of truth in their gospel was and is the fact that under industrial capitalism a measure of conflict does exist between the interests of the class of owners (and their agents, managers) and those of the class of wage-earning workers. The two "classes" have a common interest in high production, but a clash of interests over the division of the proceeds. The old economic-liberal theory of the potential, perfect harmony of all interests in the ideal free-market economy evaded recognition of the fact of "classes" and the partial conflict of their interests. On the other hand the socialist view falsely depicts that conflict as an absolute one, denies the actual bond of common interests between the "masses" and the "capitalists," and holds that democracy must in the end become incompatible with and abolish private capitalism. The socialist body of doctrine is, I believe, in definite error, and a threat to all individual liberties including those most vital to the working people. But its spread has been stimulated by the labor-capital conflict, the slowness of democracy in developing controls over business for the general welfare, and the resistance of business to the moderate controls and reforms which alone can preserve a viable union of the democratic, liberal state and the business economy.

Conservative Redefinition of Free Enterprise, and Today's Liberalism

Now it was in the reaction of business and its friends against the menace of socialism and the expanding activities of demo-

cratic governments, that, in the late nineteenth and early twentieth centuries, the old, originally liberal, economic ideal and
theory of the free-enterprise economy became, by a subtle
change, the gospel of conservatism. The reorientation involved
little apparent change in economic theory. The neoclassical
economists and the pro-business popularizers of their teachings
appeared to be only further elaborating and refining the scheme
of thought of Adam Smith and his immediate successors, the
old classical economists. But what had been the vision of a group
of liberal reformers, of a possible, ideal economy, now became
an unreal, alleged account of the mode of operation of a later,
actual system which was *not* a realization of the original ideal.
And above all, the utopia now confused with reality, now was
defended or exalted in contrast not with the original alternatives
— despotism, oligarchy, mercantilism, all business monopolies,
and the remains of feudalism — but with the new, advancing,
and dreaded alternatives — mild democratic control over capitalism and, as the frightful specter seen as looming beyond that,
socialism.

Finally, when the old economic-liberal theory had thus been
refitted to the uses of, and taken over by, conservatism, liberal
thought began its new, recent and current, still confused grop-
ings toward a new vision of a really possible and sound "middle
way" between the extremes of entirely free enterprise, and
socialism. Thus far, this latest development has attained great
importance only in this country. In Europe, socialism has become the creed of the discontented "many" and their sympathetic leaders; the main conservative forces there have turned
back to ancient antidemocratic, authoritarian ideas; and the term
"liberalism" there still means as a rule the old creed of extreme
individualism, now supported only by tiny, ineffective groups
of essentially conservative although anti-authoritarian intellectuals. But the current new or latter-day American liberalism,
despite its measure of conflict with that older creed, is the true
continuation of the old, authentic, liberal movement, in the new
conditions of today. As such it has yet to achieve, however, an
adequately clear and coherent vision, analysis, and program. One
initial source of a serious fault in much liberal thinking of the

new variety, a short time ago, was its reaction against economic theory or analysis as represented then by the reigning neoclassical economics. In their scorn for the obvious unrealism and conservative bias of that particular body of economic theory, too many of the "new" liberals became unwisely averse to all economic theory, that is, to serious analytical study of the market mechanisms, processes, and requirements of the business economy; and prone to support all reforms humanitarian in purpose without careful study of their to-be-expected, actual consequences. But this is now being remedied, because economists recently have produced much new, improved work in economic theory, of a kind fruitful in suggestions of effective and sound means to liberal ends.

Today's Liberalism and Individual Freedoms

Two questions remain now to be touched on here — of necessity, too briefly. What are the main things which our democracy now can and should do, through its government, to make our business economy work better for the general welfare of all the people? And what, in the doing of these things, may be the dangers of undue curtailment of individual freedoms, and the proper safeguards against those dangers? General answers to the first question are easily enumerated. In the first place, the worst single failure of the business economy in the past to serve the general welfare as it should has been its failure to avoid the rhythmic sequence of "booms and busts," entailing recurrent periods of depression, wasteful idleness of machines and men, and demoralizing hardships for millions. Governmental action on the lines suggested by Keynesian economics, to abolish or control and greatly mitigate the booms and busts, is now possible and can be effective, and need entail only a very minimal degree of interference with private business. In the second place, the automatic mechanisms of the market system cannot today adequately bring about in all fields of enterprise or at all times the proper adjustments of the relative prices of different goods and services and the proper, non-wasteful allocation of the nation's productive efforts and resources among different activities. Monopolies and other obstructions of the market processes at many points, in many cases irremovable, make them only incompletely effective for this purpose. We must work toward a combination of controls by the markets, and by government, of relative prices and the allocation of resources — making full use of the market mechanisms where they can be effective, and supplementing them with governmental action in special fields and at crucial times.

In the third place, a moderate change from the historic pattern of the distribution of incomes, in the direction of reducing the net, disposable incomes of the rich and raising those of the low-income classes, must be sought, through adjustments of governmental policies with respect to taxation and public spending, and policies affecting wages and prices. Care must be taken in this connection to avoid undue discouragement of private saving, investment, and enterprise; but with care this line of action can be so developed as actually to aid, not hamper, private, real capital formation and economic progress through private enterprise, by helping the consuming power of the great mass of the people to grow in step with the economy's producing power. And finally, the often excessive and useless hardships and hazards of unaided, private adjustments by workers, farmers, "little" businessmen, and others, to incessant technological and economic change — getting from vanished jobs into new jobs, or out of declining and into expanding fields of activity — can be mitigated by government in many ways; through employment exchanges, public diffusion of authentic knowledge of changing conditions and opportunities, social-security measures, and temporary subsidies. Care must be taken not to go too far in removing pressures and incentives for the voluntary adjustments to new conditions, which must go on in a free, progressive society; but the old "rugged" ideal of requiring everyone to make all needed readjustments by his own unaided efforts, or perish, cannot be defended or maintained in a modern, humane or fraternal democracy.

And now finally, how are individual freedoms likely to fare under such a program? Conservative alarmists about this generally have, I think, distorted perspectives on the total problem.

Among all the freedoms to be considered they see mainly (a) the business freedoms prized by the owners and managers of large enterprises, more than the freedoms prized or sought by most other people; (b) in general, economic freedoms, more than the civil liberties directly essential to democracy; and (c) freedoms from government, not freedoms from other sorts of compulsions or pressures having private sources. Not hostility nor indifference to, but a better balanced concern for, the freedoms of Americans marks today's liberals. Not only are they constant crusaders for the civil liberties, for all Americans; they also, in advocating new public controls over business, are seeking to enlarge the economic freedoms of the many from compulsions privately imposed by the great enterprises on their masses of employees, small suppliers, would-be competitors, and customers. Of course it is true at the same time that in some respects the new governmental economic controls are bound to impinge on the people generally, and not only on Big Business; but the dangers to the peoples' freedoms from government are of several kinds, needing separate evaluations. Some are indeed real and unavoidable, but unimportant; as they did under wartime rationing and price control, many people will suffer partial losses of minor freedoms familiar in the past, and resent this bitterly — as a rule from petty, selfish motives. One's idea of freedom may be a true moral ideal — freedom for all men, not mainly for oneself, in matters important for human dignity and free development; or it may be a mere expression of petty selfishness, or selfish pettiness — lack of the feeling of responsibility to and for others and the common welfare, and refusal to accept gracefully even merely inconvenient restrictions on oneself, for public ends however important. The love of liberty of too many Americans is too largely of this character. Some restrictions distasteful to such people are bound to be entailed in any substantial measure of positive government for the general welfare; but the loss of freedom which comes under this head will be no great loss.

In a different category are imaginary dangers to our vital freedoms — the alleged dangers of a growth, through lust for power in our public officials, of a really tyrannical, despotic government. In this country, in view of the character of its well-established political system and traditions, the notion of a sheer lust for power in our elected and appointed officials as a serious danger to the freedoms of the governed is a ridiculous myth. The prevailing fault of our officials is the opposite: excessive fear of offending voters; a timid desire to please everybody; great proneness to only follow, not lead, trends of public opinion, and to wait for clear evidence of overwhelming majority demands before acting; and the greatest reluctance to accept and exercise any new bit of power if it means having to contend with strong opposition in any quarter. The real dangers to American freedoms have their sources not within our existing government — in any power-lust in our officials — but in the precarious balance of external pressures upon the government from private blocs; and the chance that if the struggle among these leads to anarchy, or deadlock, or excessive gains by some blocs at the expense of others, aggrieved millions and those willing to exploit their frustrations may build up a frenzy against the disorder of democracy, and for dictatorship.

That brings me to the only real, potential dangers to our vital freedoms which *may* arise in or from a mismanaged "new liberal" program. Expansion of the government's sphere of action, power, and importance does intensify and multiply the pressures or demands upon it. The conflict of pressures makes it more difficult to maintain internal harmony, efficiency, wisdom, and vigor in the operation of the government. And so if the government too largely fails to overcome these difficulties, takes on too much and mishandles it and becomes "a mess," creates and disappoints diverse high hopes, and through its own disorders aggravates instead of mitigating those in the working of our economy — then indeed, in reaction to its failures, Fascism may happen here. But I think this danger can be avoided only by making our democratic government more equal to its tasks, and performing them well — not by refusing to undertake them. If it leaves the needs of the many unmet, the extreme Left will gain, and in alarm over that result the extreme Right will grow even more, and grow reckless, and Fascism will arrive by this route. Only by making a success of the "new" liberalism — the middle way between old-fashioned free enterprise and socialism — can we hope to make freedom secure.

8

ECONOMIC THEORY AND THE AGE

WE LIVE IN[1]

≈

Many readers of this *Review* may remember a past, pleasant perusal of A. G. B. Fisher's *The Clash of Progress and Security*.[2] Now we have before us, from the same author and publisher, a new book with a confusingly similar and different title — *Economic Progress and Social Security*. The latter *is* a new book (in the main), and not just a revised edition of the old one. Though we find here the same basic theme and thesis, the applications, this time, are not to the problems of the 1930's but instead to a number of the world's now current, postwar problems as they were envisaged in prospect from about 1944, when the writing was done. Like its predecessor, this newer work is well written, in an attractive style, at all points lucid and free of impediments to prompt understanding and immediate interest. And the substance is elementary but too often neglected economic theory of a now old-fashioned but still important type, together with much of the social philosophy (made only partly explicit) of nineteenth century liberalism (retained by this author in, how-

---

[1] An appraisal of A. G. B. Fisher's *Economic Progress and Social Security* (New York and London: The Macmillan Co., 1945) was the occasion for these remarks, which first appeared in the *Review of Economics and Statistics*, XXIX (June 1947) and are reprinted here with the permission of the editor.

[2] New York and London: The Macmillan Co., 1935.

ever, a somewhat unusually flexible, ingratiating, and disarming form), and much good and well used factual material on the problems discussed — all this, applied in judicious, thought-provoking treatment of some major problems of economic policy of concern to all of us now in this postwar world.

A few words of reference to the older book may, I believe, usefully precede my further remarks on the successor volume. As may be remembered, *The Clash of Progress and Security* in a measure reflected the author's earlier New Zealand background. He had been a critic of the opinion prevalent in New Zealand and Australia in the 1920's that those countries should preserve the long established pattern of their economies, i.e., continue to expand their rural, "primary" industries and not allow too much development of new, urban industries. As an economist and "economic liberal," our author saw that opinion as one expressing and supporting an unwise resistance, arising from sentimental and security motives on the part of vested interests, to a needed and in the long run inevitable adjustment of those economies to the implications of their own and the world's rising productivity; and his reflections on this case became the stimulus which led him to develop, and apply elsewhere as well, a general theory. As presented in the 1935 book this was a theory — on good neoclassical lines, though leaving statics behind to deal with the dynamics of progress — of the transfers of labor and capital into new employments, required in adjustment to technical progress and generally rising productivity and for realization of the potential fruits of that progress in generally rising standards of living; *plus* a theory of the many resistances, private and public, to the necessary transfers and adjustments, which always tend to arise from misguided devotion to security for everyone in his old position; *plus* a theory of the calamitous effects of successful resistances, in not only thwarting progress but engendering general economic instability, strife in society, contradictory public policies, and aggravation of depressions; and finally, the author's (rather few and feeble) suggestions of public measures for overcoming these resistances and stimulating, easing, and assisting the appropriate processes of structural change or continuous reallocation of resources in a progressive economy. The central application of the whole theory in this early book, written in 1934, was to explanation (admittedly only partial) of the great depression, and critical discussion of the anti-depression policies, American, British, and other, which were then developing; but the basic theory is what carries over into the new book here under review.

The latter proceeds from the immediate background of the author's more recently acquired position in London, as Professor of International Economics at the Royal Institute of International Affairs (Chatham House); and his studies there and a war-time visit to this country, in preparation for this new application of his old analysis to postwar problems seen as in prospect for Britain, America, and the world. In the title of the new book the phrase "social security" can be misleading, since "social security" in the familiar, narrow, or special sense of the social "insurances" is only incidentally and slightly touched upon (in one chapter), and is not in principle included by the author among manifestations of the evil he opposes — the general "spirit" of stubborn clinging to supposed "security" in old positions or refusing to "adjust" activities to changing conditions where losses and risks are involved. The other difference of the new title from the old — omission of the word "clash" (of progress and security) — appears to signify a slight change of emphasis; the argument as put now is more clearly not that economic progress in a society and (reasonable) security for its members are incompatible, but rather that direct *pursuit* of security as the *primary* good is self-defeating as well as inimical to progress; real minimization of insecurity for all and for each can be had only, in the long run, *through* the adaptations also involved in progress and never through resistance to them.

Before it gets to postwar international problems, the book through all its first part — well over half — restates (in a few places in the old but mostly in new words) the author's basic general theory, and illustrates it with discussions of various perennial, national, internal problems. For professional economists the new exposition of the general theory is likely to be of less interest than the one offered in the earlier book, being to a greater extent simple, popular in tone, and sketchy, and omitting the discussions of Pigouvian and other fine theoretical points which gave the earlier book a part of its interest for professional theorists. For the relatively lay readers whom the author undoubtedly has largely aimed at this time, the new presentation seems excellent on the whole, though perhaps a bit too theoretical for many and in places prolix and reiterative. On the political or ideological side, Professor Fisher throughout this book shows his admirable moderation, tact, and freedom from dogmatic narrowness — in the best British tradition. He disavows, fairly convincingly, any hostility to socialism as such, or to growth of state in the place of private action; his concern is not about formal institutions but about what is done, no matter by whom. One readily sees that in fact he fears that a socialist or semi-socialist state will usually do wrong instead of right things; but his ideal is simply any "flexible" economy in which all the (producing) parts get promptly and fully adjusted to their changing opportunities for fullest service to the world of consumers; and his castigation of British industrialists for clinging to their old positions and routines and seeking through monopoly and state assistance to avoid the need for new adjustments, amply frees him from any suspicion of being one who identifies his ideal with the private enterprise system as such. He also attacks the confusions of the varied tribe of "planners" whose "plans" disclose no economic *rationale*, and in this connection has several approving footnote references to kindred passages in Hayek's *Road to Serfdom;* but he succeeds much better than Hayek did in giving ideological opponents no apparent grounds for misunderstanding and bitter resentment.

When at last international problems are taken up, there is first a review of those of the interwar period and the mistakes that prevented any full solution of them. We are told that Britain over-concentrated on reviving her old export industries, and made no sufficient efforts to modernize and diversify her economy and reshape its pattern in the light of all currently potential consumer demands at home and abroad, and of all her currently potential productive powers. When the results of her monetary mistake of 1925 *and* of her industrial non-readjustment "forced" her into exchange depreciation, she welcomed that little device with illusory, exaggerated hopes for advantage from it, and as a refuge from the need to make fundamental industrial adjustments. Her new tariff and the Ottawa agreements were a further, also illusory, refuge of the same kind; and the bad effects of both her monetary and her commercial policies on other countries reacted adversely on herself. Likewise, the American tariff and debt-collection policies of the 1920's, and the inadequacy of the good but too limited reciprocal trade program in the 1930's, meant that Americans as well as Englishmen refused to run the risks connected with essential readjustments to new conditions. And so on; there is much more about what went wrong and why in the interwar period, but these illustrations indicate the nature of it all.

Many problems, then, of the *present* postwar period are treated effectively on similar lines — Britain's problem of righting her foreign balance and generally getting on her feet, the American tariff and dollar shortage and related problems and that of stabilizing America's prosperity for her own and the world's good, the problem of reviving world trade and in some measure freeing it from excessive nationalistic restraints, the best practicable shape for the future of international lending and investment, the problems connected with efforts to industrialize backward areas, reviving the economies of the defeated nations (vengeful treatment is emphatically condemned), and so on. All these and other problems are considered entirely from the standpoint of the author's theory of the adjustments required for progress and stability, and the paramount importance of overcoming all the fears and attitudes that prevent adjustments. By a most important extension of the principle it is argued, too, that *national* security even in the military sense is always so dependent in the end on healthy national economies and they in turn on the health of the world economy, that direct pursuit of such security at the cost of world economic progress, adjustment, and stability is for any nation self-defeating; the same thing is true here as of all the private security-seekings which prevent adjustments within the national economies, and no international problems can be solved except in so far as both kinds of obstacles can be overcome.

The general, positive proposal that emerges in the end is pathetically mild, or feeble as one likes, in relation to the stubborn forces to be coped with, but it must be granted that any stronger proposal on the same lines would be utopian. The proposal is to set up an international organization of expert investigators and advisers, for continuous study of all internationally important, national economic policies of the member nations and all changes therein and their effects; the subscribing governments would bind themselves to submit in advance all plans for changes in such policies, and to hold them in abeyance pending study and report by the international body. The advice of the latter *could* then be disregarded, but would in any case be published to the world. Adversely affected nations could also complain to this body about other nation's policies and elicit investigations and reports thereon; and the international body, without waiting to be asked for advice or complained to, could always initiate studies and reports at its own discretion. One wonders whether anything going even as far as this proposal is now deemed feasible, or contemplated, in the highest quarters.

I think that as a whole this is quite a good book, of much interest and value; but I find its value, though not small, considerably restricted by what seem to me two kinds of "bias" or only partial, one-sided vision, inherent in its author's general outlook. One limitation or bias appears, in the "scientific" field of economic theory, in Professor Fisher's evident, though barely indicated, unfavorable or entirely unimpressed attitude toward Keynesian thought and the policies advocated by its exponents. His own thinking is entirely confined within the field of the older type of theory which concentrated on the processes of attainment of the resource-allocation equilibrium, and supported the view that the one fundamental task of public policy is to maintain favorable conditions for the best working out of these processes. Hence in dealing with our postwar international economic problems, he sees them only in the light of the common need of the national economies to break down internal and external barriers preventing adequate, prompt, continuous, particular adjustments of their parts (different industries) to changing conditions of production and demand. The Keynesian thesis that present-day capitalist economies face, *in addition to* the difficulties of continuous reattainment of the resource-allocation equilibrium, a *further* set of difficulties due to a need for, and their inability without public help to attain or maintain, a *second* sort of equilibrium also, i.e., the proper balance of the over-all aggregates, saving, investment, and consumption — this thesis, and the policy-ideas it leads to, leave Professor Fisher unimpressed and receive extremely little, even critical, attention in his book. He might reply to criticism on this score that he claims only to analyze one important part (which I grant that the Keynesians, certainly, improperly neglect) of the task of getting the national economies to function and interact in mutually beneficial, instead of mutually destructive, ways. But he clearly regards the part of this task which he is analyzing as alone fundamental, and always briefly dismisses Keynesian policies as merely superficial, monetary palliatives for economic ills which leave untouched, facilitate inaction about, and distract attention from the fundamental need for adaptations of the structure of production to changes of technique and of consumer demand, and the root-evil of prevailing social, psychological, and political obstacles to the carrying out of those adaptations. Now *if* there is truth in Keynesian theory, the Keynesian policies are *not* mere palliatives merely because they are not directly aimed at fulfilling *this* need; they are efforts to fulfill another, simultaneous, and perhaps equally or even more (immediately) urgent need; moreover, if both needs are real they may well be interrelated in such a way that effective efforts to meet either one cannot be separated from but need the help of concurrent efforts to meet the other. If monetary-fiscal measures are at times required for, and successful in, preventing general depressions in the national economies, they may make possible what would otherwise be impossible in the way of success for concurrent efforts of the kind Professor Fisher urges to attain his goal; for certainly depressions and the fear of them intensify all the resistances to structural change or resource reallocation and new competition about which he is rightly so concerned. The one-sided, Keynesian view of our postwar problems is so prevalent that I welcome Professor Fisher's able presentation of the other side; but I think his view is equally one-sided in its own way.

The other bias in his thought, which I think is even more serious, lies in the field of social philosophy, and prevents him, it seems to me, from fully understanding and doing justice to the increased security-mindedness and, with that, the whole outlook which over recent decades has been coming to rule and does now rule this age we live in. As the mental context or framework surrounding his own economic thinking and controlling its focus or perspective, he retains the social philosophy or outlook on life which ruled in the culture-pattern of an earlier, now receding epoch, the nineteenth century. This philosophy idealized and largely achieved a flexible or fluid economy and society of readily detachable, mobile, adaptable, and boldly enterprising individuals, because it valued economic progress and, as means to that end, free, unrestrained innovations and adaptations to them, far more highly than it prized the other, human and social values of security, stability, and continuity of the modes or patterns of life of families, communities, and all social groups. Retaining that arrangement of the hierarchy of values as his own and the only one he can deem quite sensible, Professor Fisher works out, a little farther on the lines charted by the nineteenth century liberal, orthodox economists, his theory of economic life as the processes of adaptation to the impacts of technical and the requirements for economic progress; and he tends to assume, or even think he has proved, that the unrestrained adaptations, shown by his theory to be necessary *for* optimal results *in terms of* progress by all to fuller economic satisfactions, are in the long run necessary also in an absolute sense; and that all the human attitudes and ways of seeking first to preserve familiar and valued patterns of life, which impede or restrain those adaptations, are senseless, irrational interferences with the rational processes of economic life, which it is the main duty of public policy to overcome or break down.

Now I think it is futile to go on preaching that gospel, unmodified, to this new age we live in — not because this new

age is "crazy" as it seems to old-fashioned liberals, but because
it is groping its way, indeed confusedly as yet, to some new
arrangement of its ruling hierarchy of ultimate, human ends or
values, in which (rather centrally among other changes) economic progress will no longer as decisively outrank security, in
the sense of a good measure of stability of valued patterns of life,
as it did in the nineteenth century. It is true, as Professor Fisher
insists, that much further economic progress is still both needed
and desired by the popular majorities in even the richest countries; that people inconsistently want both this and the protections of all groups against disturbing changes and risks, which
prevent it; and also that refusals to allow or make needed adaptations to new conditions, in a world that still is technologically
and in many ways inexorably dynamic, not only impede progress
but cause multiplying maladjustments, tensions, conflicts, and
disorders, and make everyone and everything not more but less
secure. But if my guess is correct, what is under way is one of
those changes in the ruling balance of relative strengths of our
civilization's fundamental desires, which seem to occur at long
intervals in history and mark transitions to new epochs with
culture-patterns so radically altered in manifold ways as to *seem*
"insane" to the loyal heirs of older standards. Progress to fuller
economic satisfactions is still desired, yes, but not, generally
speaking, by the millions either collectively or individually, with
quite the degree of passion or of (relative) single-mindedness
which generally prevailed in the nineteenth century. Assurance
of protection or preservation of already achieved and valued
patterns of life and the means to support them is regaining something more like the great if not supreme importance it has
generally had in *most* human civilizations and parts of history,
apart from the economic liberal epoch. And the radical inconsistencies and confusions in public thought in these current
decades mean only that we are still in the chaos of transition —
the new balance of desires and new total vision of a generally
desired scheme of individual and social life have not yet found
or assumed any settled or coherent form. Absolute security cannot be had, and the many in this new age have yet to learn what
degree of it they really want at what cost in other terms, and

how to work for it in ways reconcilable with their other desires; or conversely, how to get what they want in the way of economic progress and the adaptations it requires, without more disturbance and insecurity than they can now bring themselves to put up with. While the public mind is so confused about the balance or pattern of ends it desires, economic analysis of policy problems, which must aim at discovery of the most effective, consistent set of means to a generally agreed-on set of ends, cannot do much. But it is no good urging on the public, as pure scientific truth which it *must* accept, a program that is really the best set of means to the set of ends (giving economic progress a stronger priority over the values associated with security than is now accepted) which *was* accepted in a by-gone epoch. Because economic inquiry is concerned with means to ends, it always needs the context and complement of a social philosophy, adequately specifying the pattern of ends, the conditions of fullest attainment of which it should investigate; but analysis framed in the context of an old philosophy no longer relevant to the main aspirations of a new age will not adequately serve the latter. Because the two things are interrelated — a philosophy of ends cannot be formulated without study of the means, and costs in terms of each other, entailed in the pursuit of them — I personally believe that more economists now should become also social philosophers, and endeavor to contribute to or assist the efforts of this new age to achieve a satisfactory, coherent, and stable formulation of its scheme of ends. But in any case, economists who inherit and retain unmodified the philosophy of a former age, and do all their thinking in *that* context, must expect their advice to make little impression on this age we live in.

Professor Fisher apparently has no such conception of what he is up against. In one notable passage in this book, he argues that to take account in one's economic thought of "the contemporary climate of opinion" would be to defer unwisely to a mere "fashion" of public thought which cannot usefully guide any effort to solve serious problems. It is better, he thinks, to "swim against the tide" as he is doing, because "tides have a way of turning"; surely it is *less* futile to do this (he continues) than to "kick against the pricks," i.e., resist or encourage people to resist the

stern necessities of economic readjustment to inexorably changing, objective conditions. But if I am right, the contemporary
climate of opinion against which Professor Fisher is so valiantly
fighting is no ephemeral fashion or tide that will soon turn, but
is something as durable and inexorable in its own way as the set
of pricks confronting his opponents. No doubt in the late eighteenth century, when the *now old* climate of opinion (economic-
liberal outlook) which still dominates Professor Fisher's mind,
was very new, there were many loyal adherents of the then
crumbling old regime who dismissed the new fashion of thought
as ephemeral or hopefully deemed it only a tide that soon would
turn. But it became and remained, for about a century and a half,
the climate of ruling ideals which greatly fostered economic
progress, the flexible, free society of mobile, adaptable, and
boldly enterprising individuals still idealized by Professor Fisher,
and the type of economic theory and policy which assumed and
served that form of society and its ruling ends. Today, I think,
there are signs of the coming not only of new forms of society
in the political and institutional sense, but also of some new or
rearranged pattern of ends to be better served by them — ends
among which economic progress will be less emphasized, and
security, in a wide sense, more emphasized. Professor Fisher has
enough flexiblity of mind (as I said earlier) to be willing to accept formal socialism provided it will do (what seem to him) the
right things, but not enough to see that behind the growing pop-
ularity of socialism lies a growing, *not necessarily unreasonable*,
desire of millions for institutions adapted to the doing of *other*
things, not exactly in line with his ideals. The economic-liberal
epoch did fine things, then mainly wanted, but had to discourage
and repress to a great extent the human love of preserving old,
loved, patterns of life, in order to free the currently dominant
desire for new economic achievements from the fetters which
that other motive had generally imposed in earlier centuries, and
would, where its strength persisted or revived, reimpose. Every
culture restrains some human passions with special firmness, in
order to give more scope to others with a higher standing in the
current *ethos;* and eventually, as the more freely indulged desires become relatively well satisfied and the long repressed ones

grow more starved, the latter rebel and find countless champions, and after more or less turmoil the balance changes. Part of the human cost of the great economic progress of the nineteenth century was a general subjection of most men to insecurities and a degree of mutability of nearly everything in their lives and around them, which human nature would stand only as long as getting ahead to higher economic living standards remained, generally, a very dominant, unfilled desire. That it is becoming *less* dominant, and yielding more to the again growing desire for fairly stable and well protected patterns of life, is, I think, one chief part of the meaning of the altered climate of opinion of our time. This change, viewed in a long historical perspective, is in itself a turning of the tide; but I would guess that the *next* turn lies still a good number of generations away in the future.

Nor need that, as I see the problem, seem to economists a pessimistic forecast. There is no reason why economists should think economic progress more important than it seems to other people, or be unsympathetic with popular, largely non-economic desires and values. Their business, simply as economists, is to study the conditions of attainment, at least cost, of whatever range and hierarchy of ends or satisfactions the public wishes to pursue. If the public is changing the balance in its scheme of ends, and if we as economists wish to serve it as fully as we can in our professional capacity, we must adapt the focus of our thinking to the somewhat altered problems set, in the sphere of means, by this new outlook in the sphere of ends. *This* adaptation Professor Fisher and others who share his basic convictions or ideals are unwilling or unable to make. Not to make it is of course their right, *in* their capacity as social philosophers; but they should see that in so far as their now unpopular ideals direct their economic thinking, the latter cannot lead to quite accurate solutions of the present-day economic (policy) problems set by the objective circumstances *and* the main desires of peoples in this age we live in. That is not to say that Professor Fisher's analysis of our postwar problems is by any means wholly devoid of truth that is relevant even from that standpoint. There are and will be continuing, urgent needs for countless new adaptations, often unwisely resisted, of economic activities and parts of the (resource-allocation) structures of national economies and the world economy to changed and changing conditions — whatever pattern of ends we assume in the study of what they should be and how to bring them about. But a study premised on a no longer accepted pattern of ends cannot describe for this age we live in, nor show it how to achieve, *just* the pattern of economic adaptations jointly called for by current objective conditions *and* the current desires of men and nations.

9

PHILOSOPHIES AND ECONOMIC THEORIES

IN MODERN OCCIDENTAL CULTURE[1]

◆

Introduction

Among human cultures, modern Western civilization has been distinguished chiefly by its achievements (1) in business enterprise and economic progress; (2) in natural science and technology — the development of the modern physical and biological sciences and the arts or techniques based upon them; and (3) among the social studies, in the science and art of economics. To other cultures, such as the ancient Western, the medieval Western, and native Oriental, must be credited outstanding achievements in a contrasting set of fields: the fine arts, religion, moral philosophy and codes, the ordering of life in stable and widely accepted patterns, refinement of manners in the upper classes, and the forms of philosophical and social thought associated more with art, ethics, and religion than with economics or any near approach to science in the modern sense. Now of course the esthetic, ethical, and religious interests generally predominant in those other cultures have been active also in the life and thought of the modern West; but here they have tended to be, too often, overshadowed by, and in confused conflict with, the stronger

---

[1] Reprinted, by permission, from *Ideological Differences and World Order*, ed. F. S. C. Northrop (Yale University Press, 1949).

business, scientific-technical, and economic interests. It is with manifestations of this conflict, in the related histories of modern Western philosophical and economic thought, that I am concerned in the present essay.

In philosophy, this conflict has appeared in the clashes of philosophies of two general types, which I will call respectively visionary and prosaic. The visionary philosophies, either continuing the traditions of or akin to the great philosophies which originated in the ancient and medieval periods, have been such as Platonism, Thomism, the visionary side of the eighteenth century's natural order and human rights philosophy, German (Hegelian) Idealism, and, in one aspect, Marxism. These were bold elaborations of at once cosmic or historical and social-moral visions of a resplendent order in the universe and to be achieved in all human life, transcending man's empirical but, allegedly, not his rational knowledge.

In contrast with these, the prosaic philosophies have been those with such largely overlapping names as rational empiricism, naturalism, mechanism, utilitarianism, positivism, instrumentalism — the philosophies claiming special affinities with modern science and a careful, skeptical avoidance of exciting but nonscientific, transcendental, and moral-absolutist speculations. In our culture as a whole the predominance of devotion to business, science, technology, and the economic aspect of individual and social welfare has generally given the greater competitive advantage to the prosaic philosophies; for men tend to believe that the kind of knowledge they find relevant to their more avid pursuits exhausts reliable knowledge, and that what their keenest interests make them aware of alone makes up reality. But even in the modern West there have always been countless persons — chiefly among artists, devoutly religious people, and ethically sensitive and ardent social idealists — whose predominant interests have in the same way made visionary philosophies the more persuasive to them.

My subject, however, is not simply general philosophies of these two kinds considered in themselves, but their expressions and results in varieties of economic and social thought involving general presuppositions suggested by them. Hence, before going on to discuss the philosophies in this connection, I must speak of

(1) the interconnection of the modern West's economic with its natural-scientific ardors and achievements; (2) the great prominence and development and the peculiar character this connection has given to the study of economics; and (3) how certain internal problems in the latter, and intrinsic connections of economic theories with social-moral philosophies, have brought not only prosaic but also visionary philosophic views into play in this field and into conflict within it.

Business, Science, and Economic Science

The vigorous pursuit of wealth in our culture not only has utilized but also has stimulated and supported the triumphant progress of the natural sciences. It is true that most leading scientists themselves have been chiefly motivated *not* by interest in the potentially profitable, technological applications of their discoveries but simply by love of work and discovery in "pure" science for its own sake; and I shall speak later of the philosophic significance of the experience of the scientist, which I think may be described as an esthetic-intellectual enjoyment of the patterns of order in all parts of nature, which science progressively explores. But the immense development of science since the Renaissance has required also the widespread support arising from the prevalent desire and esteem for the kind of knowledge giving power to master nature and lift human life from poverty to ever-rising planes of wealth. Probably it has been this factor which has so largely channeled the pursuit of esthetic-intellectual enjoyment into exacting work in the natural sciences, where so much prosaic, logical, and factual investigation must be toiled through, in payment for the thrilling and potentially useful discoveries ultimately won. In any event, the prevalent enthusiasm in the pursuit of wealth has clearly stimulated the advance of science; and the latter in return, of course, through its effects in the sphere of technology, has made possible the phenomenal rise of economic productivity and living standards of all classes.

Now it is no wonder that a culture thus largely dominated by business and science has tended from the outset, in the sphere of the social studies, to isolate, emphasize, and develop most fully the study of economics. Just as naturally it has tended to make this study, as far as possible, a science emulating the methods and concepts of the triumphantly advancing natural sciences — and more especially, those of physics, the first-established and in many ways the most impressive science of them all. As the study of economics, then, has developed *in its main tradition*, it has been from the outset in the seventeenth century *a physics-emulating science of the pursuit of wealth* as one abstractly considered phase of social life. More precisely, the subject matter studied by this economic science has included (1) the conditions of the fullest success in the pursuit of wealth, in the situations and on the parts of the different individual actors in an economic society; (2) the quasi-mechanical "laws" of the social-economic processes *consequent and thus contingent upon* the regular, actual fulfillment of those conditions; and (3) the national, governmental policies required for the most effective furtherance and stabilization of *general* prosperity within each nation.

As thus delimited, the subject matter of this science has in fact proved amenable *in large measure* to successful investigation by a method and through concepts broadly similar to those of physics: the method of postulation, deduction, and empirical (in the case of economics mainly statistical) verification, and the use of "mechanistic" conceptual schemes or "models." In the case of economics the models are consciously much simplified envisagements of social-economic systems as quasi-mechanical systems, in which all the parts or individual actors are always "gravitating" to the sites of, and reacting appropriately to, their best economic opportunities, and in the process exerting predictable effects upon each others' opportunities and actions. The economic science thus built up has advanced, not as triumphantly as the natural sciences but in the same accumulative way; and as the study of the conditions of maximal economic prosperity, it has naturally always attracted a wider public interest than any other social science.

My description of the character of this main-tradition economics has already suggested, however, one important respect in which it is unlike physics or any natural science: the peculiar fact that it combines inseparably a science and an art which mutually involve each other. Now this results from a dilemma which necessarily confronts any social science. In the case of a natural science and an art dependent on it (e.g., physics and engineering), the human practitioners and their practice of the art are *not* also included in the subject matter of the pure science itself; hence the latter is *not* obliged to take account of the potentialities of the art in framing its own descriptive propositions. But a social science inevitably is in the position of endeavoring simultaneously to develop knowledge which may be used to guide human actions and also to describe and explain the *actual* pattern of *the same* actions. In the main-tradition economics, the way of meeting this dilemma has been to include the theory of the art of economy among the fundamental assumptions of theory in the descriptive science; or in other words to assume — with the support of common knowledge of the character of business behavior — a natural tendency of all men in reacting to their economic situations and opportunities to act toward the wealth-maximizing goal of the economic art.

There has thus developed, through study of the requirements and consequences of effective practice of the economic art, a theory in the descriptive science of economic activities which gains increasing truth in so far as the progress and general use of this science and art reduces the gap between economically ideal and actual economic behavior. Too often dogmatic errors in economic theorizing have arisen from inadequate awareness of the implications of the peculiar, twofold nature of this type of theory; the gap just mentioned has been ignored or unduly minimized; empirical study of *actual human behavior* in business (as distinct from study of *the situations* of the actors and their economically best reactions thereto) has been neglected; and theory of a pattern of social-economic processes contingent upon universal fulfillment in fact of "ideal" assumptions, has been presented as literal description of a supposedly actual and strictly inevitable pattern. All this has involved not only neglect of an important type of empirical research which should accompany theoretical work but also a tendency to misconstrue economic theory as *just* like physical or mechanical theory. But these errors, however natural and common in the history of the main-tradition economics, have been not necessary consequences of its twofold nature as a mutually dependent science and art but failures to deal correctly with the problem.

Apart, however, from those errors and that underlying mutual dependence of the economic art and science, further problems arise from the abstractness of the purely economic subject matter and the fact that *it*, as one phase only of human life, is in concrete reality always involved with the whole. Neither as theory of an art nor as theory in a science — neither in its prescriptive nor in its descriptive aspect — can theory of the pursuit of wealth be as fully independent of other branches of social reflection and inquiry as many exponents of the main-tradition economics have imagined it to be. The economic art is neither in itself the whole art of life nor yet a special art which can be completely isolated; and the science which describes only those tendencies in individual and social life which have to do with adaptations of choices and activities to economic conditions and opportunities cannot by itself either fully or quite truly describe any actual or possible concrete activities. In each society economic life necessarily is framed within and affected by some noneconomic human and socio-cultural milieu, more or less specific to that society; and *in consequence* economic thought necessarily develops within and is affected by some wider context, or mental vision, pertaining to the rest of life and to the social order.

Despite those facts I think the main-tradition idea of a special science of the purely economic subject matter alone has fully vindicated itself long since, as most fruitful of real scientific achievements; though I shall speak later on of the contributions, and not only of the errors, of the anti-main-tradition "historical and institutional schools" of economists, who have drawn the seemingly obvious conclusion from the point I have just been emphasizing, and tried to broaden economics into forms of historical sociology. I am not yet ready, however, to discuss those efforts and the issues they have raised. Here I am concerned only with the fact that *all* economic theories have developed in wider intellectual contexts; and I think analysis of the nature of these contexts will also reveal the point of contact, so to speak, of all economic thought with conflicting views in general philosophy.

Economic Theories, Ideologies, and Philosophies

What, then, are the contexts of economic theories, and what are they about? I have so far only spoken vaguely of "the rest of life," and must now give meaning and precision to that phrase. The very assertion that all human life contains something which is noneconomic, or not included in the pursuit of wealth, may seem to come in question, if we think of wealth correctly, and in line with all recent main-tradition economic theory, as including not only material goods but all items satisfying any specific human wants or interests, and costing sacrifices of any alternative satisfactions obtainable only through alternative uses of the same "resources" — money, material goods, effort, time, or whatever. On this correct, inclusive view of the meaning of wealth it may seem that practice of economy includes all choosing, and thus everything in human life, and that nothing noneconomic is left to which the context of an economic theory can pertain. But the seeming is false. For besides all specific wants and goods, there also are in human life general desires, or ideals — desires expressed in, and producing efforts to realize, all-inclusive ideas of the good, imperative order, form, pattern, or structure of one's life as a whole and society as a whole.

The distinction I am making here, to put the matter in Aristotelian terms, is that between the "material" and the "formal" side of life. Not all wealth is material in the sense of consisting of solid, tangible things, but all is material in the different sense of consisting of *particular* items, making up in the widest sense the riches or richness of life. But life demands in addition to richness some attractive unifying pattern which will limit assertions of the otherwise indefinitely expansive and conflicting particular desires within each individual and within a society, thus assuring order in contrast with chaos and, beyond that, the type of order which is most desired. Thus economic life in any society goes on within some more or less restrictive form of order, having as its ideal expression the dominant ideology or philosophy of life in that society, and as its actual imperfect realization the institutions and generally observed mores of the society and its members. Moreover, whatever pattern of order in the scientific sense — a system of processes conforming, approximately, to predictive laws — emerges *in* the economic life, as such, of a society, is never the product of economic wants and conditions alone. It is always a joint product of those factors and the currently effective social-moral frame of order. Hence any *theory* of an economic order requires as its context a vision of the social-moral frame of order within which the adaptations of economic choices and activities to the specific wants and situations of the actors are envisaged as proceeding.

It is hardly surprising, then, that the contexts of economic theories — different systems of economic theory — generally have been ideologies — social-moral visions current in particular societies and epochs, and shared with other citizens by the economists concerned. Ideologies, to use another term, are the philosophies of life of societies through epochs, or of the dominant groups in them, or of insurgent social movements. Central in them are the general desires or ideals of their adherents; but they also include extensive bodies of beliefs supporting those desires. Among these are not only the beliefs commending realization of the envisioned "ways of life" as possible and imperative, but also overt or latent philosophical beliefs, representing either the order of nature or the past and destined future course of human history, as *necessitating* realization of the ideals in question. Now economists generally have been both citizens, and students of the current economic life, of the same societies. They have generally developed their economic theories in the contexts of the ideologies they have shared with other like-minded citizens, although often, in developing their personal variants of those ideologies, they have added important contributions. The results are compound systems of economic-scientific and social-philosophic thought.

Examples of two different types are (1) the nineteenth-century "classical" and the later "neoclassical" economic theories, in the context of the classical eighteenth- and nineteenth-century liberalism or liberal individualism and internationalism; and (2) Marxism in the nineteenth century — a special transformation and development of classical economic theory in the very different context of Marx's vision, as a socialist, of the history and destined salvation of mankind. In the former case, the ideology was already dominant, and its ideals were largely — though of course imperfectly — realized in the existing social order. Hence the economic theory consisted of analysis of those actualities and possibilities of the current economic life which were of interest to adherents of the ideology; analysis of the conditions of maximal satisfaction of all the economic interests sanctioned by the ideology, and of the pattern of processes in the *potential* economic order whose full realization was seen as contingent upon that of the ideal liberal social order. In the case of Marxism, on the other hand, the ideology was *not* anywhere dominant, nor were its ideals anywhere even partly realized in the existing social order; it stood everywhere in total opposition to the latter, and as purely a vision of a desired and predicted future "new order"; and the economic theory was chiefly analysis of the evils of current economic life under existing institutions, and a forecast of their intensification and resulting developments leading to attainment of the new order. But in *all* cases the "ideological contexts" of economic theories have affected, above all, *the fields of attention* or ranges of problems studied, and the angles of vision from which they were seen.

Is not the existence, however, of diverse economic theories tied up with rival, partisan ideologies serving as their contexts, a standing refutation of the scientific claims of economics? Not entirely by any means. The diverse biases infused into different economic theories by their ideological contexts have indeed made them all imperfectly scientific, at best; but these biases have generally *not* prevented them from attaining and including substantial scientific achievements. Facts — and economists do study facts — and logic enforce their own demands upon all conscientious, truth-seeking investigators; and few eminent economists, whatever their ideologies, have been seriously guilty of the *worst kind* of bias — distortion of evidence or reasoning in the scientific field and relating to the problems studied. What *has* infected the work of all — being inherent in the partial dependence of economic theories on their ideological contexts — is bias *in the different sense* of that direction of attention to some and not to other scientific problems, which arises from devotion to a set of social aims and pursuit of the knowledge relevant to the task of realizing them. But the effect of this has been only a production of economic theories which, while different, have all had much validity in their respective fields and been, in the main, not inconsistent with but complementary to one another.

There remains, however, a deeper, *philosophical* difficulty and source of conflict within and among varieties of economic and social thought, which reflects the general conflict in our culture between prosaic and visionary views in general philosophy. Economic-scientific thought as such shares with modern scientific thought in general a tendency to *seem* to involve exclusively prosaic, fundamental views of knowledge and reality and thus to seem irreconcilable with any visionary views whatever. But most ideologies, on the contrary, very clearly involve, or are at bottom, visionary philosophies — boldly imaginative, charged with faith and emotion, and, for their adherents, inspiring all life with a vision of the right, imperative order in all human affairs, and generally also of supporting features of the cosmic order or of the historical process. Hence the history of modern Western economic and social thought is full of instances of failures to achieve any full inner coherence in combinations of largely scientific economic theories with distinctly visionary ideologies; and also of attempts and failures in other quarters to establish satisfactory all-prosaic or all-visionary total systems.

Yet I do not believe that this dilemma is a final one or one that cannot be resolved. In philosophy and in all inquiries there are valid prosaic and other valid visionary insights; and despite the many failures of past efforts to achieve it, I think these *can* be combined in a both well-balanced and entirely coherent synthesis. In our culture the disbelief in this possibility is rooted chiefly in the conviction that modern natural science has exclusively prosaic foundations and lends no support to any, but discredits all, visionary views. Nevertheless I think despite the misleading special prominence of its prosaic side and the claims of prosaic philosophies to speak for it exclusively, natural science itself has a basic, visionary side.

At an early point in this essay I spoke of the scientists' esthetic-intellectual enjoyment of exploring patterns of order in nature; and I now make the further assertion that not only the enjoyment but also, in its primary stages, the process of discovery of those patterns of order has an esthetic-intellectual or visionary character. Before the clear-cut logical and empirical investigations which give science its prosaic aspect become possible, there must be hypotheses with implications to be elaborated and tested by those investigations; and hypotheses originate as imaginative and attractive visions, suggested by already existing knowledge *and* the scientist's *feeling for* the probable structural pattern of his subject matter. Moreover, while the vision is corrected in details in the later investigations, the *feeling* of its truth remains the indispensable basis of the knowledge that nature has an order or conforms to laws. Hume's discovery that this knowledge has no prosaic basis in definite sense perceptions or in logic should have made him skeptical not about the foundations of science but about the sufficiency of his own purely prosaic philosophy. Science involves the visionary reliance on feeling and imagination *as well as* the prosaic reliance on rigorous logic and exact observations. While in other fields we seem unable to achieve a coherent synthesis of our visionary and our prosaic insights, in its own field natural science embodies just such a coherent synthesis.

In social science, however, the task is more difficult, because here the patterns of order which must be first envisioned and later elaborated and confirmed in the realm of solid facts, are not, as in nature apart from human creations, simply existent in that realm; instead initially they are only subsistent as possibilities, realizable through human efforts. Their attractions must lead not only to the discovery of them, through feeling and imagination, as possibilities, but also to their approximate realization in actual social orders — man-made, though on a natural basis — before the study of them can be carried through in prosaic and thus fully scientific terms. And in fact, because all theories in a social science involve visions which *never* become *fully* realized and are always subjects of emotion-filled controversy, these theories never can become *fully* scientific by the natural science standard.

But it is time now to turn from purely general explanation of this situation as it affects economics to historic illustrations. I shall attempt a general sketch of much of the history of Western philosophical and economic thought, mainly in modern times but beginning with the ancient and medieval Plato-Aristotle-Aquinas tradition, mainly visionary throughout, which is both a seldom entirely discarded heritage and a contrasting background to the main varieties of modern Western thought.

II

The Ancient-Medieval Background: Plato and Economics

Both in the ancient and in the medieval European culture there was a degree of one-sidedness of the kind opposite to that which has been characteristic of modern culture. The dominant concerns were not economic and scientific-technical but esthetic, religious, and ethical. The primary stress was upon the formal, not the material side of life; not upon the pursuit of wealth to satisfy all specific wants more fully, but upon the pursuit of agreement in devotion to the right ideals, to assure well-ordered lives and societies. Hence development of science in the modern sense was neglected. As to wealth, it was held to be unimportant; not even the effort to raise living standards above poverty was thought important; the tendency was to accept and in the Middle Ages even to honor poverty, not to regard it as an evil. And the pursuit of wealth, as practiced by the capitalists or businessmen, who existed but as rather humble minorities, not only was not highly thought of; it was even regarded by the leading minds with some antipathy, as a danger to spiritual and moral health in both souls and communities — an expression and a stimulant of the always potentially overexpansive and conflicting particular desires in men, leading to disorder if not strictly curbed.

Now the great tradition of philosophical and social thought, begun by Plato and developed further, with modifications, by Aristotle and in the Middle Ages by Aquinas, expressed and by its influence strengthened all those related tendencies in those two cultures. For my purpose here, all the essential ideas in that tradition can be found in Plato's dialogues, and I need say little about their later developments and modifications. In the original

Platonic as in the later forms, the total scheme of thought was both a general philosophy and a philosophy of life for all men and societies, *and included also* the rudiments of an economic theory. For the latter had its lowly place in the scheme, though largely as a branch of social pathology—a study of the evil tendencies arising in the pursuit of wealth, which the moralist statesman should understand and thus be able to control.

Important in giving Plato's thought its direction were his three connected antipathies: to democracy, to capitalism, and to the philosophical views of the Sophists, which strongly anticipated what have been the dominant modern Western views. He grounded all three antipathies on the same foundation: a theory of knowledge, reality, and ethics according to which the condition of attainment of knowledge of reality and the consequent right ordering of lives and states is the supremacy of "reason" over the senses, appetites, and passions. Sense perceptions are of many, diverse, and ever-changing apparent objects; the task of reason is to study them with skeptical detachment and penetrate beyond them to apprehension of the stable and divinely harmonious pattern of purely general "ideas" or universals, which the sense objects *imperfectly* exemplify and which itself alone is pure "reality." Unless "reason" does this, the sense perceptions generate not knowledge but a maze of variable, confused, and misleading opinions. Moreover the sense perceptions, through the opinions they create, stimulate the appetites and passions which disrupt order and engender chaos in lives and societies. To control them reason must (1) truly apprehend the pattern of the real cosmos and thus (2) awaken the soul's potential love and emulation of that divine order; and so, finally, (3) with the help of that enthusiasm make the will or "spirited principle" in each soul and in the state its loyal, executive arm, to "rein back" all the particular desires within limits, making them mutually consistent and consistent with the proper order in each life and in the community. Now the conclusions from this whole theory which Plato applied as criticisms of democracy and of the Sophists I pass by here as familiar and not in the line of my special interest. The conclusions that I wish to emphasize are those he drew regarding the businessmen and their pursuit of wealth.

Like the Sophists and democracy, so also the businessmen in their respective ways tended to be enemies of order or producers of chaos. Seeking unlimited wealth and stimulating beyond all limits the particular desires of potential customers in order to profit the more by serving them, the businessmen embodied in themselves and aroused in others the disordering forces. And the spread in society of their "money madness" diverted all the vocational arts from their true functions in the well-ordered state to that of enriching their practitioners; reduced political life to a sordid conflict of economic group interests; and, growing into a desire of the populace for luxuries or excessive wealth, engendered greedy imperialism and wars and growth of the victorious states to unmanageable size and complexity. Thus Plato had, as one branch of the tree of his philosophy, an economic theory — a theory about "economic forces," the results of their "unfettered working," and the need to "fetter" them in order to build and preserve well-ordered states. How serious was his view of the disordering power of economic wants and ambitions is best shown by his decree of communal asceticism for the members of his governing elite — the "guardians" who must, in the state, embody reason, knowledge, and love of the real cosmic and moral order and the rational will to keep order. If the guardians were allowed to have private property, even private family lives, or any encouragements to pursue and cherish satisfaction of their own desires, the latter would expand, disorder their own souls, and unfit them for their task. But this was not all. Although the subjects, unlike the rulers, were to be allowed to own property and seek wealth within limits, the notion of a theory of the proper limits and regulations to enforce them is implicit in the whole argument of the *Republic*. Detailed development of this theory was left for Aristotle and the medieval Schoolmen, and to it belong all their ideas about usury, just prices, and the rest.

The entire scheme of thought — basic-philosophical, social-moral, and economic — thus developed by Plato and those successors was, I think, admirable in just the respects in which the bulk of modern Western thought has been defective, and vice versa. Its inspiring and largely true vision of the formal side of all existence and all proper human life — the order of the universe

and the order to be sought for in human lives and societies —
gave the medieval culture, which it permeated, an admirable set
of ideal aims, though in the circumstances of the time those aims
could not be at all fully realized. But the total scheme or outlook
was one-sided, overstressing forms, order, and an ascetic moralism, and in consequence unduly curbing and retarding economic
enterprise and progress, while also both neglecting and hampering development of science in the modern sense, and of technology. Under the influence of this outlook the many particular
desires and curiosities which must be the sources of a culture's
vitality, richness, and progressive dynamism were curbed *too
much* for the sake of social order and stability, a static harmony,
and undisturbed cultivation of the genteel virtues and graces by
the upper classes; and the "masses" remained immured in a poverty which confined them to a scarcely civilized or human existence. But modern Western culture, born in reaction against the
restrictive aspects of its heritage, has erred in the opposite way;
and so, while achieving immense economic and scientific progress,
has been deficient in the power to give men's lives and societies
any harmonious order, or to avoid that chaos which Plato feared.

Modernity, First Phase: Hobbs and the Mercantilists

The early modern revolt against medievalism and the transition
from it to modernity in the West had many phases; all of them
together produced the setting in which there appeared, in seventeenth-century England and Western Europe, the first fully
modern, complete pattern of philosophical, political, and economic thought. By this time both the Renaissance and the Reformation had made their contributions to the bold individualism
and other ingredients of the new, modern, spiritual climate. In
the social-economic sphere the great expansion and development
of commercial capitalism had been long under way and now was
booming along at a great rate; and in the political sphere there
had been a great change — the rise of the modern centralized and
fully independent national states. Individuals and nation-states
were now the important units; the unity of Christendom under
Pope and emperor was gone, small region localism was declining,

and there had begun a progressive loosening of many social bonds. And along with the economic, social, and political transformations an intellectual revolution also had by this time reached its floodtide: the rise of modern science, following and using both advances in mathematics and the earlier growth of a new interest in faithful, empirical observation of nature.

The development of the new science, thus far mainly physics, had involved a revision of methods and fundamental concepts which entailed a break with — though there was also much unacknowledged indebtedness to — the scholastic Aristotelian kind of science. And with the new physical science had come, too, with Descartes, Bacon, and others, a revolution in philosophy, having two main aspects: in theory of knowledge, empiricism, and in theory of reality, the belief that "all is mechanism." Meanwhile, advances in many practical arts — such as military engineering, accounting and business management, and the arts of technical statecraft including large-scale bureaucratic administration — had done perhaps even more than the advances in pure science to develop and spread the modern spirit of close study of causes and effects or of means to ends, and minute accuracy in the required joint logical and factual studies. And finally, with all these social and cultural changes went a change in both economic and political life and thought from general prevalence of belief in the need for a predominance of religious-moral over wordly aims in all activities to wide prevalence of a very worldly point of view. Both the pursuit of wealth by individuals and, even more, the pursuit of national wealth and power by ambitious rival nation-states had taken on new vigor and expansiveness, thrown off restraints, and become accepted, primary preoccupations.

With the background of all those developments in mind, then, let us notice the characters and coherence of, first, the philosophy and political theory of Hobbes and, second, the economic theory of the merchants, bureaucrats, and scholars of that epoch who supported the set of policies for promoting national wealth which in retrospect we call mercantilism. To speak first of Hobbes, his philosophy was at all points antithetical to Plato's. (1) His sensationalist empiricism and nominalism stood in exact opposition to the Platonic rationalism and, in the medieval sense, "realism"

— the doctrine of "real" or objective ideas or universals. (2) His mechanistic materialism, again, was antithetical to Plato's cosmic-ethical teleology, or view that "reality" is a cosmic harmony — a harmonious pattern of real universals — which "lures" all particular, actual, active entities toward participation in it through actualization of their own real-ideal or best possibilities and functions. And (3) in the ethics and politics founded on his sensationalist-mechanist epistemology and psychology, Hobbes' central doctrine was that not reason, as in Plato, but only a ruler or ruling group with overwhelming despotic arbitrary power can subdue the chaotic conflict of desires and men and produce social order.

Let me slightly elaborate those points in turn. (1) All knowledge originates in sense perceptions; universals or concepts are only signs invented to designate our groupings of sense objects; and reason is only a power of "calculating," with the help of these signs, what sense experience adds up to. Thus reason cannot apprehend (intuit) any primary, nonsensory, objective ideals or premises of ethics, and therefore cannot govern conduct independently of or in any opposition to the sense-linked desires — appetites and passions — which are the only desires men have. Being merely a power to draw inferences from sense *data*, reason can only serve active life instrumentally, by discovering the conditions of satisfaction of the nonrational, inevitable and actual, sense-linked desires. (2) The only "reality behind" the sense perceptions is matter in motion; *all* existents are in last analysis simply physical mechanisms; and what humans know as their mind-states are, as Hobbes put it, only "phantoms" of brain-states. External events, through the sense organs, produce in our nervous systems "internal motions" which occur in "trains," and of which the phantoms appear to introspection as trains of experiences, thoughts, desires and aversions, and resultant volitions — all leading to our actions, the end results of this mechanical process. There is reasoning which tends to make actions "logical" in relation to the desires and situations of the actors, but this reasoning, too, is a part of the mechanical process. Finally, (3) the sense-linked desires are — as Plato also taught — conflicting and expansive without limit; hence, if not curbed, they inevitably drive men into mutual conflict — in Hobbes' picture a frightful, intolerable "war among all." And reason, in Hobbes' view of it, cannot itself directly curb the desires or quell the conflict and produce social order; being in each man only — as Hume was later to express the same view — "servant, not master" of his sense-linked desires, reason itself is a tool of the disordering forces. What alone makes order possible is the predominance among each man's desires of the desire for saftey from the aggressions of his fellows, and the discovery that this can be had only by joining in submission to an almighty despot who restrains all and thus protects all. Thus the human "natural" mechanisms are impelled to organize political (nation-state) societies, despotically governed, which are "artificial" mechanisms — mechanical monsters, "Leviathans," omnipotent over their subjects, members, and creators. Finally, one last corollary has for us here a special interest: in international relations, the several independent Leviathans *remain in* the "state of nature," i.e., a state of war, and each must simply carry on its conflict with the others with all possible vigor and resourcefulness, and no hampering scruples.

Thus on the foundation of a purely prosaic philosophy Hobbes logically erected an utterly grim and hard-boiled view of the basic, practical necessities inexorably controlling all human life. Now, although as a rule in economic writings it was mainly implicit, not explicit, I think essentially the same tough view of the necessary aims of individual and national life and imposed despotic order in the state was the ideological context of all the mercantilist economic theory which flourished in that epoch; and with one exception all the elements of the philosophy which Hobbes spelled out as the basis of that outlook were presupposed in the mercantilist writings — in *both* their economic theory itself and its ideological context. Hobbes himself, in the twenty-fourth chapter of *Leviathan* on "Nutrition of the Commonwealth," produced a bit of perfectly good and typical mercantilist economic theory, obviously fitting perfectly into his system. Indeed, the best scholar among the seventeenth-century English mercantilist economists proper, Sir William Petty, professed admiration for and indebtedness to Hobbes. Most other writers in this group, however, were not philosophers and undoubtedly owed nothing to Hobbes; they were merchants or public officials or both, men with more practical than speculative minds and interests, and unlikely to draw ideas from such a book as *Leviathan* or to express their own ideas on the same — the philosophical — level. Nevertheless, being also entirely hardheaded realists in the modern sense, with logical and matter-of-fact minds and cause-effect curiosities like those of the physical scientists of the time, and a keen interest in the search for effective ways of increasing national wealth and power through governmental stimulation and control of trade, the mercantilist economists all went at this search with a way of thinking which presupposed fundamental notions nearly identical with those of Hobbes.

While not apt to formulate in philosophical terms the empiricist theory of knowledge, the mercantilists were in method generally better *practicing* empiricists than Hobbes himself. He, philosopherlike, announced that empirical evidence must support significant reasoning but scarcely bothered to gather and present any facts to support his own. But they were pioneers of the statistical as well as of the theoretical branch of modern economic science, and avid seekers and users of economic-factual knowledge; they generally theorized in the light of their information and in a very matter-of-fact spirit; and unlike the later liberal economists have never been accused, to my knowledge, of neglecting facts and relying on unverifiable, a priori premises.

Nevertheless, as regards the other basic doctrine of Hobbes, mechanistic materialism, I think a division must be made. The Mercantilists in general theorized constantly in mechanistic terms, but I see no ground for ascribing to them as a presupposition the metaphysical doctrine of materialism. Though the two ideas, "all is mechanism" and "all is matter," seem inseparable in Hobbes and to most philosophers, I think they are not; some of the philosophers and physical scientists of that epoch who shared the former idea were Cartesian dualists, not materialists, and Leibniz, for example, called the "soul" a "spiritual mechanism" — *automaton spirituale*. In any case, this question of the ultimate substance(s) need never arise in economic theory, and as far as I know never did among the mercantilists; nor is any one answer to it necessarily involved in supposing that all events, including human thoughts and actions, occur in mechanical patterns or can be explained with the aid of mechanistic conceptual models. The latter were certainly in the minds of the mercantilists; they all reasoned constantly in mechanistic terms about interdependent changes of prices, supplies, demands, etc., in the markets, and expansions or contractions of "branches of trade" and effects of governmental measures on them — long before Sir Dudley North, near the end of the century, wrote that "since Descartes, natural science has become mechanical and the *chimeras* of the Schoolmen are done away with; and to become as clear and solid the science of Trade also must become mechanical."

Unlike their liberal successors, however, the mercantilists thought of the national business economy as a mechanism *to be manipulated* by the state through policy devices — taxes, tariffs, bounties, controlled interest rates and other prices, subventions to favored trades and penalities against obnoxious ones — to *make* it work for maximal enrichment of the national state as such. Theirs was *not* the later idea of an automatically, socially beneficent, self-adjusting, harmony-insuring economic mechanism. They implicitly shared with Hobbes the assumption that not harmony but conflict of the interests of men and of nations is the fundamental fact; and hence shared also the resulting views about the practical necessities of despotism at home and war abroad — and strong governmental control of the national economy, and direction of its processes to maximization of *the national wealth significant as the basis of military power*. Their stress on amassing a national treasure of the money metals through a favorable balance of foreign trade was not, as later liberal critics supposed, the result *merely* or mainly of a simple confusion of wealth with money; neither was it due mainly to the natural tendency of a business community in which merchants, not physical producers, were dominant, to stress the money gains from shrewd trading rather than efficiency in physical production. The *main* foundation of their special concept of national wealth was the fact that not the liberal, humanitarian aim of higher living standards for all men, but readiness for war, *had* to be the supreme aim of all economic policy in their Hobbes-like view of struggle for security as the essence of life. In those times national security required an ample treasure of the money metals, strong home industries, and subservient colonies to make the mother country independent of markets and supplies in potentially hostile countries — precisely the objectives of mercantilism as a set of actual policies. And the body of economic theory which culminated in ideas of the most effective means to the ends of those policies was in the main, sound though rudimentary economic-scientific theory, empirical and mechanistic — in an ideological context and involving philosophical presuppositions closely similar to the political theory and underlying philosophy of Hobbes.

This whole pattern of thought, then, of Hobbes and the mercantilists, was, in my terms, all-prosaic and, internally, admirably coherent — not, like later systems, full of inner conflict between the economic-scientific element and a visionary ideology. But its grim assumptions of the iron necessities of despotism and war — a merely forcibly imposed and arbitrary order within nations and none in the world of nations — denied men's hopes and insights concerning the possibility of a more complete and better kind of human order — international as well as domestic, and in both spheres more largely spontaneous, truly harmonious, compatible with fredom, and based on reason, justice, and fraternity, not arbitrary might. A new expression, however, of these hopes and insights — modern liberalism, involving as we shall see a revised and weakened revival of the Platonic-Stoic vision of a divine-natural, cosmic, and moral order — was growing up meanwhile in other quarters and became dominant through much of the West in the next long epoch. The economic science which began its growth in the context of the outlook best expressed by Hobbes was to reach its maturity in the very different context of liberal thought; and to this I now turn.

Economic Theory and Three Forms of Liberalism

In its long career from early modern times to the present, liberalism as a quasi religion with varying creeds has had three successive, general phases. In the first phase, which culminated in the eighteenth century, liberal thought relied in part upon ideas with a Stoic and thus ultimately a Platonic origin, current also in the Middle Ages: ideas of ethical-juristic natural law and the natural rights of all men, and the harmonious natural order of the universe, realizable in the world of men through conformation of their institutions and conduct to natural law or morality. It was in the context of this form of liberal thought that the physiocrats and Adam Smith developed the first formulations of the economic theory of the self-adjusting mechanism of the free, competitive economy. In the second phase, extending through the nineteenth century, the bulk of liberal thought discarded the natural right and related ideas as nonempirical and nonscientific, and tried to replace them with the supposedly scientific principles of utilitarianism. This change did not lead, however, to any great alteration of concrete objectives or the liberal program; and the theory of the free economy continued its development, through the nineteenth and into the twentieth century, in the context of utilitarian liberalism. The classical economic theory of the early nineteenth century, however, although its chief architects were friends and co-workers of the first utilitarian liberals, did not apply Bentham's idea of calculations of amounts of "utility" for "happiness" directly to the problems of economic theory itself. Only in the great new development of economic theory after 1870, led by Jevons, the famous Austrian School, Walras, Marshall, and others, was this done; and even then only Jevons acknowledged the connection of the new utility economics with utilitarianism. Meanwhile, there began a change in not only the philosophies but the practical objectives of the liberals and a growing division of their movement into conflicting wings.

Both the eighteenth-century natural-rights and the early nineteenth-century utilitarian reformers had supported the classical, liberal program — liberal individualism and internationalism. That is, they stood for maximal freedom of all individuals from external dictation of their views or actions, limited government, and a voluntary comity among nations. And they relied mainly on general "enlightenment," spontaneous morality, the interdependence of all men and nations, basic harmony of their major interests, and the "natural" processes of a free, unregulated world economy, to insure order and a steady progress and general diffusion of prosperity and happiness. But in urging this program they had been strongly reformist in temper, being not defenders of a status quo, but crusaders for a new, free world order, in opposition to the traditions of oligarchy, despotism, and mercantilism — the *first* modern, predemocratic and preliberal regime. In a degree of contrast, the Victorian liberalism of the later nineteenth century and quite early twentieth, while it still supported the classical, liberal platform and especially the planks of free enterprise and limited government, took on a conservative tone and became largely a business class gospel; being oriented now not against the original alternatives but against the rising menace of socialism and the expanding activities of democratic governments. And this change produced another: the original, humanitarian idealism and reforming fervor in the movement began to pass, and has since passed mainly into development of a new, third phase or form of liberalism in general, which is still inchoate — the semisocialist, more democratic (for mass welfare) than individualistic, liberalism of our time.

The philosophy, as well as the program of this new liberalism is still inchoate, but tends generally in the direction of pure pragmatism, avoiding formulation of any system of abstract social-moral principles, even of the type of those of utilitarianism, and aiming to develop "experimentally" institutions and policies found to "work" in terms of satisfaction of majority demands. Hence the "new" liberalism may be called pragmatic democracy. And the latest developments of economic theory in the liberal (nontotalitarian) world of recent years have been and are at least loosely related to that outlook. The theory of monopolistic competition tends to undermine the old faith in free enterprise and the automatic social beneficence of "natural economic laws," by refining the analysis of the "competitive" economy in a way which finds it to be full of "monopoly elements" working generally, in results, against public welfare, and thus by implication requiring either destruction or public regulation if the latter is to be best served. And more trenchantly and positively in another direction, Keynesian economic theory directly implements the new liberalism with ideas of a technique for making the business economy serve democracy or mass welfare by using governmental fiscal operations to control and stabilize it.

Now the instability over time of the philosophic base of liberalism has been due I think to an inner conflict present from the start, between the visionary element, originally boldly expressed in the natural-law and harmonious natural-order ideas, and the prosaic element of empiricist and mechanist ideas associated with modern science. In the long development I have just outlined, the prosaic element has become more prominent in each new form of liberal thought, while the visionary has come to be denied philosophical expression; but I think this increasingly submerged, visionary element necessarily remains, all the same, the source of whatever the liberal movement retains of vigorous idealism and clarity in its goals or direction. Clarity of aims, in particular, requires an accepted, philosophical expression of the vision — of the pattern of the potentialities — of nature and human nature, and the good society to be achieved. But although modern liberal thought began its career with a philosophy which in a fashion supplied all that, the included and essential metaphysical and moral ideas in that philosophy were marred and weakened from the outset by their conflict with the even more emphasized, but mistaken, purely empirical and mechanistic formulations of modern scientific ideas. As these latter ideas have increasingly prevailed, the clarity of the liberal ideals or vision has declined.

The loss of clarity has become conspicuous in the present-day confused pragmatic liberalism, in which the idealism is only an emotional, vague humanitarianism, and the intellectual content is only a *mélange* of variable and often mutually conflicting, purely empirical and mechanical ideas of ad hoc remedies for diverse, particular social ills. And this state of liberal thought has adverse effects on any economic theory of which it is the ideological context. Thus the Keynesian economic theory, though it has much merit, analyzes only an unduly restricted range of features of the working of the present-day business economy, because it is solely intent on developing the knowledge on which to base ad hoc remedies for one particular, urgent evil — mass unemployment. And the Keynesian economists tend to be "political" economists of the worst kind — active in politics on behalf of their favorite policy devices, and lacking in this role a political philosophy or unambiguous vision of the type of social order they regard as desirable, and a theory of all the conditions of its realization, to guard them from ignorance and unconcern about the broader, institutional changes which may ensue from general adoption of their policy program.

Nineteenth-century utilitarian-liberal thought and the classical and later neoclassical economic thought connected with it were not as bad in those respects, because in the former and thus for the latter there remained the fairly clear vision of the good society and economy embodied in the classical-liberal program. But already the logically required philosophical foundation of that vision and program had been disavowed, in the effort to achieve a purely scientific, logical-empirical, and mechanistic way of thinking. The utilitarian formulas did not really in themselves prescribe the liberal program. The conditions of the greatest general happiness — simultaneous satisfaction of the greatest number of desires — in a society depend on the character of the desires of its members. If desires of a certain type predominate in the great majority, a bellicose, totalitarian despotism may best satisfy them. The utilitarian liberals, despite their denials, really presupposed a general if not universal agreement of men's spontaneous desires with their real needs or "true interests," and of both with that vision of the natural society of free men respecting one another's natural rights which the eighteenth century and earlier liberals had dared to formulate in half-Platonic, metaphysical and moral terms. But even that original liberal vision was made defective by the inconsistent mixing with it of the ideas which were to cause it to fade out or be disavowed in later explicit liberal thought.

The pioneers of liberalism of the sixteenth to the end of the eighteenth century were thinkers who did not depart as far from the ancient-medieval tradition as did Hobbes and the mercantilists. They carried on but modified its ideas. One modification made was only the rejection of one that Christian dogma had imposed on medieval thought. The latter held that sinful, fallen man's uncertain grasp of natural law and his still more enfeebled love of the good order in life to be had by obeying it must be helped and supplemented by supernatural revelation and grace if his evil passions were to be controlled. The founders of the modern liberal revised version of the natural-law philosophy rejected the supernaturalist additions. They asserted the full capacity of the natural reason in all men to apprehend and bring them to agreement on the rules of natural law, as well as the predominant attractiveness of the ideal natural order to all human nature — when the latter should become enlightened with modern knowledge or properly educated and freed from the corrupting influences of bad environments. Then, too, in rejecting the Christian-supernaturalist additions, the liberal revision went further and discarded also the austere and pessimistic element in the original views of Plato and the Stoics — the distrust of the desires connected with the senses and regarded as too "naturally" predominant in "the many," and the belief that chaos could be avoided and the natural order be realized only through a repressive control of society by a ruling, wise, and good elite enforcing an authoritative formulation of a body of natural law, rather highly restrictive in relation to the mundane, "natural" desires of ordinary mortals.

What was retained was only the optimistic side of the ancient vision — the belief in the reality of the ideal pattern, the capacity of mankind for direct apprehension of it, and its great attractions for all human nature. Thus eighteenth-century liberal thought had a tendency to slide into a superficial and egregious optimism, almost identifying the *spontaneous* natural with the morally ideal behavior of mankind. And this was supported by the influence of the empiricist and mechanistic element in that mixed way of thinking, which tended to cause confusion of the characters of the moral, the Newtonian physical, and the social-economic natural laws. Yet those confusions and that overoptimism were not always as pronounced as they are often said to have been. Thus in the total systems of thought of the physiocrats and Adam Smith, the included ethical and economic theories were really tolerably distinct, and related in the sense of being complementary. Deliberate reforms, directd by moral insight, to make the actual social order and legal system and effective moral code conform more closely to the ideal, rational, natural order were seen as preconditions for that socially beneficent operation of the mechanism of the free economy — free only from nonmoral, arbitrary controls and internal obstacles due to machinations by selfish special interests — which was envisaged in the economic theories.

Romantic and Positivistic Alternatives, and Marxism

In most of the intellectual life of the nineteenth century the visionary and prosaic halves of the eighteenth century's composite outlook came apart, so to speak — with some change in the process — and went on developing to new results in, respectively, the romantic movement, and the trend in most nonromantic circles to pure positivism. Romanticists and positivists, while thus holding mutually opposed positions, were often mainly conscious of their oppositions to the full tradition and to all even relatively full continuations of the eighteenth-century way of thinking, in which each group tended to see only what it rejected. Now while, as I indicated in the last section, the development of liberal, and of economic, thought itself increasingly conformed to the positivistic or prosaic trend, it nevertheless remained visibly enough indebted to the entire composite eighteenth-century way of thinking to encounter opposition not only from romanticists but also from a few (in precept) thorough positivists.

The romantic opposition developed mainly in Germany, and is best represented by the line of German scholars including — in temporal order from the early nineteenth century to a very recent time — Adam Mueller, Frederick List to some extent, the first economists of the "historical school," and such recent figures as Werner Sombart and — on a lower level of ability — Othmar Spann, who was active at Vienna in the years just before the rise of the Nazis and had, intellectually, very much in common with them. In differing degrees and ways all those scholars were romantic-conservative nationalists and statists; opposed to liberal individualism and internationalism and the theory of a free-world economy; inclined to cherish romantic visions of a state-led German national society and economy. And the latter, they insisted, must be conceived as a unique and unitary spiritual "organism," having as members not separate individuals pursuing their private ends within a framework of agreed-on rules but persons and groups bound together as organs of the whole, with natures and functions formed by and serving the unitary, traditional, self-evolving national spirit — *Volksgeist*. Hence, with their opposition to the liberal ideology of Adam Smith and his successors, they joined inseparably a radical opposition to the character, method, fundamental concepts, and alleged philosophical foundation of the "science" of the liberal economists. And their primary object of attack in the latter was the ideal of emulating physical science. All declared this ideal to be wholly out of place in a social science, and to involve the metaphysical ideas of atomism and materialism and, as their corollaries, "practical materialism" in the sense of the sordid, mercenary view of life as only the pursuit of material goods, and "social atomism" or individualism in contrast with the romantic idea of "social organisms."

Also, they attacked the effort to discover or believe in a universal, timeless pattern of economic laws, and the predominantly postulational and deductive method — with its attendant stress on, and conception of theory. They insisted that each local or national culture in each stage of historical development does and must evolve, under the joint influence of *Volksgeist* and *Zeitgeist*, its own unique and unitary concrete pattern of all, including economic, institutions and activities; and along with that its own body of both economic theory and policy, entirely and solely valid for itself. Thus on a larger scale the only true method of economic study must be historical, and must aim to understand each local, temporal culture and economy through study of its special history. Furthermore, this study must be of a new type, investigating the facts of record only in order to reach intuitive or sympathetic "understanding" (*Verstehen*) of the special "spirit" (*Geist*) or set of ideas and feelings which produced the objective phenomena as its manifestations. Finally, in their attacks on the thought of economic liberalism and of liberalism generally these writers always emphasized its origin in the "wretched" philosophy of the Franco-British eighteenth-century "enlightenment," in which they saw only the prosaic elements.

That the liberal vision of societies of free men living on a basis of mutual respect for each other's rights embodied a moral idealism and involved a visionary metaphysics which modified its prosaic side, was never recognized.

In contrast with this romantic opposition to economic and philosophical liberalism, which exhibited itself for the most part in German eastern Europe, the positivistic opposition appeared mainly in "the Western democracies," where the number and influence of its representatives have been limited by the increasing conformity of economic and philosophical liberal thought itself to the prosaic trend in this part of the world. However, in company with others of no great importance, two widely separated, and in many ways dissimilar, representatives of positivism were not satisfied with that conformity. These two were August Comte and Thorstein Veblen.

Comte, as is well known, attacked the classical political economy as a mere continuation in its field of the eighteenth-century kind of thought which he called metaphysical or prescientific. By metaphysical he very clearly meant precisely what I call visionary thought — taken in its rationalistic, not its romantic form; thought positing, and seeking to grasp and reason from, abstract but real universals, forming a pattern and serving both to explain all nature and to define the ideal pattern for all human life. Only this element could Comte see in economic and general liberal thought; the stronger positive scientific element in classical economics and even (in aim at least) in utilitarian liberalism he could not see at all. In his view the economists and utilitarians reasoned not from observation of men's actual circumstances and behavior but only from a priori postulates about a universal human nature. Moreover, the attempt to keep economics a separate special science entailed, he thought, its nonempirical or metaphysical character. In empirical social life the economic and other elements are so interdependent that positive social science must be all one single, unitary science — the sociology Comte sought to found. This must truly emulate the methods and concepts of natural science, in essentials, but in details develop its own variants adapted to its subject matter; thus it must be in part historical, in part descriptive of each society in each stage of its

development. Above all, like natural science, social science must
develop into or support a scientific art — of government, or the
proper ordering of life in each society by a body of experts. Here
he missed or fumbled the distinction between a scientific art and
a philosophy of ends; his social science would also prescribe the
moral code to be enforced in his "positive polity," which, in
contrast to liberal individualism, would emphasize not rights
but duties. The "metaphysical stage" had only destroyed the
outmoded moralities and political systems developed in the first
or "theological stage" of human development; liberal thought
logically culminated in pure anarchism — a doctrine that everyone must obey only the promptings of his "nature" — and could
not create a new social order. Positive social science would in
its way fill the place once filled by religion and create a new,
scientifically controlled society. Comte's kind of positivism,
although philosophically at the opposite pole from German
romantic idealism, likewise led to antiliberal authoritarianism.

Veblen's partial agreement with Comte is obscured by important differences, and by the wholly different, informal character of the former's writings. But although it has never, to
my knowledge, been pointed out before, I think the degree
of agreement about nineteenth-century liberal "orthodox" economics, and what, for Veblen, should replace it, is fairly striking.
To Veblen, also, the classical and neoclassical economics seemed
a continuation in its field of the eighteenth-century, prescientific
mode of thought, elaborating the vision or mythology of a universe ruled for good ends by natural laws — including human
societies thus ruled by economic laws — the philosophy of which
was bound up with that of the natural rights of property and
contract, dear to businessmen. Oddly, Veblen thought the up-to-
date kind of science was half a product of the machine age and
half a product of Darwinism. How the machine age got started
is not wholly clear, for his account of the features of eighteenth-
century thought which made it prescientific would seem, as an
earlier critic of Veblen has noted, to condemn Newtonian physics
along with classical economics. In any event, the new age was
habituating everyone having intimate contact with machines —
working men and engineers — but not businessmen, preoccupied

with rigging markets to make money and not familiar with the new ways of making useful things — to thinking of *all* processes in impersonal, mechanistic terms, as having no inherent purposes but only causes and effects which become new causes. Darwinism was diffusing into all sciences the idea that there is no immutable, timeless pattern of "kinds" of entities with appropriate relations and ways of interacting; there is only the temporal process of ceaseless change of all the kinds, and hence of all relevant categories and concepts. The "evolutionary" idea, to Veblen, meant only this and not the particular theory of "natural selection," which was suggested to Darwin by the work of Malthus and was used by Spencer and others to bolster up the economic and general social theory of "free competition."

Economic science then, according to Veblen, should get over being a laggard, still prescientific theory of the fixed categories, values, wages, etc., and their apropriate relations, and the beneficent, "natural" processes of a static or unchanging business economy. It should become a modern mechanistic evolutionary science of the temporal process of unending, goal-less social change. Actually, his new economic science as represented in his own writings was a kind of sociology, or cultural anthropology, applied to "modern" as well as to "primitive" societies. As such it was often highly perceptive and suggestive, but wholly unlike economics as conceived in its main tradition. More important, as "science" it wholly lacked any "vertebrate" structure of either precise or systematic theory, and also any statistical or other "exact" studies of particular facts; Veblen's writing was all intuitive and impressionistic, not scientific. Nonetheless, his gospel was science only, and his complaint against traditional economics was that it merely carried on the eighteenth century's prescientific, visionary, metaphysical moralism.

Now in turning, finally, to Marxism I apologize for having saved only an insignificant fraction of my space for comment on that imposing, complex, and in every sense important intellectual system. In this crumb of space I can only faintly suggest how I see it in relation to the others I have just considered.

Like eighteenth-century liberal and economic thought it combines, but again not coherently, I think, prosaic and visionary elements. The former include not only Marx's special transformation and development of old classical economic theory but also the solid, factual part of his own historical investigations which — I am told by experts whom I trust — were in and for his time excellent and highly relevant to economic science. The visionary elements include both the socialist vision itself, of the future ideal society, and the "inverted Hegelian" *philosophy* of history.

In the latter philosophy, termed "historical materialism," the so-called "materialism," it is my impression, does not quite conform to any non-Marxian, familiar meaning of the word. It is of course not the classical, mechanistic materialism, for its dialectical theory of history is a different, nonmechanistic idea of process. Further, I would say it has little more in common with classical metaphysical materialism than the fact of being metaphysical, in contrast with positivism in the sense of antimetaphysical "phenomenalism." The latter opposition is made clear in Lenin's essay "Dialectical Materialism vs. Empirio-criticism." Not subjective human sense impressions but an absolutely objective reality the Marxian philosophy does insist upon; but in precisely what sense the reality is "material" may be open to question. I suspect that it is so only in the sense literally got by simply "inverting" Hegel: all that is "objective" in a concrete society through a given time — in the people and their social and total environment — is *not* a product or manifestation of their spirits, feelings, ideas, etc.; on the contrary, the objective social world is the reality which generates the subjective, the states and contents of the people's minds. In any case, a more serious error is to be avoided: Marxian "materialism" is not and does not imply or produce the practical "materialism" of aiming only at a society rich in material goods, or supposing wealth in the latter sense to be the main end of life, *or* the main actual aim of most human beings. This calumny is no more fair or true when aimed at Marxism than it was when aimed by romanticists at the nineteenth-century liberal economists.

The economic determinism in the Marxian theory of history is the notion not that "economic motives" are all-controlling but that objective, economic (and with them all social) *cir-*

cumstances engender, by psychological conditioning, the feelings, views, etc., and thus the aims of the human beings who live in those circumstances. For example, rich men and poor men, generally speaking, are sure to have different outlooks, because they have different experiences.

But the dialectic, in the form of the class struggle and, more generally, the dynamic temporal ebb and flow of "contradictions" or conflicts within a society as the behavior patterns and ideologies of diversely conditioned groups clash with and change one another and produce "evolution" — this concept, derived from Hegel who put ideologies in the primary causal position, I think retains in Marxism its romantic-visionary character. For it remains the notion of a process which occurs *in order* to realize an ideal; the idea of an "inherent logic" in history whereby the world "must" (ought to, and will inevitably, fused into one idea) become rational at last, free of contradictions (human conflicts), a perfect harmony. There is the relation to eighteenth-century liberal and economic thought that here too is self-enforcing, ethical natural law, only now in the historical dimension; the existing order is *not* natural, rational, harmonious, hence self-maintaining, but full of evil or conflict, hence fated to destroy itself and in so doing generate the harmonious order — in the ultimate historical long run. But this visionary and the prosaic side of the system are unreconciled; the whole claims to be a science but, as was the case with economic liberalism, it is half a science and half a religion in some mutual conflict.

10

THE ECONOMICS OF A "FREE" SOCIETY:

FOUR ESSAYS[1]

❧

In the political climate of today in the western democratic world, economists and laymen alike are more than ever involved in the old, perpetual debate over economic freedom *versus* governmental and group controls. Unfortunately, the quality of this debate is too often marred by the failure of participants to recognize the nature of the general question at issue. It is not a question which the progress of knowledge tends to "settle," by making possible a conclusive demonstration of the "right" answer. There is an ever growing mass of *relevant* knowledge, both in economics *and* other sciences; but even in its fullest sum this knowledge can never become *decisive* for the question. The reason is that all opinions on the matter necessarily involve, in addition to whatever knowledge they may partly rest on, inherently unprovable value judgments, which are often mere prejudices but, at best, are reflective, philosophical convictions.

All the great questions of political economy — the complete

[1] John Jewkes, *Ordeal by Planning* (London: Macmillan, 1948); Henry Simons, *Economic Policy for a Free Society* (Chicago: University of Chicago Press, 1948); J. M. Clark, *Alternative to Serfdom* (New York: Knopf, 1948); and David McCord Wright, *Democracy and Progress* (New York: Macmillan, 1948). This article first appeared in the *Quarterly Journal of Economics* (November 1948), and is reprinted here by permission from the editor.

inquiry as to what are the "proper" ends and means of public policies affecting the economy — alike share this nature. Political economy is a much broader subject than economic science; it involves the latter *plus* all other social or human sciences, *plus* philosophical, ethical and political reflection, *plus* thoughtful study of human history. And like philosophy, into which it overlaps, it must forever remain in essential part a theater of controversy, and never can become entirely a branch of research leading to agreement on the truth. That is why, as one of the central controversies in this field, the debate about the proper spheres of individual freedom and collective control in the "good" economy is eternally recurrent, wherever thought and discussion are free.

Nevertheless I cannot agree with those strict positivists within and beyond our profession who on that account depreciate this (and every such) debate and all contributions to it, and urge that economists should confine their range of professional work to the limited domain of their science proper — adopting as their motto "science only, and political neutrality." On the contrary, I share with the majority of economists, including the authors of the books before me, the belief that it is a part of our professional task to venture, at times, beyond the frontiers of our science, as widely as we must, in order properly to form and express our considered judgments on the great public questions to which it is relevant although it cannot be the whole foundation of our answers to them.

Here again, it is impossible to prove that either view is "right" because value-judgments — this time concerning intellectual values — are involved. The positivists advocate "science only, and political neutrality" because they value only contributions to established knowledge, and are allergic to all inherently inconclusive, philosophical discussions. On the other hand the rest of us — political, and thus, whether knowingly or not, philosophical, economists — while likewise valuing science, also value, no less, the full, uncircumscribed pursuit of what may satisfy each individual, group, and society as being the inclusive "wisdom" which "ought" to govern active life, or policy, or conduct.

Now no one can hope to persuade all mankind to accept his

"wisdom"; and what to one man, circle, society, or epoch is wisdom is to others folly and *vice versa*. Yet everyone, and every society in each new epoch of its life, must seek a viable and satisfying faith to live by; a faith which without unreason can be held as true, with enough conviction to give life stability and vigor, and yet with enough flexibility to permit adjustments to new conditions, desires, and insights. And the non-positivist holds that in this vital quest there is always intellectual work to be done, which, though it must transcend the limits of any one science and even of all sciences and cannot lead to wholly provable results, is of no less value than more purely scientific work. Its function is to bring all available relevant knowledge and rational reflection to bear on old traditions and new gospels in the sphere of policy; to test the elements or doctrines in them which turn on questions of logic or of fact; and to challenge the elements which are value-judgments with reasoned criticisms, and expression and support of the value-judgments of each critic.

Too many economists in the past, however, have undertaken writing of this kind without an adequate awareness of its special demands, and without using adequate equipment and procedures. Until not very long ago, all were involved in the error of identifying economic "science" with the whole of political economy; and this confusion led politically differing "schools" of economists to confound the science with their social-moral policy creeds, to do less than fully objective work in the former, and falsely to claim its authority for the latter; and led, not least, to erection of the policy creeds on too narrow an explicit basis of solely economic knowledge and considerations. For some time now there has been within our profession a growing awareness of the fact that our genuine science can develop only a limited body of abstract, partial knowledge, by itself inadequate to determine what is "sound" public policy; that a wide variety of political creeds may be alike compatible with its findings; that it needs much supplementing with other kinds of knowledge and reflection if one is to develop and support any one such creed against the others on an adequate basis. But there still is no universal acceptance of this fact and its implications.

Thus, of the few "die hard," old style economic liberals among us, some are still prone to defend their position and attack the alternatives in the old dogmatic and narrow way; as though they could fully prove the unique, universal, and eternal validity of their liberal gospel by sound (scientific) economic reasoning alone, and as though economic nonsense and only that was the necessary basis of every opposing gospel. Nor are sinners of this type to be found only in that little group; the strict Marxian economists are no less guilty of the same kind of error — Marxism being another rigid unification of economic science with a complete philosophy and political creed; and today a good many zealous "Keynesian" economists are by way of joining also in *their* way in the repetition of this same old error. As a reaction against all this it is easy to understand the "science only, and political neutrality" ideal.

But finally, even those many economists of today who neither accept that ideal, nor are guilty of perpetuating any form of the old confusion, too seldom fully realize how broad a basis is required for wise critical or constructive work in the whole arena of political economy. Such work is not only not the same as purely scientific work in economics; it is far more difficult work. It calls not merely for a popular style and the addition of some modifying "common sense" to a simple version of some economic theorems; but rather for ability to draw, for the purpose, on all the disciplines concerned with human life and affairs — psychology and sociology, political science, history, and philosophy, as well as economics. It calls further, and above all, for full possession and use of an authentic sense or feeling for the total, concrete realities of social situations and developments, which in some degree elude all types of intellectual, abstract categories. These can be apprehended only with the help both of a touch of practical experience, and of the native gift or bent of mind that alone can profit by it.

These general considerations suggest the standards that I think we should apply in judging essays in political economy, like the ones before me. These four books seem to me of especial interest because — unlike so many efforts in this general field — they all do, in various degrees, approach fulfillment of the large, exacting requirements of this kind of writing. In substance, the general positions taken up by all four writers are different shades or modifications of economic liberalism in the old sense — ranging from the fairly strict "orthodoxy" in that quarter of Jewkes and of Simons, through J. M. Clark's limited, conscious departure therefrom, to the rather different, independent position of Wright, who is perhaps not less but a trifle more "conservative" than Clark, but goes beyond him in the sense that he is the freest of all these writers from the compulsion to defend *or* attack the old set of doctrines, or to conceive the problems that concern him in terms dictated by them. But I am as much interested in the question of the adequacy of each writer's (utilized) equipment and "approach," as I am in what he says. And in this respect again I array them on a scale from Jewkes and Simons, who barely avoid the dogmatic narrowness too often typical of such strict believers in the "free" economy; through Clark, whose explicit basis of argument is broader than theirs, but I think still inadequate, being tied too exclusively to social "science"; to Wright, who ably takes account of everything in any way germane, in his search for wisdom. In still other respects the four books differ a good deal, and no conclusion that they are alike should be drawn from the fact that this article reviews them as a group. I shall now discuss them separately, and in the sequence already indicated.

I

Ordeal by Planning is a British "liberal" economist's critical attack on his country's current adventure into socialism — a good tempered but vigorous defense of old liberal capitalism, and attack upon the "planning" ideal of the socialist leaders. The author, John Jewkes, launches this defense and attack from an appropriate site and chair — he is Stanley Jevons, Professor of Political Economy at the University of Manchester.

The book is brief (243 pages), concise, lively, very well written, and very readable. It is bound, of course, to be compared with Hayek's *Road to Serfdom*, and indeed bears a certain acknowledged relation to that essay, which Professor Jewkes in his introduction praises highly. But while the general point of view is the same, the particular aim and "line" of argument are unlike Hayek's. The latter was "warning" the British and other western democratic peoples in advance about the likely, ultimate consequences of abandoning their own individualistic traditions for socialism or any form of state-ism, i.e., for ideals having their main historic roots (by his account) in central and .eastern Europe, where they had already led to dictatorial police states. And the Hayek argument was centered in the fields of intellectual history, political philosophy, and social-psychological forecasting — not in economic theory, and not in the analysis of any actual events under any professed regime of democratic socialism.

By contrast, the aim and claim of *Ordeal by Planning* is to show, through analysis of the actual record, how British socialist "planning" is producing economic chaos and decline, and is already beginning also, with respect to every sort of freedom, to fulfill the grim Hayek prophecies. And the argument traverses ground on which the average economist feels more at home; it uses some simple, "popularized" economic theory, and much illustrative evidence concerning the confused and changing views and deeds of the socialist Ministers, their schemes and failures in dealing with various problems, and the ensuing events. Thus while the book may be called a logical successor to the *Road to Serfdom*, it is complementary, not similar, to the latter.

I find it on the whole a good book, well worth reading, but marred by the faults of a zealous, polemical, political pamphlet; and by inadequate understanding of what it attacks, inadequate realism in the judgments supporting faith in the present and future viability of what it defends, and an inadequate sense of the complexity of the modern economic, social, moral, and political problem. I hold no brief for English socialism, but this attack upon it goes, I think, to unfair extremes; and the author's own alternative position is in my judgment not only too extreme — too close to a laissez-faire position — but also at bottom, unclear.

As illustrations of these two points I take two contentions that appear already in the author's introduction. In the first place, at the very outset he sharply minimizes — without presenting any evidence or argument — the importance of the commonly recognized historic causes of Britain's present economic plight, and holds her socialist government of today responsible, in a major degree, for all her current ills. This seems to me unfair and untenable. No doubt the government's mistakes, and the disturbing effects which the transition toward actual socialism would have in any case, must bear some (within wide limits debatable) share of the "blame" for the present hardships. But Professor Jewkes does not debate the question of how great that share is; he only asserts, dogmatically, that *not* all the older, general causes together, *but* the deeds of this government, are "largely" to blame — and thereafter treats "largely" as equivalent to "mainly." This is an unsupported, and surely an unsupportable, overstatement of the economic case against the government.

A little further along in the introduction, the other contention I have referred to appears, in a passage defining the (good) "free economy" and the (evil) "planned economy," and discussing the difficult problem of drawing the line between the two in the range of actual "mixed" systems. I have space only for attention not to his fairly good definitions, but to his view about drawing the line. He admits that it cannot be drawn sharply; that the economic freedoms of individuals cannot be absolute but are always limited, diversely under diverse circumstances; in short that, in his words, "every sensible economy is a 'mixed' system." But, he hastens to add, ". . . everything turns on the mixture . . . There is a watershed . . . where . . . the difference between . . . liberty and slavery is being irrevocably determined. I submit that there is no question in which direction the current has started to flow for us." In other words there *is* a line across which England's socialists have pushed her on to the definitely evil, perilous side. And his proofs or "tests" are two: that in England today all economic freedoms have been gravely narrowed, and that nobody accepts the present arrangements as satisfactory or stable — all agree that England must either go back to more freedom or on to more planning. Now it seems to me that all this is logically a weak discussion of the "line" problem, which lacks any real criterion as to how far individual freedoms can properly be limited, *because freedom is the only moral value that is recognized as relevant.*

That always has been the central dilemma of the old, or classical, liberalism. If one thinks of freedom as the only good, or the sufficient source of all goods, one can accept as limitations of it only those required to maximize, in general, for all men equally, the thing to be limited in each special case; and this view leads to no clear conclusion but only to a suspicious bias against all particular, proposed limitations.

For a clearer result the problem must be conceived as one of finding the point of best "balance" among a number of equally valid but in part conflicting ideals or imperatives. Freedom, justice, order, progress, stability — all the goods to be included in a sound conception of the common welfare — must be the joint goals, or parts of the goal of an adequate idealism; none absolute, each limited by, and imposing limits on, the others. Different ideologies differ in their distributions of emphasis among these goals, or "balance" them diversely; and what should be central in any reasoned defense of one ideology and criticism of another, is a full comparative discussion of their value patterns. But an author whose zeal for freedom too largely blinds him to all other values is bound to be hampered in defending freedom: though forced to acknowledge that it must be limited, he cannot derive from other values (the only possible source) the grounds and measures of the proper limits. And he must be hampered also in attacking the rival "planning" ideology of socialism. Seeing only the large restraints on freedom which it implies, he cannot recognize and proceed to appraise the other values which lure his opponents and make them regard those restraints as justified. An inadequate understanding of the socialist value pattern, of its roots in the history of our culture and in the experiences under capitalism which have turned millions of men into socialists, and of the complex nature and great potency of its challenge to old liberalism — inadequate understanding of all that, is, I think, the central weakness of this book.

After first appearing in the introduction, in the passage I have just discussed, that same weakness immediately again appears in

Chapter I, entitled "The Spread of the Fashion." This chapter
purports to examine the historical and mental background of
the "planned economy" idea. But it first belittles the idea as a
mere contemporary fad, in the author's view peculiarly dangerous, but in all other respects in the same category with all
the many historic "crackpot" ideas — each briefly and widely
popular in its time — of economic cure-alls. In my judgment,
this view puts the modern "planning" aspiration definitely into
the wrong category, and betrays a serious underestimation and
misunderstanding of its place in modern history.

After thus belittling the "planned economy" idea, the author
goes on to attempt to discredit this particular "fad" with English
readers by asserting that its first origins — allegedly quite recent
— were (1) German — in German projects after World War I
for turning the (retained) national "war economy" into a permanent socialistic "planned economy"; and (2) Soviet Russian —
in Lenin's projection of the first Five Year Plan. Now this, I
think, is a piece of superficial history, which may possibly be
technically correct as regards the first uses of the term and the
precise, articulate concept under discussion, but is seriously misleading through its failure to refer at all to the old, widespread,
long developing, profound, general basis of the idea in the entire
history of modern Occidental culture — the culture of the entire
"age of modern science." From the Renaissance to now there
has been endemic in our culture the ideal or vision of a rationally
designed, human world, to be deliberately constructed by and
for collective mankind in the light of social-scientific knowledge
of all human needs and situations, and of the real conditions of
fulfillment of the former, imposed by the latter. I submit that it
is clearly this old, general aspiration, profoundly rooted in our
whole civilization, which in our time has ripened into the
"planned economy" ideal that Professor Jewkes is attacking. He
later argues persuasively, and I think rightly, that the idea in
this ("scientific") aspect is fallacious and illusory; but the illusion
involved is so old and central in our culture that the idea cannot
be dismissed as a mere ephemeral, contemporary fad, nor viewed
as in any significant sense the peculiar property or creature of
state-worshiping Germans and Russian Communists.

In the body of the book, beyond the first chapter, there is much interesting matter. Chapter II, "Is the Business Man Obsolete?," is a fairly cogent refutation of Schumpeter's thesis about the decline of capitalism as given in the latter's *Capitalism, Socialism, and Democracy.* This is followed by a fairly good, but I think overoptimistic, chapter about the problem of monopoly. Then we come to one — "Is Mass Unemployment Inevitable in the Free Economy?" — which outlines and supports the case for a cautious form of "Keynesian full employment" policy, and boldly claims that this can assuredly be successful; but disavows and attacks the version of, and additions to, the program advocated by Sir William Beveridge. The claim is emphasized, I think with much justice, that the "Keynesianism" of Keynes himself was a liberal (in the old sense), and not at all a socialistic, gospel; and that it is distorted when stolen by socialists and semi-socialists and fitted into or combined with their planning programs. But while this view is tenable, I think Professor Jewkes overstrains it by ignoring the anticapitalist touches (hostility to interest and to the *rentiers,* and failure to credit the business class in "mature" capitalist economies with much of the bold spirit of creative enterprise) which appear in Keynes; and also, dubiously, by greatly minimizing the amount of governmental control of things economic which a full employment program need entail.

After this chapter come two others of generalized attack on the "planners" — one on "Planners as a Species," discussing the different varieties and their special confusions of thought, and one on "Planning as a Scientific Method," endeavoring to demonstrate that it is and can be no such thing. The remaining chapters develop the attack on current English socialist "planning" by discussing its consequences for prosperity, economic stability, all human freedoms, the general morality and culture of the people, and international relations. Effective points are made on these topics, but they are unlikely to convince readers not already favorably disposed to the author's point of view.

In conclusion, I repeat my over-all estimate: a book worth reading, but one which exaggerates the tenable case against English socialism; evinces no deep understanding of it as an historical phenomenon; defends as the alternative a regime too little removed from *laissez faire* to be feasible in this epoch; and presents its whole argument in what is too nearly the narrow, doctrinaire spirit of the liberals of a century ago, who imagined that their program was conclusively and exclusively sanctioned by economic science, and that every departure from it could be shown to spring from economic fallacies and nothing else.

II

Economic Policy for a Free Society is a volume in which are collected the principal short writings of the late Henry Simons, who, in the decade before his recent death, became well known (though deserving to be still better known) to his fellow American economists as a bold, stout, and able, though extreme, defender of the pure old liberal gospel. His University of Chicago friends have performed a real service not only to his memory but also to the profession and to the country, in bringing together his scattered articles, pamphlets, speeches, etc. in this well arranged and edited volume. I warmly recommend its purchase and perusal by every economist keenly interested in the great controversial questions of our time in public policy.

The extreme doctrinaire positions so sharply and logically presented by Simons, generally seem to me to be impossible, and deserving of severe criticism; but I know of no better stimulant to careful thinking about the problems he discusses — which include all the major public problems that we face as economists and citizens. His central error lay, I think, in his rejection of "the middle way" of compromise between the strict old-liberal utopia and full collectivism. He insisted that all, even the slightest, compromises, departing ever so little from the former in the direction of the latter, must impel us on *to* the latter in the end; that totalitarian dictatorship could be avoided only by a drastic revival, rebuilding, and unyielding preservation of the "libertarian" society and economy as conceived in the eighteenth century. I believe, on the contrary, that the salvation of liberal democracy (and capitalism or private enterprise) must lie hereafter on the path of compromises of the kind condemned by his inflexible, too simple logic. But it is true that this "middle way" is too commonly conceived only in excessively vague, confused, and non-logical or illogical ways, which are indeed full of dangers. We who favor it need all the help and prodding we can get toward the achievement of an adequately clear, thorough, and coherent analysis and program — an objective extremely difficult to achieve in view of the extreme complexity of the real world and its policy problems. And despite his oversimplifications, the sharp logic and often good, though always incomplete, insights of Simons can both prod and help us to that end; by revealing real flaws in the sloppier compromises that may tempt us, and by offering in support of his own extreme views arguments the refutation of which is often a salutary, and never an easy, task.

An excellent feature of this volume, for which credit is due both to its editor and to Simons himself, is the fact that it begins with a not exclusively, nor even primarily, economic essay entitled "Introduction: A Political Credo." This is the way in which every book supporting a general position in political economy *should* begin — with a candid, clear, and reasonably full statement of the social-moral and political philosophy involved in that position. Here that requirement is fully met in what seems to me a piece of philosophical, political writing of high quality; although in good measure I dissent from its tenor, premises, and conclusions. What it expounds is Simons' personal variant of the traditional American form of the eighteenth- and nineteenth-century liberal — or "libertarian" — idea of the good society. Explicitly it asserts that individual liberty for all is the basic, all-sufficient civic good, including in itself or assuring as its corollaries all other goods; and especially that growth of freedom is both the condition and the sign of all social progress.

The author clearly cared even more deeply for all the civil liberties, intellectual and spiritual freedoms, etc., than he cared (for their own sakes) for the economic freedoms directly bound up with "free enterprise" and the competitive market system; but the essay insists that all are bound together — that if men lose those economic freedoms they are bound to lose all the others too. At the same time, an unmistakably genuine tone of warm, democratic, and humanitarian feeling pervades this essay, more clearly than it appears in the writings of such modern English and Continental old style liberals as Jewkes and Hayek. No reader could easily confound Simons, as so many did, though unfairly, confound Hayek, with the "reactionary" business men who make an interested use of some of the same slogans, but are in no sense "liberals." And one practical fruit of this spirit in Simons' "Credo" is his strong advocacy of a marked reduction of existing inequalities of wealth and power, to be achieved through sufficiently progressive taxation, appropriate governmental spending for mass education, public health, consumer subsidies, etc., and through antimonopoly policies — *not* through direct regulation of wages, prices, and profits or "interference" with the "free market system." His peculiar faith that highly progressive taxation and redistributive fiscal policy as a whole, in complete contrast with governmental efforts to influence wages, prices, etc., for the same egalitarian purpose, need have no harmful effects at all on the vigorous functioning of the business economy, is a piece of economic theory I would question here if I had the space. But it is one of many evidences that his heart lay with "the people," not with "the interests." Much of this introductory, political essay is an acute discussion of the philosophy and problems of political democracy, of which he proves himself to be a radical and firm supporter. Yet good, and original, though this essay is, one might almost suppose it to have been written in the eighteenth century. Its general flavor, intellectual method, and basic assumptions are most strongly suggestive of the Age of Reason, and scarcely touched by anything in our culture of more recent origin.

Next after the "Credo" comes the most widely known product of the author's pen — the pamphlet, "A Positive Program for Laissez Faire." To readers familiar with that only, I may say that it is typical and in a way almost all-inclusive. Most of the views of Simons are in it, succinctly stated in the good, vigorous style characteristic of all his writings. But a number of the other pieces in this volume more adequately express, clarify, and support his full position on particular subjects, and they also should be read by everyone desiring to know Simons' thought and to be able to judge it fairly.

Since it is so well known, I shall make only a few brief comments on the "Positive Program." The title seems paradoxical only to those who share the always prevalent misconception of what *laissez faire* meant to the old liberal economists. As the pamphlet insists, they did not mean it to suggest a wholly "negative" or do-nothing kind of governmental policy. Although the unfortunate slogan put all the emphasis on *not* "interfering" *directly* with market processes, a good number of positive or active policies, designed to create and maintain the conditions under which the market economy would work well for all *without* direct regulation, were always consciously inherent in the program. There is no question but that Simons was right historically in emphasizing this, and none that he was right on the two further points: that the "positive" side of the old liberal program never has been carried out consistently or thoroughly, and that today in the resulting (?) state of our actual "system," some very drastic "positive" reforms would be necessary to make *laissez faire* in the original sense desirable and feasible.

What I do question is whether the historic failure of the old liberal program on its "positive" side ever to get itself realized in practice has not been a result and an evidence of inherent faults which justify the now general repudiation of it. It was never really thought through in such a way as to become an adequately clear, realistic, cogent, and persuasive program. In the main it was popular in its *heyday* only because it was so easily and generally misunderstood as imposing no onerous "positive" tasks upon the government or restrictions upon the governed. And when the misunderstanding is corrected as thoroughly as it is in this pamphlet, I think any mind less austerely devoted than the author's to this abstract utopia, or more tolerant of human nature as it really is, can readily see why the stringent "real" economic-liberal program never was, nor is ever likely to be, widely popular. The tasks and the restrictions actually involved are *too* onerous for human nature. To control money and credit so firmly as never to allow any inflation or deflation; to devise and enforce effective measures to prohibit and absolutely prevent all possibly serious private monopolies; to refuse all special favors to all pressure groups; to oblige all men as in-

dividuals to make all their own adjustments to economic change
and never seek, through government or through organized group
efforts, any protections from its pressures which would possibly
be injurious to anyone else — to do all this we would need a
government with superhuman wisdom and virtue, and a citizen
population mainly composed of individuals able to combine
ideally rational pursuit of their self-interests with an ideally self-
less readiness to accept, obey, and support all the rules required
to make the "free" economy a perfect servant of the common
welfare.

I pass over such other pieces in this volume as "The Requisites
of Free Competition," and "For a Free-Market Economy,"
which largely re-state and re-argue portions of the thesis of the
"Positive Program," and turn now to the author's particular
views in two special fields — that of money and finance, and that
of labor policy.

His monetary-fiscal doctrines were very individual, neither
traditional nor currently popular, and in one sense radical (extreme or drastic). Their general quality may be gathered even
from the "Laissez Faire" pamphlet just discussed — readers familiar with that will recall its advocacy of the one hundred per
cent reserve idea, and a fixed quantity of money. But the present
volume offers a much fuller and better presentation of his entire
position in this field, in four additional essays: "Rules versus
Authorities in Monetary Policy" — the "key" article in this
group; "Hansen on Fiscal Policy" — a vigorously hostile, critical
review of Professor Hansen's *Fiscal Policy and Business Cycles;*
"On Debt Policy" — a short paper on the federal debt problem;
and "Debt Policy and Banking Policy." From these may be
gathered the following list of his central contentions in this area.
The supply of money in the widest sense, or all means of payment, should be issued and controlled directly by the government alone; the deposit-creating, commercial banking system is
pernicious and should be gradually abolished. The authority in
charge, along with Congress, of the country's monetary policy
should be, not a central bank, but the Federal Treasury; and
the latter should be guided strictly by a fixed simple rule, or set
of rules, understood by the public, and having the force of a

monetary "constitution" and "religion," removing for business all uncertainty about the monetary future. There should be no gold standard, however, but only a stable "fiat" currency — government paper money, not bank credit, with a rule to control its quantity. As far as possible all near-moneys and in general all short term debts should be abolished. Ideally, all debts should be perpetuities, and equity (stock) financing should be overwhelmingly the main reliance of all business enterprises.

In sum, Simons demanded a very drastic simplification of the whole financial system, in order to make it amenable to democratic comprehension and control, and to replace what he saw as a "chaos" containing the sources of recurrent inflations and deflations with a rigid, simple "order" in which both could be prevented by a monetary policy adhering to fixed rules. As to what the master rule should be, however, he wavered and seems not to have made up his mind. The rule of a fixed quantity of money, advocated in the "Laissez Faire" pamphlet, he later in these further essays abandoned as impractical, admitting that its purpose might be defeated by uncontrollable changes of velocity. But he retained a hankering for it, and encumbered his unwilling acceptance of the substitute rule of price level stability with so many criticisms that his advocacy of this had none of his usual decision and vigor. His dream of a system through which the government should give business complete security about the monetary future obliged him to wrestle vainly with insoluble problems. He should have recognized that in this field as in all others, there can be no complete security in a free economy.

The most remarkable piece of all in this volume, however, is the devastating attack on labor unionism entitled "Some Reflections on Syndicalism." The truly drastic position, ably supported, in this piece is not at all "anti-labor" — Simons' social sympathies were all that any humanitarian could ask for, and are fully evident to an unprejudiced reader throughout this essay — but it is anti-union in the most thoroughgoing way. We may grant that readers who will see a sheer contradiction here are wrong, without granting the author's thesis. The latter is supported by much good economic theory, showing how the policies logical for unions in the interests of their memberships are bound to distort the allocation of resources among industries and regions; to limit employment in the unionized labor markets and depress wages in other markets; and in short to bring monopoly gains to limited labor (and employer) groups at the expense, not of the employing class, but of other labor and the community as a whole. And there is also a challenging, if obvious, bit of political theory, as much emphasized as all the economic theory, showing how unions become organizations of power used in their own special, and against general community, interests, how they infringe the state's proper "monopoly of violence," and how they may outgrow the power of a democratic state to control them at all without destroying them, and itself (as democracy), in the process.

Simons' reasoning, both economic and political, about unions, is cogent reasoning, on his plausible and not wholly incorrect premises. But it all ignores the human, psychological and sociological considerations which make unionism inevitable under capitalism; inevitable, and a vehicle of values — among them group solidarities, coöperation, and security of various kinds — which are worth some costs in terms of the values or elements of community welfare that enter into the economist's calculus. And it also ignores the considerations that make it possible, as well as necessary, for a capitalist democracy to achieve the compromises whereby the powers and policies of unions can be confined to zones of tolerable compatibility with the general needs of other groups, the state, and the economy. An abstract perfectionism in terms of his own simple, "pure" idea of the individualistic, free society and economy lay at the root of Simons' anti-unionism, and of all his views. The real human world is too complex to be able to conform to any such simple, rigid pattern.

III

Despite all their merits it is on the whole a relief to turn from the partisan, doctrinaire contentions of Jewkes and Simons to the well balanced, judicious wisdom of J. M. Clark. *Alternative to Serfdom* is the publication in book form of a series of five lectures delivered by Clark on the William W. Cook foundation at the University of Michigan in March, 1947. Apart from its title, the book contains no other allusion to Hayek's *Road to Serfdom*. But the thought behind the title clearly is, that, while the danger is real that we may fall into the new serfdom or become a totally regimented state, return to *laissez faire* is *not* an open alternative. To avoid the danger we must develop a *new* alternative — a somewhat novel social order adapted to meeting the needs of our times, and avoiding both the extremes of pure individualism and of full collectivism.

The first lecture, or chapter, attributes the totalitarian danger to the alleged fact that our society — the type of society thus far produced by the joint effects of industrialism and democracy — is no real community. It is, on the contrary, a collection of aggressive, special interest, power groups — corporations, labor unions, farm organizations, etc. — the relations among which so nearly approximate a state of war as to keep us unsafely near to a forced choice between the extremely coercive state and chaos. And this condition of our society is said to be the product of the laissez-faire era, which lived under the illusion that the truly great organizing power of the free market system was *so* great as to be able to accomplish all needful organizing of society as distinguished from the state.

The attempt to get on without any other, less external bonds of social union beyond those provided by the market economy and a limited "policeman" state — without further inducements to mutual service and mutual justice among men beyond hope of profit and fear of the law — has been breaking down in the formation by particular groups of unions, filling the void, in a fashion, within each group, and converting ruthless self-interest into ruthless, narrow group interest. And we still have achieved no over-all moral or spiritual union and constitution of our whole society, able to restrain the conflicts among the groups. So now, as those conflicts grow increasingly acute with the growing power and sophistication of every group and increasingly disrupt and distort the operation of the market mechanism, we tend to enlarge the coercive powers and functions of the state and look to it to control the groups.

This route to order, however, endangers liberty. Liberty can

be saved only by an adequate growth of responsibility in its
exercise by all individuals and groups. And responsibility requires
the existence of a common, shared loyalty to a definite, social
constitution — a structure of groups included in larger groups
up to the all-including whole society — leading all men to feel,
on consistent lines, both their responsibilities to their special
groups, and their shares in the responsibilities of these to all
other groups and to the whole community. Thus our basic need,
in Clark's view, is not merely a limited enlargement of the state's
sphere of action, although he favors that, but agreement on, and
creation of, a social constitution to support our political and
economic constitutions.

I have been tending thus far, however, to give an exaggerated
impression of the degree of prominence in this book of the theme
suggested by its title — the totalitarian danger and the author's
prescription for avoiding it. Though definitely present, and emphasized by the title chosen, that special theme appears only as
an incidental part of a very general discussion of present-day
American desires and problems — what Americans in the mass,
today, want in and from their society and economy, and how
by a balanced set of compromises among their conflicting desires
they can best formulate and carry out a coherent program. The
central idea is that of a program for building "a society of
responsible individuals in responsible groups," to make freedom
and order compatible, and to strengthen both; but this is presented not only as our sole or best "alternative to serfdom," but
primarily as our central need and task in any case. And around
this central thread is woven a loose texture of discussion, over a
wide range of problems. The first lecture asks what are the main
American desires which are to be "balanced" or adjusted, and
jointly satisfied so far as possible; the second, what is possible
or advisable in the way of steps toward our goals in view of
the capacities and limitations of our human nature as biology and
psychology may help us to understand it. Then follows a discussion of narrower, more particularized problems. The third
lecture, in a way the heart of the book, asks how we Americans
can best deal with the problems implicit in our common, simultaneous approval of competition, disapproval of monopoly, and

approval of "security" for everybody. The fourth topic is what to think of "Keynesian" economic thought and policy, and how to integrate what is valid and useful in it with our older economic wisdom. And the fifth, concluding lecture returns to the central theme of how to "balance," in a generally accepted "social constitution," the asserted rights of free action and the accepted responsibilities and powers of groups, members of groups, individuals in the same categories who prefer not to join organized groups, and the government.

In the initial discussion as to what results Americans of today in general desire from their economic and social system and public policies, one key point is the position taken that they are, actually and rightly, rather less eager for increasing abundance of economic goods than they are for some intangible, non-market "goods." These latter include, above all, those vaguely covered by the word "security": an improved stability of the economic system and of their own and others' positions, incomes, etc., some guaranteed or protected *minima*, and the psychological "security" or comfort of a sense of "belonging" to groups and to a community both friendly and powerful enough to relieve them in a measure of the strain of pure, lonely self-reliance in a world full of hazards. I personally agree with Clark in both the factual and the value judgments here involved — that such in fact is the most widely prevailing "balance" of these desires in our society today, and also that it is reasonable. This, as much as anything, underlies our moderate deviations from old liberal orthodoxy in which a key element was and is the austere conviction that all men *ought* to be extremely self-reliant individuals and individualists, and "sensibly" more eager for the fullest freedom, opportunity, and economic progress than for the consolations of "security." Clark recognizes the potential dangers in excessive developments of the quest for "security" — dangers to a still desired and desirable continuance of economic progress, to individual freedoms, and to society's freedom from the exploiting monopolies which groups, aiming at "security" for their members, too easily become. Indeed, what seems to me especially sound in his approach to all these matters is his firm attitude that *of course* we all have conflicting desires or ideals, and must do our best to resolve their

conflicts *not* through absolute either-or choices, but through
wisely balanced compromises, aiming at partial satisfactions of
all needs together.

I pass to the second, bio-psychological lecture on "human nature's" equipment for getting what it wants, and its liabilities to
err and fail in that endeavor. This seems to me an interesting and
a moderately illuminating treatment of its subject; properly modest in its claims to knowledge in this difficult "outside" field,
broad and balanced in the range of knowledge and ideas actually
drawn upon, successful in showing that (political) economists
who ignore psychology are wrong and miss important, available
insights needed in their work, and far superior to most attempts
by other economists to grasp and utilize psychological insights.
The main emphasis is put not on the doctrines of any one school
of psychologists but on the broad implications of biological "evolution" theory. Man is an animal with impulses, an intelligence, etc.,
evolved in past ages to adapt him for survival in a struggle with
nature and his fellows, and adaptable only with some difficulties
to the altered and complex tasks that face him now in the civilization they have caused him to build, but may or may not enable
him to preserve and to go on improving. This is of course a well
worn theme, especially beloved by Columbia scholars, but Clark
handles it well and fruitfully. And he throws in a good number
of additional insights taken from psychologists ranging from
Thorndike through Freud to Karen Horney. The main broad
result for his economic and social thought is a sound and substantial modification of the traditional liberal faith, handed down
from the eighteenth century, in the good and "rational" natural
man. Clark at least knows, as Simons for example did not, that
we cannot design a workable society if we expect its members to
be fully "rational," and spontaneously, socially good (at once
competitive and coöperative in the right ways and measures), and
without inner jungles of strong impulses requiring careful social
control, and certain, if *wrongly* controlled, to produce grave
mental and social disorders.

Some economist readers, however, may be impatient with the
very broad and somewhat vague generalities making up the first
two lectures, and able to read with keen interest only the third

and fourth, which at last come to grips with familiar, largely economic, problems. It is in the third lecture, on "Competition and Security," that Clark's general theses find their chief, specific applications in a definite field of economic policy problems. This lecture attempts to resolve the dilemma, or basic confusion, in American thought and policy, which arises from the fact that as a people we believe in a competitive economy and oppose monopoly, and yet incline to sympathize with and approve group efforts and political demands for "security" or protections from the extreme pressures of competition — protections which merge insensibly, and often develop, into the foundations of the worst monopolies. As might be expected, Clark's line about this problem is that we need fine distinctions and a careful compromise; that competition does often develop forms and go to extremes which make coöperative and even governmentally assisted efforts to mitigate or modify it desirable; and that drawing and holding the lines or limits required to make this consistent with general enforcement of real competition or prevention of exploitive monopoly (on the part of labor and farm groups as well as of business firms) is possible and necessary, although difficult. His discussions of particular types of cases in the labor, agricultural, and business sectors, and of the relevant range of economic theories about competition and monopoly, I find always interesting and generally fairly sound and penetrating. He is adversely critical of "monopolistic competition" theory and I think less than fair to it, and at some points guilty of not understanding it; but I cannot here go into these matters.

The fourth lecture, on Keynes, etc., is good — neither pro- nor anti-Keynes in any partisan or one-sided way, and yet, I think, clear, consistent, and firm: an attempt to indicate how to "put together" the valid contributions of the older, and of this newer, body of economic theory, and to "balance" the policy ideas suggested by them. The final lecture, on the approach to ways and means of making our medley of groups and individuals responsible, and a true community, admirably summarizes and develops farther this main theme of the book as a whole, but still leaves it, inevitably (in so short a book) and regrettably, in a stage of being only a set of suggestive but vague generalities.

As is evident by now, I think very well indeed of this little book. Although inferior to Simons in analytical clarity — a bit "fuzzy" at many points in the exposition of its reasoning — it far more than compensates for this by the superior breadth, balance, realism, and ripeness of its judgments. What economic science as such has to say on the problems considered is admirably combined with other relevant insights in the fields of psychology, sociology, and politics. I think it too bad that *in* doing this Clark refuses to recognize that he *is* going definitely beyond the province of economics alone; that he quarrels with the "narrowness" of the usual conception of the scope of economics, instead of insisting only on the need to supplement it in approaching the great problems of policy or *political* economy. There is some advantage in keeping one's categories clear and distinct even when attempting a wider "synthesis." But that is a minor criticism. My major criticism is that the book does not recognize the necessary role, in its inquiry, of philosophical in addition to all social-scientific thought, or include a conscious and careful philosophical approach to the ethical problems it is centrally concerned with. Adherence to the belief that "science" alone can solve all our problems involves, after all, precisely that "eighteenth-century idea" of scientific, and yet at the same time moral, "reason" which Clark in his psychological chapter properly repudiates. Any program or inclusive outlook as to policies involves a faith which transcends knowledge. And in order to be as "rational" — sane and wise — as possible, it needs to be developed into a philosophy which transcends science. Too many of even the best representatives, such as Clark, of present day American liberalism (in the now politically current sense of the word), have not outgrown the old naïvely optimistic reliance on social science alone for social salvation, which in its earlier form inspired and marred the old classical liberalism.

IV

As a book free of even that fault, and for other merits, David McCord Wright's *Democracy and Progress* seems to me the best of all among these four. As will appear in due course, that does not mean that I agree with everything in it, but my partial dissent from the central one of its several themes does not diminish my great admiration for the book as a whole. As the title indicates, what is here presented as the central problem facing us is not *simply* the problem of where to draw the lines between private freedoms and public controls in developing our economic policies. It is rather that of how to preserve both the democratic and the *progressive* character of our (American) civilization through a present and visible future which the author, with some pessimism, sees as full of hazards to both — and especially to the particular qualities of both which, at their best, have bound them together in a relation of harmony and mutual furtherance. In the ominous trends and confusions of our time, Wright sees a danger not only that our freedoms may perish in a new age of despotisms, but also that all the economic and general progress so well begun over the last few centuries may be coming to a halt in the imminent arrival of new static, hierarchic, rigid, and ossified societies. Democracy and progress may be dying together — and in the process acquiring perverted characters which make them tend to destroy each other. In the main, the source of these dangers is held to be located in the sphere of ideas and attitudes — developments, not of our old "objective" economic and social system or institutional heritage, but of things in our *cultural* heritage inimical to that and to the real conditions of its preservation and further improvement. With all its physical power, America is suffering a deep moral confusion, due in some part to the complex conditions and problems of the time which bewilder us, but mainly to the current growth in our culture, from historic roots, of certain pernicious, false beliefs and wrong attitudes, which are causing all minds infected by them to view our problems in false perspectives. *One part* of the complex thesis which Wright develops on these lines *does* pertain to economic freedoms and controls, as they affect economic progress, and *this* aligns him *in a measure* with the heirs and champions of the old economic liberalism. But the other strands of his thought, interwoven with, and modifying this one, make his total vision, analysis, and remedial program markedly original and superbly rich in illuminating insights.

Underlying the whole there is, besides the heritage of economic-liberal thought and other things, a conscious philosophy, mainly indebted — by Wright's own acknowledgment, and apart from that, visibly to any reader already acquainted with it — to the philosophy of A. N. Whitehead. I must freely confess — if it be a confession — that my own enthusiasm for the latter contributes not a little to my enthusiasm for this book. No reader, however, who is *not* in rapport with Whitehead need be at all deterred by this from reading Wright! The connection, nevertheless, is important enough to justify a few words about it here.

Central in Whitehead's thought is a general metaphysical theory of progress — its great importance, its relatively rare, never guaranteed occurrence, its nature and requirements, and the ever present danger for all life of relapse, after temporary bursts of progress, into the *rigor mortis* of stagnation. According to this theory, progress is achieved by adventurous, creative vitality, which successively abandons its old achievements when they threaten to become mere automatic, repetitive routines, and goes on to new achievements. The latter are novel creations, converting abstract possibilities into concrete actual objects of enjoyment, though in the other non-actual, non-temporal realm there eternally exist all the mere possibilities — Platonic "ideas" — of largely (but never absolutely) harmonious, rich combinations of values, goods, or delights. Increasing richness (internal variety) and exquisiteness of the relative harmonies, always including enough contrasts or subdued conflicts to preclude dullness, mark the sequence of achieved, new patterns of life, so long as progress continues. The urge to progress is the response of creative vitality to the persuasive attractions of the felt or conceived, but as yet unrealized, possibilities. But the process always involves adventure, risks of failure and disappointment, and the relinquishment of secure and familiar old routines, or resistance to the counterurge to mere passivity and acquiescence in control by the past — safe automatic repetition. Thus progress ceases and stagnation ensues whenever adventurous vitality "tires," or declines to an intensity less than or barely equal to that of the opposing timid and nostalgic feelings which bind us to the past.

This cosmic theory of progress reciprocally adjusts to each

other and combines essential elements of Platonism and of the nineteenth-century liberal idea of social progress. It eliminates from the former the idea of pursuit of a final, static, perfect, harmonious order, but retains the ideas of "final causality," or the persuasive lure of ideal possibilities, and of life as pursuit of realization of aesthetic harmonies. And it frees the latter (liberal progressivism) from its hampering entanglement with the merely mechanical philosophy of nature and historical determinism. Now Wright builds on the Whiteheadian theory of progress, or "applies" it in the sphere of his interests, without overemphasizing it or ever using any mere deductions from it as a substitute for independent study of his own materials. And its influence, merely as one part of the general background of his thinking, broadens, deepens, and otherwise improves his personal version of the (old school) liberal theory of society's economic progress — its required method and inevitable costs or disturbing concomitants.

Even in his version, the latter theory is only one strand of his thought, though it stands alone in the first part of the book and is central throughout. The others, more original and distinctive, modify it as they appear in succession, and to me they are more interesting. In itself this first theory deals with only one aspect of progress — economic progress in the simple sense of generally rising productivity, real incomes and wealth, and living standards. Insisting that, despite its depreciators, future continuation of this economic progress still is generally desired, desirable, and important, the book begins with an analysis of the conditions which have accounted for it in the past. The origin of modern economic progress, in the industrial revolution, is ascribed to the fortunate, mutually favorable interactions in that period of advancing science (with its application in technology), of capitalism, and of democracy. The defining feature of the "capitalism" concerned was the general prevalence of free competitive innovation (the influence of Schumpeter is apparent and acknowledged) in types of products and methods of production. Such innovation was no longer repressed by a ruling, security-conscious and tradition-loving oligarchy — social groups of all kinds and a government intent on preserving a stable order or *status quo* — and by a network of restrictive customs serving that purpose. Progressive capitalism first arose from the disintegration of the post-feudal oligarchies, mercantilist "planned economies," and guild regimes; and it thus arose in sympathetic interaction with the rise of democracy. Furthermore, it had, as its own democratic aspect, a new and wide diffusion of opportunities for economic achievement and social influence, which weakened the powers of the old vested interests to resist disturbing change, and enabled the creative enterprise of a multitude of new men, rising out of obscurity, to triumph over all such resistance. And there was *mutual* dependence too between this social evolution and the simultaneous progress of science and technology. The latter made possible the new progressive industrial capitalism, but also the new type of society (in contrast with the old) uniquely and fully encouraged inventions, and above all the industrial use of them — being not too much concerned over the upsetting effects on the economic positions of the people dependent on the continuing use of old products and old methods.

At this point, the second chapter takes up the "moral dilemma of progress" and meets the objection that capitalist progress was and is a brutal, immoral affair of ruthless and greedy competition or conflict, by attacking the ideal of a world free from conflict as a miserable illusion — one of the pernicious elements of our cultural heritage from the over-optimistic side of the eighteenth-century "enlightenment." Diverse utopias suggested by the ideal are in turn examined and rejected as certain, if tried in practice, to prove either unworkable and incapable of lasting, or prisons confining life to a very meager and grim level. In part, the core of the argument here is familiar simple economic theory: human wants in the aggregate are insatiable and no amount of economic progress can satisfy them; yet the alternative, ascetic limitation of wants, forbids the endless progressive enrichment or enhancement of life, and is no solution. But with this is combined a wider view, again suggested by Whitehead, in a saying quoted in the preface of the book: "The deliberate aim at Peace easily passes into its bastard substitute, Anaesthesia; in other words, for the quality of life and motion is substituted their destruction." The creative vitality essential for progress is inseparable from a degree of selfishness and conflict; no perfect harmony is attainable or desirable; some conflict is inherent in the nature of the universe, of life, and of value. The final conclusion drawn however is not that capitalist competition should or can be wholly unrestrained. Proper mitigation and civilization of its conflicts, making the competitive economy a not perfect but relative harmony in which in the main each prospers by serving all, requires — and we have been developing as a part of our progress — an improving code of standards for competition, *i.e.*, for the selection of individuals for advancement in society.

From the points so far made about the conditions of economic progress, on the whole best fulfilled in the nineteenth century, it follows that certain present-day developments are increasing threats to its continuance. For one thing, established, now security-conscious, capitalist firms and groups, *and* labor unions and all other vested-interest groups alike are with increasing success defending the "security" of their existing positions, and hampering the process of competitive innovation through private action as monopolies and through political pressures for governmental help. In addition, our "advanced" (!) intellectuals in growing numbers have Platonic visions of a perfectly harmonious and stable order to be achieved by comprehensive governmental planning. Short of this latter, we are reducing the incentives for new creative capitalist enterprise by imposing types of governmental controls and taxes designed to lessen inequalities of wealth and income in our society and to stabilize the economy, but actually carried to the point of destroying the mainsprings of progress. Finally, in our large business and other organizations, where the spirit and pressures of our democracy oblige managers to pay tender heed to the wishes, envies, and susceptibilities of all concerned, there is a spreading perversion of the democratic ideal of equal respect for all persons into one of no distinctions of merit or value offensive to anyone's pride. This perversion is leading to the replacement of competitive performance tests for the selection and promotion of men, by mechanical "objective" standards such as seniority, to the serious detriment of the opportunities for able men to rise by contributing to progress.

Other themes in the book go beyond this largely orthodox-old-liberal preoccupation with economic progress as commonly conceived. As a complex whole the "progress" which Wright is concerned about includes much more than just the abstract, quantitative economic progress which increases "wealth" *per capita* — "wealth" of which the contents and quality are in this concept entirely unspecified. He is equally concerned for progress in improving tastes and the quality-standards expressed in the demands to which business caters; progress in improving all (including the aesthetic) qualities of all such specific items of our "wealth" as houses, clothes, furniture, cars, works of art, literature, journalism, entertainments, etc. As he says, quoting Ruskin about "illth" with approval, "pure competition can be competition in the production of pure garbage." And along with progressive, aesthetic and general qualitative improvement of the products of our economic system, we need also a progressive improvement of the morals and manners with which all activities involved in operating it, are carried on. The two things are not unrelated — both depend on the prevailing level of tastes or of culture.

I suspect that Wright's emphasis on, and extremely interesting discussion of, these matters (rarely considered by American economists) may stem in part from his personal background and artistic interests; and partly also, again, from his reading of Whitehead, whose entire philosophy of value in every sense is basically aesthetic, and who constantly stresses the importance of concrete, particular things and qualities and the inadequacy of abstract, scientific thought alone to guide our decisions in action, policy, or conduct. At all events, his interesting thesis about this phase of progress, in public taste, in products and in behavior, is that it has been and remains the function in our society of a "censor class" to bring it about. In older European societies the "censor class" was to a great extent the aristocracy; in our American society it has consisted of our best educated, professional groups — the ministers of religion, professors and teachers, men of letters, high grade responsible journalists, etc. The democratic-capitalist mode of economic and general progress, depending on the continual rise through competitive success of new, ambitious and able, but initially uncultured, crude, philistine men and families, out of "lower" into "higher" social strata, makes it especially necessary that these oncoming leaders in the business and social world, and the mass of the people, be educated and led in matters of culture, taste, and morals by the "censor class." But we need a balance of the creative, though rude, vitality of the builders of new enterprises, with the harmonizing influence of the exponents of good taste and culture — not domination and suppression of one lot by the other. Today too many in the American "censor class," misled by the unsound elements now mainly emphasized in the cultural heritage they especially guard, are developing a wholly anticapitalist attitude and a wish to make themselves as a class the actual governing or ruling class. And at the same time, performance of and respect for the proper function of this class — discrimination among values and persuasion of others to accept the standards arrived at — is being rendered impossible by one of the worst developments in our intellectual culture — the growth of exclusive respect for "science" alone or contempt for everything else in the sphere of thought, which logically and actually tends to spread as a consequence the view that all values, aesthetic and ethical, are purely "relative" to each person's whims.

I still have said almost nothing about the book's treatment of the other half of its general subject — democracy, which is as much the object of Wright's concern and attention as is progress, the two themes being interwoven throughout. Like his full concept of progress, his concept of democracy also is ample and complex, including far more than the mechanism of political democracy. Distinguishing "ballot box democracy" and "ethical democracy," he insists that the former is of value only insofar as it helps to realize the latter. And by the latter he means the ethical humanism which demands respectful good will and full, generous justice from, toward, and among all members of the human race — the classical-and-Christian moral idealism which, for Americans in general, has come to be embodied chiefly in the complex of ideals they mean by "democracy."

But even on the level of imperfect, actual, institutional democracy — the mechanisms or vehicles for movement toward realization of the democratic ideals — the political mechanism of the democratic state does not stand alone. The competitive market economy or mechanism, Wright maintains, in its own nature is a no less democratic institution, in and through which enterprises compete in catering to the tastes and demands of the democratic multitude in the whole wide sphere of economic, including many cultural, goods, just as parties and candidates compete in catering to them in the other sphere of political goods. Moreover, the "democracy of opportunity" in the economy which is essential for its progress also is an essential support for the preservation of political democracy. For if an oligarchy of vested interest-groups in the economy-and-state can restrict new, outside competition and the rise of new men in large numbers to substantial wealth, they can thereby also restrict attainment by those not of their party or clique, of substantial, social and political influence.

Again, comprehensive economic planning by the government, if it aimed and managed to continue economic progress in its way, not only would be likely at best to slow it because the "ins" would intrench themselves and fall into stereotyped ways, not being under the pressure of new, outside competition; but this enfeebled, "planned" progress also would be at best difficult to reconcile with the preservation of democracy, because the "ins" would have control of the economic bases of political power, and the "outs" would lack the economic independence and means required for independent political action. Moreover, as some current tendencies are threatening to slow up economic progress or to change its method to one unfavorably, instead of favorably, related to democracy, others are threatening to change or pervert our democracy into a *milieu* hostile instead of favorable to progress. As with any "religion" there are democratic "heresies" — corrupted versions of the true faith; and these, Wright fears, are gaining ground. Democracy throughout, economic and political, is essentially competitive, and healthy competition requires not only that the winners play fair with new challengers, but also that the losers be good sports. The false egalitarianism — proud, envious refusal to accept advancement of others relative to self, through superior achievement — which grows out of the worst perversions of democratic idealism, erects all sorts of barriers to progress through competitive innovation and achievement. One part of the discussion is devoted to the errors of modern "pro-

gressive" education through which it fosters the democratic heresies and weakens the attitudes on which sound democracy and
social progress depend. But enough! — though there still is much
more in the book which I have not mentioned.

My concluding criticism will be brief. I think that Wright is
somewhat unduly fearful in viewing as great dangers to the future
of American democratic progress the now current strivings in the
country for more "security," more (in the popular sense) demo-
cratic-governmental control of our capitalist economy, and more
reduction of both the major inequalities of wealth-and-power,
and the major instabilities in the economy. In other words, I think
he is somewhat unduly "bound" in his thought by, or to, his admiring vision of the particular nineteenth-century mode — goals
and method — of democratic-capitalist progress, and prone to be
sure that any extensive deviations from it, such as are now developing, must necessarily portend a return to static despotism, and
cannot possibly instead be moulded into a good, new phase of
progress.

The fact that there are real analogies between very modern
and medieval social aims and devices does not necessarily argue
against my less pessimistic view. A degree of order, stability,
security, and coöperative harmony not wholly but largely restraining competitive strife — a degree of all this sufficient for the
emotional needs of the people can be in itself a good, or part of
the society's and of each member's "wealth" in the widest sense,
and a creative achievement signifying progress, too, if brought
about after a period of excessive disorder, instability, insecurity,
and prevailing strife. Wright of course would not deny this; we
differ only on the question of degree, as to where is the point of
best balance combining "enough" of these things with "enough"
freedom for, and progress through, competitive innovation. The
medieval civilization overdid the pursuit of order, stability, etc.,
and too largely inhibited progress; but I think the nineteenth
century went to the other extreme, evolving a society so intensely
competitive, and so little ordered by collective agreement, custom,
and control, that it finally became, for all its great economic and
other achievements, intolerably chaotic. We are now in the reac-

tion against that extreme and outcome, and although there is danger of swinging too far and again throttling progress for the sake of security, there is I think the better possibility of working out a new, modern compromise superior in its balance to either part of the past.

11

SCHUMPETER AND MARX:

IMPERIALISM AND SOCIAL CLASSES

IN THE SCHUMPETERIAN SYSTEM

~❧

I

An event has occurred. The late Professor Schumpeter's two, long famous, and hitherto much neglected essays, which had been available in German only, have at last been made available in English — together forming one small, attractive book.* The gratitude of all is due to the "entrepreneur" and editor, Dr. P. M. Sweezy, and the translator, Dr. Heinz Norden. The excellence of the translation is reliably vouched for by Dr. Sweezy, and the result is certainly an English style which can be read with pleasure and a secure feeling that the author's thought is coming through with entire clarity. A word of praise must be said for Dr. Sweezy's brief, felicitous, and delightful Introduction. As the latter says, it is regrettable that these two monographs — always regarded by Schumpeter as among his best and most important

* Joseph A. Schumpeter, *Imperialism and Social Classes* (New York: Augustus M. Kelley, Inc., 1951). "Zur Soziologie der Imperialismen" appeared first in the *Archiv für Sozialwissenschaft und Sozialpolitik*, 1919; "Die sozialen Klassen im ethnisch homogenen Milieu," *ibid.*, 1927. The present article first appeared in the *Quarterly Journal of Economics* (November 1951) and is reprinted here by permission of the editor.

works — have been so generally neglected in the world of Anglo-American scholarship. And it is to be hoped and expected that in this easily accessible form they will now be widely read and discussed, will stimulate and aid much new research in their important fields, and will be studied by all economists interested in Schumpeter's work in general *in conection with* all the other parts of the great, many-sided structure of his thought.

The present article attempts a "broad," though inadequate, discussion of them in that latter connection, and thus also of Schumpeter *and* his structure of thought as a whole. The interpretation herein developed bears some relation — or is my reaction — to that suggested by Dr. Sweezy in his introduction, in a passage with which I partly agree and partly disagree. Hence by way of "preface" to my own discussion, and for the reader's benefit, I begin by quoting the essential parts of this passage. Dr. Sweezy writes:

> Economists who conceive of their science in traditional and rather narrowly restrictive terms — and that means most of the economics profession in this country today — will naturally be inclined to treat Schumpeter's essays on imperialism and social classes as forays into other fields — essentially unrelated to his main work on business cycles and the theory of economic development. Thus, for example, R. V. Clemence and F. S. Doody have written a (very useful) book entitled *The Schumpeterian System* (1950) without ever mentioning either of these essays; and both Haberler and Smithies set them apart as representing Schumpeter's "sociological" views.[1] No doubt there is much to be said for this position, and I am sure that it would be possible to find support for it in Schumpeter's own writings and still more in his oral teachings; no one made a sharper distinction than Schumpeter between economic and non-economic phenomena, when it suited his purpose to do so. But at the same time I think it would be possible to construct a broader "Schumpeterian system" — comparable in its scope to Marxian social science though not to Marxism as a whole — into which these essays fit as integral parts. I . . . think

[1] Note by O. H. T. Dr. Sweezy's reference here is to two memorial articles on Schumpeter, in the August 1950 issue of the Q.J.E. (Haberler) and the September 1950 number of the *American Economic Review* (Smithies). It is true that both authors classify these essays as sociological — and I agree; but I am sure that neither Haberler nor Smithies meant thereby to set them *aside*, as Dr. Sweezy implies, as if of only minor interest to economists. In fact the Smithies article goes even further than I would go in the opposite direction, in commending Schumpeter's sociological work to economists *more* highly than his technical work in economics.

it may be useful in "placing" these works to indicate . . . the main lines which such an attempt might take.

Schumpeter's central concern throughout his entire scientific career is best described by the subtitle to *Business Cycles* . . . "A Theoretical, Historical, and Statistical Analysis of the Capitalist Process." The core of the analysis . . . is set forth in his *Theory of Economic Development*. But there are many aspects of capitalist reality which are not explained by this theory. Some of these, of course, are of . . . minor significance. But at least one such aspect, comprising the phenomena of imperialism and war, is obviously of crucial importance. Any theory of capitalism which leaves it out of account is unquestionably incomplete. More, it is *prima facie* inadequate and even wrong. Now Schumpeter's theory of economic development not only does not explain imperialism and war; it leads to the expectation that the advance of capitalism will push them further and further into the background and eventually relegate them to the scrap-heap of history. It is perfectly clear, then, that unless this contradiction between theory and reality is resolved, Schumpeter's whole system would be, to say the least, suspect. The essential point of the essay on imperialism is precisely to resolve this contradiction, and in this sense it forms a crucial part of his entire structure. . . .

The theory of social classes occupies a different position. . . . To Schumpeter — and in this respect as in others, he was undoubtedly deeply influenced by Marx — capitalism is, like all social systems, a transitory phenomenon. It had a birth, it is now living its life, and sooner or later it will die. A complete theory of capitalism . . . would have . . . three parts: the theory of origins, the theory of functioning and growth, and the theory of decline. Most of Schumpeter's work concerns . . . functioning and growth, but he was perfectly conscious that this is not the whole story. . . . At the risk of being somewhat overschematic, I would say that the essay on social classes in Schumpeter's central work on the theory of origins, while *Capitalism, Socialism, and Democracy* occupies the same position with respect to the theory of decline.

This estimate of the essay on social classes will certainly not impose itself on the reader as self-evident. . . . The essay . . . has the form of a general theory . . . and its conclusions are relevant to all of recorded history. But the substance . . . is based upon an analysis of two classes, the (western European) feudal nobility, and the modern *bourgeoisie*. Now . . . the origins of capitalism can be treated in terms of the decline of the nobility and the rise of the *bourgeoisie*. These problems are in fact aspects of the transition from feudalism to capitalism. . . . Schumpeter does not deal with the transition systematically . . . but the broad contours of his thought can, I think, be clearly discerned . . . here. . . . No more need be claimed . . . to substantiate the view that the essay on social classes occupies an important place in the over-all structure . . . and is not a mere excursion into the "foreign" realm of sociology. . . .

Now as will be evident in what follows, I go a considerable distance in agreement with Dr. Sweezy's general view as expressed in these paragraphs. Thus I agree first of all that economists, equally with sociologists and others, should find these essays — as well as *Capitalism, Socialism, and Democracy* — of great interest, even though all these writings may (and I think must in the main) be classified as work in sociology, not in economics narrowly defined. I further agree that these sociological works are by no means unrelated to their author's theory of economic development and of business cycles, but do stand in fairly definite relations thereto and round out a "broader Schumpeterian system," which it is indeed worthwhile to construct and consider as a whole. Thus in a sense my effort here will be to carry out in a measure in my own way — which doubtless may differ even more than I know or guess from what would be his way — Dr. Sweezy's suggestion. But on a number of very crucial points, my reading of Schumpeter's thought diverges rather widely from Dr. Sweezy's, largely I think in consequence of the facts that the latter is a Marxist; that Schumpeter as everyone knows had a complex, discriminating attitude to Marx and rejected many elements of Marxism while accepting others; and that my own standpoint is even more largely un- and anti-Marxian than Schumpeter's was. Thus it seems to me that Dr. Sweezy, by implication, exaggerates the degree of resemblance, or unduly minimizes the marked dissimilarities at essential points, between the "broad systems" of Marx and of Schumpeter. That applies I think first of all on the preliminary "scope and method" question, and the *modes* of relatedness of the economic and sociological parts of the two "systems." And it applies again in even more important ways on the substantive questions concerning the natures and relations of economic capitalism and the bourgeois civilization, the transitions and overlappings connecting capitalism with "feudalism" and with socialism, the connection or non-connection of "imperialism and war" with capitalism, and what should be stressed about Schumpeter's theory of social classes, in comparing him with Marx.

II

Like Dr. Sweezy I reject and deplore — both in general and as applied to Schumpeter's works — the too common, narrow and absolute idea of the restricted field of economics and its isolation within the broad, general area of social science. But it will not do I think, in approaching the question of a "broader Schumpeterian system," merely to mention in passing and then to ignore the fact that Schumpeter himself always insisted strongly on at least a relative, clear separation of economics from the rest of social science; and proceed to construct his broad system as though we could suppose it to embody or agree with the Marxian idea of a single, unified, and all-inclusive economic-social science. Not only is it "possible," as Sweezy admits, "to find support" in Schumpeter's teachings for a view which insists on dividing social science into a number of dissimilar sciences, economics and others, and consequently on dividing the whole work of a Schumpeter — or, as in his practice, of a Marx — at least into work in economics, and other work in sociology. The record, it seems to me, of Schumpeter's constant, consistent, emphatic insistence on such a view decisively forbids us — in the absence of overwhelming evidence that his practice violated all his precepts — to assume that the contents of all his diverse writings together form one *fully integrated, homogeneous, monolithic* system.

Schumpeter always taught that economics and sociology are different sciences, dealing with different elements of social reality and using different sets of concepts, data, and procedures, and that it is injurious to both to fuse together a theory of economics and a theory of sociology into one rigid "synthesis," claiming an absolute unity. And in the first part — on Marx — of *Capitalism, Socialism, and Democracy*, he criticizes the Marxian system as a whole *for* being or attempting just such a rigid "synthesis." [2] Hence we must beware of the idea of a "Schumpeterian system," *closely similar in this respect to* that of Marx — a complete and

[2] See chap. iv, pp. 1–5 especially, of this essay on Marx, which appears both as Part I of *Capitalism, Socialism, and Democracy*, and as the first essay in Schumpeter's *Ten Great Economists* (Oxford University Press, 1951).

unified theory of the entire life history of the capitalist economy-and-civilization. At the same time I think there *is* a broad "Schumpeterian system," in its own way covering *much* of that ground, but having unmistakably a two-part structure consistent with his teachings about the two sciences — which never implied that they are entirely unrelated to each other. It is, however, unfortunate for our purpose here that — as far as I know — he never told us fully just *how* the two subject matters and types of problems were related to each other in his mind. Thus what immediately follows expresses views of my own about economics and sociology, which I *think* are in substantial agreement with his teachings and may be of use in analyzing his "broad system"; but I do not claim his authority for them.

The central, main, and peculiar part of the subject matter of economic science may be described as the patterns of relations *inter se*, of functional dependence or co-variation, in which the economic quantities occur and change, in the functioning and development of economic societies. By "economic quantities" I mean the changing input-flows of work and resources into the production processes and their output-flows of products; prices of all kinds; and the money-flows — of old and new money and credit into circulation, sales-receipts of enterprises, incomes, liquid balances, and outlays, of all types. Such are the items, variables, or phenomena which can be studied by economic theory and the collection and analysis of economic statistics, which together make up almost the entire mass of strictly "scientific" work in economics. At the same time, however, it is of the utmost importance that economists should always bear in mind, with all its implications, the obvious fact that "behind" and interacting with what is metaphorically called the "behavior" of the economic quantities, lies all the real human behavior going on in the economy-and-society concerned.

Now of course there cannot be an *absolute* restriction of economics to a study of just the pattern of related, changing economic quantities and *nothing* else. To have any means of explaining that set of phenomena, the science must include also a volume and selection, sufficient for its purpose, of ideas and facts about human motives and the economic behavior of all actors in the social economy, and the changing institutional framework and socio-cultural milieu affecting that behavior. But about these matters, precisely the best "working notions" for use in economic theory as such do not try or pretend to go much below the surface of these human social phenomena; or do much *to explain them*, in contradistinction to merely *using* appropriate *data* or assumptions about them, to explain its own peculiar subject matter — the relationships in which the changes of the economic quantities occur. For a study of economic developments within a given society and epoch, the main facts about the institutions of that society and behavior-tendencies of its members during that epoch are of course parts of the essential *data*. But the task of explaining how these behavior-tendencies and institutions and their changes in historic time are engendered via the emotional and mental processes in the human beings and the evolution of their social order and culture — *this* task by its nature belongs not to economic science but to the group of psycho-social sciences, which need development by specialists with skills and equipment quite unlike those of the economist as such.

Moreover, that remains true no matter what may be true in the last analysis about the interactions upon each other of economic conditions and developments, on the one hand, and socio-cultural, institutional, and ideological developments, on the other. And so for example, whatever measure of truth and even if complete truth be assigned to that great sociological hypothesis, "the economic interpretation of history," the point made above remains unaffected. For even if the economic conditions and developments within a society are the basic, initial causes of all the later-appearing features of (and changes in) its entire social order, way of life, and civilization, *the long and complex, intermediate, psychological and social processes* — through which economic changes at length engender the new institutions and behavior-tendencies of which, when they mature, economic theory itself must again take account — are processes, the study of which by its nature belongs to psychological-and-social science, not to economics. It is one thing, however, to insist on this point and quite another to infer that between these diverse sciences there is no border zone of potentially, mutually beneficial, or instructive contact and even necessary overlapping; or that economists lack valid reasons to be interested in, to study, and even to contribute to this other kind or part of social science. From the fact that economic science has a limited scope it does not follow that economists should be economists only or absolute specialists. Breadth of horizons of interest, reading, reflection, research, and creative work is in general a valid, admirable, though not compulsory ideal for scholars whatever their main specialties. The only restriction is that one should know when he is "crossing over" into a new field, with distinctive problems, and take the trouble to acquire the distinctive equipment, skills, and viewpoint required for effective work on them. And it is generally a mistake to aim at a full synthesis — unification under one conceptual scheme — of results arrived at in the domains of different sciences. The powers of "adjoining" and "related" studies to throw light on each other's problems can be real and important, but it is rarely if ever possible to solve problems in one field entirely or mainly through application of ideas or knowledge "brought in" from another science.[3]

Thus to describe one part of Schumpeter's — or of Marx's — work as belonging not to economics but to "psycho-social" science is not at all to describe it as consisting of mere "forays" into a field entirely "foreign" to the interests of the author as an economist, and unrelated to his work in economics, nor as necessarily, in contrast with the latter, of less interest to other economists. But a bit more needs to be said now about this field of psycho-social science, and the common species but differing varieties of work done in it by Marx and by Schumpeter. And in this connection, first, a contrast of that species with another, younger one that is now perhaps more vividly familiar in our environment may be suggestive. Today the conspicuous, rising kind of work in this general area is being done by collaborating groups of specialists in psychiatry or clinical psychology, social psychology, cultural anthropology, and a modern sociology having affiliations with all those specialties. And in all this work the great aim is to develop

[3] Some evidence that Schumpeter's views were at least consistent with all I have said here about economics and sociology may be found in, among others, the following places in his writings: *Theory of Economic Development*, chap. I; his essay on Marx in *Capitalism, Socialism, and Democracy;* and his essay on Pareto in *Ten Great Economists.*

truly "scientific" studies — really similar in principle, in the matter of attaining close empirical verification of theories, to the experimental "natural" sciences — of the conscious and unconscious, emotional and mental processes of human individuals and groups, and their resulting reactions to all kinds of stimuli, situations, problems, etc. Avoiding the irrelevant digression and the presumption that would be involved in any general appraisal here of this kind of work, let me say only two things about it. On the one hand, whatever its deficiencies thus far, I think it is a great mistake for scholars in other fields — including economists, whose own science could well use much more and better knowledge *about human beings* than economic thought in general has ever yet reflected — to despise this very modern, fledgling type of social science. And on the other hand, whatever its special value and promise, this species of social science does not seem at all likely in any visible future to entirely supersede or make obsolete another, quite different, more old-fashioned kind of scholarly and reflective work, which may be called *speculative historical sociology*. While not *in the same sense* scientific, the latter can be something hardly more insecure and far more apt to deal impressively with really large, important themes; by combining at once broad and thorough historical research with good intuitive-and-logical theoretical work, developing theories consistent with all the historical evidence adduced to "explain" the origins and careers in history of social systems and civilizations or important social and cultural phenomena. It is in this category that we must place Marx's, and Schumpeter's, contributions to sociology; though unlike Schumpeter, Marx thoroughly combined and fused together his sociology and his economics. In an effort now further to illuminate that difference and bring to light some other differences between the two "broad systems," I turn, in comparing them, from the formal structures to some matters of substance.

III

In Schumpeter's "broad system" as in that of Marx, the sociology has as both its own basic element or core, and its link with the economics, an "economic interpretation of history." That phrase, however, may designate either a bare general hypothesis only, or a complete, particular way of carrying out in specific studies, the program or task which needs much beyond that hypothesis to define it fully. Now in the first sense the Schumpeterian and the Marxian economic interpretation are the same; both authors used the same general hypothesis, conceived and understood in the same way. To state it at once, their hypothesis is: that in history as an on-going process, "economic development" is in a substantial measure "autonomous" and is the chief "prime mover" of other social and cultural change, though of course in its turn it is not unaffected by the repercussions upon it of the changing institutional and cultural milieu. But although Schumpeter accepted that hypothesis from Marx, he discarded and replaced with his own original and quite different alternatives some essential elements — additional, subsidiary hypotheses — in Marx's way of implementing and applying it; and thus developed his own largely different "economic interpretation" in the full specific sense of the term. On the complex question, *how* the changes of phenomena in the other spheres of social life are brought about by "autonomous" change in the economic sphere, the Schumpeterian theory as a whole is not more than half Marxian, and in several important respects is decidedly un-Marxian. To spell this out is the purpose of this section.

First of all, a few words must be said on their common initial assumption of autonomy of the primary causative process, economic development; with reasonable fairness to both authors I think, this assumption may be explained as follows. One thing which generally goes on through time in human societies, however slowly under some conditions, is economic progress in the sense of technological advance and rising efficiency in the physical production of material goods — together with all necessarily consequent adjustments of all economic quantities. Eventually the earlier, inefficient tools and methods get improved or superseded by other, more effective ones; changes in this sphere occur, with some rise of output per unit of input as one general purpose and result. Ideas of motives and causes behind this tendency and historic trend need not detain us at this point beyond quick mention of some that are obvious. Population pressures and other pressures of unsatisfied wants, ambitions of some individuals for wealth and power and proceedings to gain them which (often) include steps to improve production, initiatives of governing groups or leaders with military or other ends in view, ingenuity and enterprise in whatever quarters, and the slow, accumulative growth of experience and knowledge, skills, technical know-how, and eventually scientific knowledge — all doubtless play their parts. Full recognition of the extensive powers of differing regimes, institutional set-ups, social structures, and culture-elements (ideas and attitudes) of many kinds, to accelerate or retard the process, is entirely consistent with the assumption of autonomy, and explicit in both Marx and Schumpeter. Thus for example both emphasize the great, new, immense invigoration and liberation of the process of improving production that came in with the rise of modern industrial capitalism along with the bourgeois culture and social order. The hypothesis that economic development has some autonomy means not that its pace and mode of occurrence are independent of the influence of non-economic factors; but only that to some extent, never or rarely negligible, it goes on anyhow, one way or another, under almost all conditions. Though the speed and the manner do, the mere occurrence of this process does not require explanation by reference to any particular types of external non-economic causes.

Now to outline Marx's theory — which up to the point of divergence to be noted when I come to it, is Schumpeter's also — of the external, or broader social and cultural, consequences. First, economic-technical change carries with it, as a more or less precisely determined necessary concomitant, change of social-economic organization and the general pattern of human "social relations" within and around the process of production. Use of a set of techniques of production, in a given stage of their development, largely determines the organization of production and distribution, and thus the main social relations among the producers and all in the society. And that organization or pattern of relations together with the techniques makes up the "mode of production," which as a whole is the foundation of the entire related social system and civilization. All the rest of the latter — the political and legal system, all non-economic institutions, and the entire intellectual, aesthetic, and moral culture — is "superstructure," built or growing up (originally at least) upon that "foundation" and subject, throughout, to profound influence by it in two ways. In the first place there must occur a good deal of practically necessary or highly expedient adaptation of much in the society's whole organization or many of its institutions, folkways, etc. to the requirements imposed by its techniques and entire mode of economic production. And in the second place, the psychologies of all elements of the population are profoundly affected by their places and roles in, or relations to, the society's and period's mode of production and their economic circumstances, environments, and tasks. Men's economic life-situations in that sense largely generate or determine the basic attitudes and outlooks or mentalities which they carry into all spheres of life and all their contributions to the character of everything in their society and its culture.[4]

All those propositions, however, about the social relations included in the mode of production and the ways in which the latter affects the superstructure have been stated thus far, carefully, in terms so general as to express only what is common to Marx and Schumpeter. And in the two authors' respective theories they all receive quite different types of additional, more specific contents or meanings, because the economic interpretation hypothesis is implemented, in Marx's theory entirely and in Schumpeter's not at all, by the former's great, second or further hypothesis — his "class struggle theory" of all history. Let me now "go back" and insert this at the proper point in Marx's theory, and complete my account of the latter with the understanding that the next few paragraphs do *not* refer to Schumpeter's theory, which I will take up presently.

According to Marx, at every point of time in all history either past or to come, *up to* the arrival of his dreamed-of, future, socialist utopia, it would be true to say as of that time: in every existing society the set of social relations — social structure — inherent in its mode of production, includes as the central feature

---

[4] See Schumpeter's explanation of the "economic interpretation" in the essay on Marx.

some class-structure consisting chiefly of a dominant, owning and directing and a toiling, oppressed class; and in every case the antagonistic relations between those classes form the central focus of the entire pattern of all social relations in that society. And further, in every case the entire "superstructure," mainly influenced by and serving the dominant class, operates to sanction, enforce, and crystallize the existing pattern of all social relations. But precisely by doing so it, in time, becomes and makes the latter a set of "fetters" impeding further technological-and-economic progress, in so far as that requires as its complement appropriate, continual change of the economic-social organization, relations among owners and workers in production, institutions to enforce those relations, and ideas or beliefs sanctioning those institutions. Institutional and cultural change, though induced and eventually compelled by economic-technical change, lags behind and increasingly obstructs the latter; and in history at long intervals it has to be and is speeded up, temporarily, by revolutions. The lag is always due to resistance by the dominant class to changes in the "superstructure" which are needed to re-adapt it to its changing economic "foundation," but which are feared by the class as threats to its familiar power-position and advantages. And the effect of the lag is always *not mere* retardation and arrest of progress, or stagnation, *but* an accumulation of tensions, conflicts, and growing, eventually fatal, and explosive "inner contradictions" in the entire productive-and-social system.

Eventually a revolting class initially below the "top" — e.g. the bourgeoisie in the early-modern period — destroys the old ossified and now intolerably restrictive social system and creates a new one, which makes its creators the new dominant class and frees them to improve production and in general perform the socially useful tasks that were not allowed to be performed as well or at all under the old senile system. Those tasks meanwhile have become urgent and well understood; hence the new system at its birth is well designed for its initial functions, and there follows a period of economic and all-around social progress. But in time the evolving society again develops new internal tensions, conflicts, and dilemmas due to the defects, relative to new conditions, of the institutional framework — its bias in favor of one class — and increasing rigidity as that class grows more conservative or concerned with consolidating and protecting its power. And the dominant class resists the increasingly needed institutional reforms, *not only* in the effort to preserve its own economic advantages, *but also* because the minds of its members have been so conditioned by their situations and one-sided experience of life in the society that they sincerely identify the entire institutional and cultural *status quo* with all civilization as opposed to barbarism. Just because they have that sincere, unchangeable, emotional conviction, rational persuasion of the dominant class to voluntary acceptance of the increasingly necessary social changes is impossible. Adequate change by any method is impossible until the deterioration of all conditions of life in the society, due to the self-hampering system's growing, unresolved dilemmas and malfunctionings, becomes intolerable to the suffering, oppressed class — meanwhile converted by its sufferings to a new ideology or social vision of its own — and brings on revolution. All history according to Marx has been a series of repetitions, with endless variations of details, of this cycle: revolution, period of progress, rise of need for and resistance to institutional change as a part of further progress, period of degeneration or growing evils, and again, revolution. Only the final revolution, victory of the "proletariat," and inauguration of the "classless" society, will destroy the internal barrier which has caused every civilization in history to develop, deadlock itself, decline, and perish in that manner.[5]

That in bare outline, as I understand it, is Marx's general theory of the process and pattern of all history. No anti-Marxist need deny that it contains some important, largely valid insights. But its too simple and too rigid formula exalts one set of tendencies, which actually are modified by many others — diversely in diverse societies and epochs — into the universal, sole, and invariant determinants of all social evolution. This oversimplification has three related aspects. The basic one is the already emphasized assumption that "class struggles" are the sole vehicles through which economic changes produce all social and cultural changes.

[5] I believe that my summary of the familiar Marxian theory of history is non-controversial, and that little beyond the *Communist Manifesto* need be read to confirm it.

But further, in the second place, the resulting picture cuts up history much too sharply into a series of discrete, self-contained, internally uniform, and entirely dissimilar economic-social-and-spiritual period-systems, neatly separated by the intervening, all-transforming revolutions. For example, virtually as soon as the economic system of the feudal period is superseded, in any country, by industrial capitalism, the entire civilization of that country in all aspects supposedly becomes a pure, typical bourgeois social order and culture. There is no adequate recognition of the frequent, continuing, active powers of very long-lived traditions. And finally, in the third place, Marx's theory of history assigns the same, fixed, general form to the life cycles of all period-systems — again because it makes class struggles the sole converters of economic into social change, and assumes that in all the successive systems alike, their "dominant" classes are bound to display the same intransigent conservatism.

Now just these three features of the Marxian are entirely absent from the Schumpeterian development of the economic interpretation. For in the first place, Schumpeter entirely discarded Marx's theory of social classes and class relations.[6] His own radically different views on that subject will be described below, in my discussion of his essay on social classes. Here it is enough to say that in answering the question, how *economic* evolution brings about *social* change, Schumpeter made no use whatever of Marx's class struggle theory. Instead he implemented his own economic interpretation far more broadly, flexibly, and subtly, in a variety of ways for different problems, societies, and periods. One example, to be more fully considered shortly, may be mentioned now: for Schumpeter the chief link between the evolution of the modern capitalist economic system and that of its complement, the bourgeois culture and social order, was the full formation — first within business life as such and under its discipline — of the utilitarian-rational mentality, and the "spread" of that into all life and culture. And we shall meet another, different example below in considering his essay on imperialism, which shows how in many ancient, medieval, and early-modern

[6] See his highly critical discussion of that theory in the essay on Marx, parts 2 and 4.

societies and some down to the present time both social structures and mental attitudes, *originally* formed by non- and pre-capitalist economic systems and conditions, in turn produced the phenomena of imperialism and militarism.

Nor is replacement of "the class struggle theory" with other ways of implementing "the economic interpretation" the only difference from Marx. In the second place, in contrast with Marx's sharp division of history into discrete period-systems with nothing much from the earlier living on in the later ones, there is Schumpeter's recognition of great continuities throughout all history, due precisely to indefinite prolongations of the lives and influence of parts of ancient civilizations, retained within their modern successors despite full change of the economic "foundations." Here again, the most striking illustration will be found in the essay on imperialism; but apart from that, there are also in Schumpeter's other writings many expressions of his general belief that otherwise fully developed modern capitalist countries have retained to the present time, in their civilizations, important remainders of old "feudal superstructures." Obviously this means that in dealing with many a problem of explaining this or that group of modern social-cultural phenomena, one may find that their basic, original, economic causes existed and perished centuries ago, leaving behind these products which are still active in their own rights, in a new modern economic world to which, however, they may owe nothing of their being or their powers. It begins to be evident how the un-Marxian character of Schumpeter's economic interpretation — involving no simple, uniform, rigid, always fully and promptly effective economic determinism — agrees with and further explains the *relative* separateness of his economics and his sociology and their semi-independence of each other.

Finally in the third place, I believe it follows that Schumpeter also rejected the third feature of Marx's theory of history which I criticized above: the idea that as history moves on, every economy-and-civilization in its turn must as a matter of course pass through a complete life cycle of the same general form — birth, progressive evolution, decline, death. Now Dr. Sweezy in the commentary which I quoted above, interprets the main part of all Schumpeter's work, his theory of the evolution and decline of modern capitalism and the bourgeois civilization, as an application of that general idea. But the latter as an idea about *all* historic systems *including* capitalism requires the full Marxian basis discarded by Schumpeter: the historic series of discrete and definite period-systems, and within each, the process of change determined through the class struggle. Dr. Sweezy, however, without referring to that basis or the question of its agreement with Schumpeter's views, tries to represent this general idea as a simple, self-evident truth. This he does through what seems to me, in effect, a fallacious syllogism: every (specific) social system that endures for a certain time in history is transitory; capitalism is *a* (specific) social system; therefore, capitalism is transitory. (And here the life cycle form is slipped in without argument as though covered by the adjective "transitory.") The fallacy, I submit, is that capitalism is not a specific but a wide, generic concept, admitting of an indefinitely great variety of forms and degrees which might together fill most of all past and future history, without violating the rule that everything definite is transitory, or history is perpetual change. Actually, there was more capitalism in many places in remote antiquity, and there has been more of it scattered widely through most of history, than Marxists can readily admit. And on the other hand that special industrial capitalism, which was rampant in England in the early nineteenth century and identified by Marx with capitalism in general, is today already dead and buried some time since, in most of the world. In particular the American capitalism of today is considerably different, and departs a good deal in many ways from Marx's predictions. And while this too will of course go on changing, that fact in itself proves nothing against a speculation that perhaps *some* form of largely private capitalism may still be flourishing widely on this earth in remote future centuries. The Marxian reading of all history and the resulting prognosis of the fate of capitalism does not follow from the mere observation that all is transitory. Its validity depends on that of the entire Marxian theoretic structure including the parts rejected by Schumpeter.

It remains possible of course that some penetrating, economic and sociological analysis of just the historic processes of change within the capitalist world of the last few centuries may have established a strong case, independent of views about history as a whole, for believing that *this* economy-and-civilization is nearing the end of a full life cycle and a "death" which will be that of all capitalism and a transition to socialism. *Marx's* analysis, to this effect, of modern capitalism was a vast elaboration for this special case of his general theory of all history or all the period-systems he "saw" within it. *Schumpeter's* was a very different, clearly divided, two-part analysis without that background, of a progressive evolution of the modern capitalist economic system "seen" as inducing, and in time being ruined by a concurrent, degenerative evolution of its complement, the bourgeois culture and social order. And while this analysis leads to a general result similar to that of Marx's analysis, it does so in a way and on grounds of its own, diverging widely from and owing little to the ideas of Marx. I must now complete this section with a direct comparison of these two analyses of modern capitalism.

Marx's general theory which I outlined above was all in the domain of sociology — dealing not with the inner mechanics of the process of economic development itself but with its institutional and cultural consequences. Only for the special case of modern capitalism did Marx develop a detailed theory of the basic, economic side of the complete social process. And even here, in his theory of the structure, working, evolution, and prospective self-destruction of the capitalist system, the part that really is economic theory and that which is sociology are interwoven and dependent on each other at every point. Marx's capitalists are not like those of most other economists — simply individuals, like all others, reacting rationally to their economic opportunities and to nothing else. In everything that they are and do they are the members of the dominant class, which has created and intends to preserve a legal property system through which it "exploits labor," and a political system controlled by itself to develop in detail, enforce, and preserve that legal system, and a special, complete, intellectual and moral culture existing mainly to idealize and sanction that existing order. The individual capitalists in their business activities are driven and directed by a

profit-and-accumulation motive which again differs, in its foundations, nature, and results, from what the profit motive is supposed
to be by bourgeois economists and by the common sense of the
bourgeois culture. As conceived by Marx that motive in the
capitalists does not arise from their wants as consumers, is not a
matter of mere rationality or prudence, and does not operate
merely in the mode nor within the limits of passive response to
existing opportunities. Its objective, material foundation is the
alleged, objective fact about "the system," that its central process
— exchanging money investments for products of labor and those
products again for money — has point only if the capitalists
regularly get back more money than they invested, and reinvest
the enlarged sums with only fractional deductions for their own
consumption. In its subjective character the resulting motive
is supposed to be a passion to grasp and accumulate as new capital
every possible cent of profits in order to increase, within the
capitalist class, individual and family shares of power, prestige,
social weight or influence, and self-esteem. The bourgeois culture
makes those final ends emotionally all-important while it, together
with the economic system on which it is based, makes financial
success and accumulation the sovereign road to them. In Marx's
vision the resulting, frenzied passion for profits and accumulation
is what makes the economic system extremely dynamic and the
capitalists world-changing Titans.

For as they go on amassing ever more capital in the aggregate,
Marx's capitalists are driven also, by their passion and the resulting exigencies, into all needful acts of aggressive enterprise to
enlarge or create investment outlets and combat the tendency of
the falling rate of profit. This they do, during the history of their
system, by a series first of technological revolutions, then of great
monopolizations, and finally — in the modern-Marxist theory of
imperialism — of foreign ventures into backward areas, backed up
at need by the political and military power of their own domestic puppet governments.[7] Meanwhile the great dynamism of the
economic system itself is in growing conflict with the more static

---

[7] The last mentioned proposition — theory of imperialism — was of course
developed by successors of Marx, not by Marx himself. See discussion
below, part IV.

superstructure or power-system. In spelling this out, Marxian economic theory with the indispensable help of the sociological ideas united with it, about the power-system and power-lust of the capitalists, produces the following well-known chain of doctrines. However productive the economy may become, it continues to withhold from its labor force all the excess of the value of output over bare subsistence wages. Relentless accumulation of the bulk of that surplus as new capital continues no matter what happens. There is chronic deficiency of total consumer demand in relation to the ever-growing potential output. Prosperities are brief and separated, occurring only when swarms of new innovations and preparatory plant expansions temporarily expand employment and consumer income more than current finished output.[8] The intervening, successive depressions are increasingly severe and the last one will mark the breakdown of the system. Meanwhile, preparation for socialism goes on in the shape of progressive concentration of assets and production in the hands of ever fewer and bigger firms and combines, not only because there is no limit to the increase of efficiency with size of the business unit, but also because competition in the always inadequate total market is ferocious and means ruin of the weak by the strong. And finally along with all this goes also preparation for the revolution, in the shape of growth of the proletariat and progressive awakening by labor to the meaning of its growing miseries.

Now in contrast, Schumpeter's theory of modern capitalism's economic evolution is a theory constructed not in close union with, but rather in full abstraction from, his sociological theory of the civilization and its changes through time — which in any case is very different as we shall see from Marx's sociology of the capitalist power-system. Hence the Schumpeterian economic theory too is in the main unlike the Marxian, and the few similar elements have dissimilar grounds. The innovative and expansive dynamism is there, but is not due to power-lust and the exigencies created by relentless snowballing of the mass of capital. It is due simply to the creative spirit of the great entrepreneurs; and capital-growth is a response — largely by the credit-creating

---

[8] Of course Marx contributed to business cycle theory much besides the one idea here alluded to.

banking system — to the growth of demand or investment outlets first created by the entrepreneurs, not the other way around. Also as the system's productivity and output rise, so do real wages, and the whole effect of the growth of production is benign, going mainly into raising the living-standards of the great majority. There is no general tendency to over-saving and under-consumption, and, since enterprise leads and capital-growth follows, no great nor growing difficulty in continuing to achieve a sufficient growth of investment-opportunity. The business cycle is due to "swarms" of entrepreneurial innovations, but is merely the system's not at all unhealthy way of achieving progress; and the depressions have their beneficial aspects and function, do not grow worse over time, and with the rising level of wealth can eventually be robbed of their sting of hardships, without eliminating progress. Concentration into fewer and bigger business units does go on, but makes the system work better, not worse, for the general welfare,[9] and does not entail for big business itself any dilemmas of a kind to drive it into imperialism.[10] In short, nothing in this theory of economic progress under capitalism suggests any reason why either the process or the system should ever end, decline, or lead to socialism.

Schumpeter's theory of the decline and transition is identical with his separate sociology of the bourgeois culture; the latter grows rotten, destroys the vigor of and stifles the economy, and in the end makes the transition to socialism acceptable to everyone and the only way left which offers hope for a workable economy and a new, perhaps healthy, civilization. Now it is true as we have seen that in Marx's theory too, in a way, it is the sociology which really "explains" the system's decline or self-destruction and the change to socialism. But the quality which, according to Schumpeter, develops in the spiritual or cultural and institutional "superstructure" and makes it fatal to the economy and to itself is *the exact opposite* of the quality which does the damage according to Marx. In the Marxian theory the source of the damage is the inflexible will of the dominant class to re-

[9] See *Capitalism, Socialism, and Democracy*, chapter 8.
[10] See 4th part of essay on Marx, as well as *Imperialisms* essay, discussed below.

main dominant by maintaining and refusing to change its oppressive power-system, or allow even necessary adaptations of the
institutional framework to the changing requirements of its own
economic system. There is of course also the point that in Marxian theory the power-system is and makes the economy inimical
to the welfare of labor and the mass of the people, giving them
real, serious, and growing grievances which eventually goad
them to rebellion. But they could not triumph were it not for the
system's self-inflicted injuries, due to the growing incompatibility
of the static superstructure with the dynamic economy and its
changing requirements. Schumpeter's theory comes to just the
opposite conclusions on both questions, thus also on the welfare
of the masses including labor; the benignly progressive economy
continually improves their lot, and they grow discontented only
because, by doing so, the capitalist system raises their expectations and demands even beyond its own possible performance. But
again this would not be fatal were it not for the growth, meanwhile, within the culture and attitudes of the business and whole
"upper" class itself, of "suicidal" tendencies *opposite in kind to*
that excessive will-to-power and fanatical intransigeance assumed
by Marx. Instead of excessive resistance to all reforms, what
develops according to Schumpeter is a flabbiness which weakly
yields to and even joins in supporting all kinds of "crazy," injurious "reforms" and nostrums, which enfeeble and stifle the
economy. Schumpeter's decadent bourgeoisie loses all faith in
itself and its own traditional values, institutions, and economy,
and indeed all faith in anything, all will and ability to defend
or preserve anything; and becomes, along with the populace, a
crowd of victims of the variable, noxious winds of doctrine
propagated by "the intellectuals" or dreamers and agitators, who
acquire a vested interest in promoting and "leading" subversive
movements.

Where then in all that is Schumpeter's economic interpretation
— explaining how the progressive economic evolution brings
about the degenerative cultural and institutional evolution which
overtakes and conquers it? This too is there, and takes the form
which I mentioned at an earlier point. The discipline of business
life fosters, and diffuses into all life and culture, the mentality or

mode of thought which tries to solve all problems and reach all decisions solely by applying analytic reason to the study of empirical facts, cause-effect connections, and means to ends, and by foreseeing and comparing costs and benefits, evaluated only in the terms of individual, subjective preferences. Schumpeter of course in one way entirely approved this in itself, and many of its consequences. It belongs I think to the logic of his whole position to say that the rise and development of the modern business economy and civilization has carried with it, as products of the economy and parts of the civilization, the whole development of all modern science and all free, critical, rational, nonreligious, and unmetaphysical inquiry; emancipation of thought and life from the ancient stranglehold of theological and metaphysical dogmas; and growth of free, pragmatic pursuit by all individuals of worldly goods and pleasures, and satisfactions of their own desires of all kinds. But all that, I think Schumpeter felt, has had a negative side also: loss of the vigorous, emotional and imaginative faith, conviction, and ardor required in a ruling class to enable it to rule and maintain itself and all it needs to stand for; loss of the "glamor and passion" out of life, and the heroic virtues, and the will and capacity to govern, manage, and lead society, to ends and by standards fully, firmly believed in.[11] Schumpeter was a European conservative with divided loyalties, partly to the pre-modern, aristocratic civilization of the pre-industrial age, and partly, only, to the modern bourgeois civilization; and he saw in the latter, along with great merits, enfeebling qualities which he thought would become its nemesis.

I do not at all mean to imply that his analysis and prediction was a *mere* result of romantic nostalgia for the "glamor and passion," heroic virtues, etc., of old aristocracies, and a resulting "low opinion" of everything by which the modern bourgeoisie and its culture betray their lack of those qualities. I do think it hardly to be questioned, however, that — despite his too absolute, impossible ideal of *completely* independent "science" — his value judgments had some "influence" in helping to lead him to his

[11] See, in A. Smithies' memorial article on Schumpeter in September 1950 *American Economic Review*, evidence of the latter's views on bourgeois culture's lack of "glamor and passion," etc.

particular insights (and not others) into factual qualities and their connections, origins, development, and consequences. But I do not, in any sweeping way or large measure, impugn those insights and their claim to much independent, objective validity. The influence of value judgments, which seems to me always unavoidable in studies of this kind, is influence simply in directing one's keen attention as observer and analyst to questions, facts, and implications which strike him as important. The "bias" involved need be nothing worse than some limitation of the range of awareness, or failure to improve one's actual discoveries by also discovering, and taking account of *all* other relevant, additional, modifying and supplemental truths, including those more likely to be discovered by some other student whose interests and attention are directed, in part, by a different set of value judgments. *Absolute* objectivity is impossible; that is to say, omniscience is impossible. But the element of objective knowledge, supported by independent evidence and analysis of that evidence, may be there and have major importance, whatever has been the role of a particular set of value-feelings in leading to perception of all that, and non-perception of some other, evidence. I am sure that much of what Schumpeter saw as going on in our civilization is going on, and to some large extent has causes of the kind, and tends in the direction, indicated by his sharp analysis of the great array of evidence he found. The central argument of *Capitalism, Socialism, and Democracy* can by no means be dismissed lightly in my judgment. At the same time I am not fully convinced by it as a whole and do not regard the prediction it leads up to as proved. But another different facet of Schumpeter's high, relative objectivity as observer, historian, and sociologist of civilizations, must be noticed now in transition to a new topic. Although he saw great, growing, and destructive weaknesses in modern bourgeois civilization and admired much in various premodern and ancient societies and their civilizations and ruling classes, he could also see and analyze objectively, in those more glamorous antique worlds, traits and tendencies to which — though insistent on excluding his value judgments from a scientific study — he no more gave full approval than do most of us. Thus he did not always prefer above their purely modern bourgeois alternatives all the elements of modern culture-patterns that he saw as survivals from those same antique worlds which on the whole he tended to admire. All this I think should be borne in mind as I turn, at last, to his essays and take up, first, the essay on imperialism.

IV

Superlatively brilliant, packed full of an amazing range and wealth of knowledge of ancient, medieval, and modern history, and displaying deep insights on every page — Schumpeter's essay *The Sociology of Imperialisms* is magnificent reading. The subject is not the relations of "advanced" with "undeveloped" and dependent countries, but the problem of the nature, varieties, and causes of imperialism in the most general sense — the inclination, bent, or drive in imperialistic tribes, nations, states, or governing groups toward aggressive war, conquest, and extension of their own dominion over other peoples and territories beyond their own original frontiers. After thus defining its problem at the outset, the essay starts with a "look" at England under the leadership of Disraeli, as an example of "imperialism as a catch phrase" *only* — perfectly harmless, no reality in action — because (Schumpeter argues) the full development of England's capitalist civilization had made that impossible. Then the central, main part of the essay builds up its argument — diagnosis of the real thing in its many historic varieties — by delineating and analyzing in succession, each in a few pages but incredibly fully, a numerous, full series of concrete examples, extending all the way from ancient Egypt, Assyria, and Persia down through Alexander, Rome, the Saracen empire, the Merovingians, Carlovingians, etc., to the France of Louis XIV and Russia of Catherine II. And finally its concluding section, "Imperialism and Capitalism," directly examines, and sums up the answer to, what has been in the background throughout as the opposition thesis, viz., the modern-Marxist theory of imperialism as a product and trait of "the last stage of capitalism." Only the earliest and best form of the latter argument, the Bauer-Hilferding theory, was as yet extant when Schumpeter wrote his essay, so that theory is of course what is examined in it. A few valid details are found within it — e.g., a part of its analysis of "export monopolism," aggressive forcing of exports by cartels in alliance with governments — and fitted into a quite minor place is Schumpeter's own theory of modern imperialism as, in the main and essentially, a long antiquated, lingering aftermath of the far past, in the time and world of full blown capitalism, but owing nothing to and opposed by all the main, inherent forces in the latter. There is no doubt at all that the purpose and achievement of this essay was to counter the essence — the sweeping, fundamental thesis — of the modern-Marxist (Bauer-Hilferding) theory of capitalist imperialism, with a radically different as well as far more complex and adequate theory of imperialism, overwhelmingly supported by analysis of all the most relevant, historical evidence. But the mood and manner, and some accompaniments of the execution of that undertaking, reflect the environment and state of mind in which the essay was written — in Austria in 1919.

Today we are all familiar to the point of great weariness with the now current, Soviet-propaganda version of the modern Marxist theory of "capitalist imperialism." It may be assumed that all readers of this *Journal* know also, with varying degrees of thoroughness, the history and substance of the underlying piece of analysis which gives the doctrine its "scientific" pretensions. Were anything more to be said here about the present day, orthodox Stalinist version of the latter I think it would be correct, and I think Schumpeter would agree, to speak of a "descent" in every sense — degeneration as well as derivation — via Lenin's as well as later contributions, from that earlier Bauer-Hilferding theory — the original and relatively sanest form of that piece of analysis, added after his death to Marx's scientific structure by those disciples, leading Central European Social Democratic figures in the period just before the absurdly misnamed First World War. Now as that war came on, that theory, then still relatively new — and to Social Democrats a brilliant completion of Marx's structure and its power to explain contemporary history — was in wide vogue and under widespread discussion in that part of the world. And for many of those Marxian socialists and traditional pacifists it must have played a welcome, small role in helping them to "reconcile" their antiwar principles with their stronger patriotic and anti-British feelings. Was not England, the first, most developed, classic land of capitalism, also (in consequence) the chief embodiment of that monstrous evil, imperialism, and as such the great enemy to be hated and fought in the name of justice to all humanity as well as in defense of Germany? Such emotional "reasoning," claiming a logical foundation in Marxian "science," must have appealed to a good many fully Marxist and other Marxward inclined students and professors; but it did not appeal to Schumpeter. Well known to them all as an eminent, admiring student and authority on the science of Marx, he was yet not at all a socialist or political Marxist, nor a pacifist, though as a humane man and a lover of the high cultural life which flourishes at its best only in peace, he hated war. At the same time, though by no means devoid of patriotic feelings he was no jingo-patriot, and he always deeply loved and admired England. Living throughout the war in the Germanic world, he did not much conceal the fact, which accordingly was known, that his feelings were in sympathy with the British and Allied cause and discordant with the war spirit of the Central Powers.

Moreover and above all, apart from as well as in its relation to that war question, the theory that modern imperialism is essentially a product and phase of maturing and degenerating capitalism was to his mind nonsense. It is not accidental nor unconnected with the main point (but it is not the main point) of his essay that it freely reveals his Anglophilia. The main point is the appeal from what he regarded as the errors of Marx and even worse errors of those neo-Marxists, Hilferding and Bauer — whom he had known as fellow students and friends — to what he regarded as the valid method, created by Marx and capable of leading to the true explanation of imperialism as well as to the true explanations of most social phenomena. To Schumpeter that method or great tool was economic interpretation of history, *minus* the class struggle theory and everything connected with it, and all the mistaken, additional and restrictive notions including much of the analysis of capitalism under which Marx had buried his real great discovery. Hilferding and Bauer had built their theory of imperialism on superficial and erroneous elements of Marx's structure, plus new errors of their own, and not by a proper, sound, thorough, independent use of that fundamental method. Though he almost "leans over backward" to be fair to them, or give full credit for and salvage and use all the grains of sense he can find in their writings, he everywhere explicitly, completely, and emphatically rejects their essential theory of intrinsic connection of imperialism with capitalism. And along with that he explicitly rejects and labels as such all the errors of Marx which it relied on or utilized: the theories of pressure of incessant, automatic, immense capital expansion on investment outlets, non-improvement of mass living standards, underconsumption, *forced* acquisition of new, distant markets and investment outlets, unlimited growth of monopoly and decline of competition within national economies, full and continuing control of all politics and state policies by capitalist interests, and the total, ridiculous misconception of the bourgeois character in its full development as aggressive, ruthless, and domineering. Discarding all that, the essay is a sociological analysis, by the method of economic interpretation of history in the broadest sense, of virtually the full history of all imperialism in the western (and ancient near eastern) world, from remote antiquity down to the twentieth century. The method is to pick out unmistakable "strong" cases in which either entire societies (peoples) or the groups in control and counting for the purpose were imperialistic, that is, continually pursued *as their main aim in life and for its own sake* expansion of dominion by war and conquest; and to show in all these cases how the social structures and group attitudes immediately responsible for that behavior were formed, by economic environments and modes of production including the social relations involved therein and, in the modern cases, by all of the relevant social inheritance of old ideas and attitudes formed by earlier, but still operating in the newer, economic environments along with the new influences arising from the latter.

Unfortunately there is no space here in which to describe any of the case studies, the precise applications of the method and the results arrived at in them, or any of the general conclusions of the essay except the chief one: that all the "modes of production" or "economic systems" which ever generated real imperialism were pre-capitalist in the Marxian sense. The whole effect, according to Schumpeter, of everything inherent in modern capitalism and its development and of the social structures and the culture created by it is to undermine, diminish, and eventually banish all support for imperialism and aggressive war in any quarter. The continuing possibility, in the modern age, of existence or appearance on the scene of imperialistic states, regimes, and foreign policies is due entirely to the fact that much of the world, including much of what is commonly but mistakenly supposed to be the fully, maturely, and purely modern capitalist part of it, is actually still largely or partly pre-capitalist or enough influenced by internal tendencies, carried on from the far past and not yet extinguished by the influence of capitalism, to be susceptible still to the appeal of imperialism as a policy and even able to pervert local forms of capitalism into its service. All that is made unmistakably clear as the main thesis of the essay. There is thus no basis whatever, it seems to me, for Dr. Sweezy's idea that this essay is a corrective supplement to Schumpeter's *Theory of Economic Development*, repairing the latter's omission of any explanation of "imperialism and war" as one large aspect of "capitalist reality." [12] To think in terms of pure period-systems and therefore designate as capitalist reality, i.e., due to and part of capitalism *all* that exists or occurs *in the period* "of modern capitalism," is to follow Marx but *not* Schumpeter and entirely miss or rule out the whole point of this essay. It is not the *Theory of Economic Development* which "leads to the expectation that" capitalist development "will eventually relegate" imperialism and war "to the scrap heap of history," for the *Theory* has no implications in the field of this topic. It is entirely and precisely the essay on imperialism which not only leads to, but explicitly affirms and supports, that expectation — with stress on *eventually*, and the proviso, *if* there proves to be enough time and opportunity for all the tendencies inherent in capitalism as such to produce and make dominant their full, potential, socio-cultural consequences. The essay does supplement the *Theory* but not in the way alleged. Within its field the *Theory* finds the economic development of capitalism to be a process having in

[12] See the second paragraph of the quotation from Dr. Sweezy's introduction to these essays, p. 259 above.

general only beneficent results for mankind. And the essay adds a sociological analysis in one area, extending back into all pre-capitalist history but including the "period of capitalism" too, and showing that in the matter of the whole basis of imperialism and war also, the long-run effects of capitalist development as such are entirely beneficent. The only catch is that the essay does this in considerable part by emphasizing *the same* socio-cultural results of capitalist development, which the theory of decline of the "system" in *Capitalism, Socialism, and Democracy* regards as likely to bring about, before very long, the "death" of all capitalism and the arrival of a worldwide, "culturally indeterminate" socialism.[13]

It may seem to some readers that the thesis of the imperialism essay — advance of capitalism means decline of imperialism and war — must reflect merely, or in a degree fatal to its merit, the optimistic illusions which still were possible in 1919 and have been discredited by subsequent history. But I think on the contrary that it would be possible and very illuminating to extend and apply to the world events of the decades since it was written the line of thought and method of research and analysis of Schumpeter's imperialism essay and, by so doing, to explain all the fascisms and the Second World War, and also Bolshevist Russia and the present situation. Not only long persistence but possible revivals or bursts of renewed vigor of the forces having ancient, pre-capitalist origins and conducive to imperialism were explicitly provided for in his essay and its theory and heavily conditioned forecast. He found real imperialism already dead beyond any possible revival in England, due to her relatively high capitalist maturity, and still more completely absent in America as the most purely capitalist country in the world. He did not go so far in an essay written in Austria in 1919 as to say explicitly that the heritage from pre-capitalist times, full of elements apt to breed imperialism and war, was very much more alive in Germany than in England, but I think such a judgment is clearly implicit in the essay. It is not without significance that all the Fascist movements triumphed only in countries still partly pre-

[13] Regarding "cultural indeterminacy" of socialism, see *Capitalism, Socialism, and Democracy*, part IV.

capitalist by Schumpeter's criteria — in their civilizations if not their economic systems — nor that Russia is even closer to its pre-capitalist past, and certainly profoundly influenced by that heritage as well as by its new socialism — the cultural, moral, and political consequences of which according to Schumpeter can be anything, depending on other influences not inherent in socialism. It is true that the tenor of these suggestions is in some conflict with some of the known, orally expressed attitudes of the Schumpeter of the 1940's, but I doubt that they were intellectually well matured judgments, deserving to weigh in the balance in this connection.

At all events, *The Sociology of Imperialisms* is certainly an important, integral part of Schumpeter's largely un-Marxian, though in one respect Marxian, "broad system," consistent and coherent with all the rest, and forming one section of its sociological part, concerned with explaining non-economic, social phenomena by the method of economic interpretation of history, *minus* the features as developed by Marx which involve his class struggle theory.

And now I come at last to the other essay which reveals not only why he rejected Marx's theory of social classes but what his own positive views on that subject were. This essay — *Social Classes in an Ethnically Homogeneous Environment* — is a stiff piece of purely sociological research and analysis, instantly recognizable as such by, and sure to evoke admiration from, any first rate professional sociologist. Again its method is economic interpretation of history, but in Schumpeter's, not Marx's form. And as to its significance and place in Schumpeter's "broad system," there is truth in Dr. Sweezy's view as far as it goes, but I think he has made only a minor, not the major point to be made in this connection. It is true as he says that this — as well as the *Imperialisms* — essay deals with both the pre-capitalist feudal and the modern capitalist era, and with some aspects of the transition — by no means so clear-cut for Schumpeter as for Marx — from one into the other. But it seems to me that from almost any standpoint and above all from that of an effort to grasp the essay's main contributions to its author's "broad system" and to compare the latter as thus completed with Marx's system, the nature of the essay's theory of its subject is what needs the main emphasis. Though hardly as important in the Schumpeterian "broad system" as Marx's "class struggle" theory is in *his* system, the theory of social classes worked out in this essay is I think quite important in and to the former. And it is a radically un-Marxian theory of what classes are, what causal factors account for their existence, behavior, and changes through time, the elements and grounds of coöperation and conflict among them, and their roles in all the processes of society and history or social change. It is impossible here, however, to cover that ground, outline the theory, or touch on more than a few of its major themes.

As the prefatory note to the essay explains, the phrase in its full title, "in an ethnically homogeneous environment," means only that a complicating factor — "race" differences — is abstracted from to reduce the subject to manageable proportions. But it is significant that while explaining that point Schumpeter immediately goes on to emphasize his view that "racial" or "blood" stocks and their differing, innate capacities and qualities *are important and by no means entirely extraneous* to the subject (social classes), and would have to be dealt with too in a fully adequate treatment of it. He had, he says further, in the earliest, youthful stage of his interest in that subject leaned to the "racial" theories, which tried to trace all class distinctions everywhere back to origins in "race" differences. And though he had found that approach to be erroneous and abandoned it, he remained convinced that such differences in all mixed populations generally play important roles in helping to account for many of the concrete phenomena of class divisions or groupings and much in the behavior and fortunes of the different groups, although they are not the "heart" of the explanation of what classes are and why they exist. Now as I read his essay, it seems clear to me that, while by assuming "an ethnically homogeneous environment" he ruled out of consideration in his theory the part of the range of biologically determined, human inequalities classifiable as "ethnic," his belief in the importance of all such inequalities, in general, in a way underlies the whole essay. And I think there is no doubt that the basic attitudes which disposed him to this belief affected both through that and in other ways, also, the choice of his lines of inquiry. It is even suggestive in this connection that the essay deals exclusively with *upper* classes — feudal nobility, and nineteenth-century capitalist entrepreneurs. It is true of course that historical data of the kind — in considerable part, family genealogies — relied on in the study, are mostly non-existent except for such upper classes. But it also is true that Schumpeter's interest was primarily in upper classes; and that is not unconnected with the importance he attached to blood-stocks and hereditary differences.

Like many other men with strongly conservative predilections on all social questions, he held firmly that all high abilities and human excellences are relatively rare in any large population and tend to be confined to a minority of good family stocks in which they are hereditary. Also he believed that the "families" (enduring through many centuries), having generally superior traits, eventually rise from wherever they start to high class positions, and inferior families (if once temporarily highly placed) fall in time into low class positions — this in almost every kind of society that ever existed anywhere, however great the apparent obstacles. "Vertical mobility" in the social scale always has been far greater — in the long run, over a series of generations — than modern sentimental radicals believe; and the effort *to prove this* for the societies, periods of history, and class-groups examined in the essay is its most central undertaking. Families, not individuals, the essay insists, are the units of which social classes are composed; families endure through centuries though individuals die; and families over any few generations rise or fall, both within and across class boundaries, in accordance with the excellence or not of their abilities and "drives," and their consequent successes or failures in performing the tasks and coping with the conditions confronting them in their successive generations. The objective validity and scientific interest of the study are high and independent of this fact, but it is a fact I am sure and of interest that Schumpeter *liked* the clear implication of that line of argument: that roughly, to a great extent, any upper class and its members in a given, "normal" society and time are "upper," most fundamentally, because by innate endowment they really are the superior people; and the "masses" consist chiefly of their real — by nature, not mere convention nor lack of opportunity — inferiors. Changing economic systems and conditions determine the natures of particular class structures, class functions, and objective requirements to be met; but the abilities and traits of character inherent in family stocks go far to determine — "given" those objective factors — the successes or failures of families and groups of them in meeting the conditions, fulfilling the old and at need adapting to new functions, and achieving and maintaining high positions in the social scale.

There was also another well-known judgment of Schumpeter's which I must mention here although it is mainly expressed not in this essay but in other writings of his — another side of his view about all "lower" classes. He believed that in general peasants, workingmen, and other members of "the masses" not only have inferior, i.e. quite limited, native capacities of every important kind, but also tend normally to have only corresponding, appropriate, limited aspirations — unless indoctrinated from the outside with absurd dreams of grandeur by meddling, radical "intellectuals." What the workman himself genuinely, spontaneously wants is never more than to become a small bourgeois. Ambitions as well as abilities are "by nature" small in the large majority of mankind everywhere, and great in the great people who compose the upper classes. Hence "the class struggle" idea of Marx was nonsense to him, not only as regards the overtones of indignant feeling about injustice, domination, and oppression, but also as an idea of a real, important, strongly motivated, dynamic process that is bound to develop and operate as the mainspring of history, so long as there are classes of the mighty and the humble. To Schumpeter a stable, social equilibrium would necessarily *include* a well marked hierarchy or social pyramid, with superiors — in both capacities and largeness of desires and aims — placed "above," and the larger numbers of inferiors in both respects, hence satisfied in their positions — "below." Moreover, his ideas about "power" on the part of upper classes over the lower and over whole societies — the nature, foundations, instruments, uses and abuses, and limits of such power, and the place of the will-to-power among upper class motives — were in most respects profoundly un-Marxian. But I cannot go into this, except to touch on one line of considerations related to it and affording opportunity to bring out a particularly important comparison with Marx.

One of the rather few value feelings which Schumpeter and Marx did have in common beyond doubt I think, was a strong admiration of "power" in the sense of the forceful, potent, driving ambition and will and energy as well as ability, seen as lying behind and essential for all great achievements. That admiration in Schumpeter's case clearly underlay his admiring interest in the classes studied in his *Social Classes* essay — both the feudal nobility and the great entrepreneurs who, he held, have built and sparked modern capitalism. That Marx had the same admiration for the latter, at times overcoming his hatred, is well known, e.g., from the "hymn of praise" in the *Communist Manifesto*. But one of Marx's fundamental mistakes — to Schumpeter's mind and surely in fact — was to take that "power" and "will to power" of the captains and generals of industry of the early and middle nineteenth century to be outstanding in the character of the entire, much larger class, the bourgeoisie as a whole, and sure to continue to characterize it in undiminished degree as long as the class should exist. For Schumpeter on the contrary, the forceful or potent character was always confined to the group of leading entrepreneurs, a small minority within their class, and further as we know he believed it to be in recent times declining and vanishing in most members of the class, including those modern successors of the great entrepreneurs of old, big corporation executives. And again as we already know his theory of that decline involved the idea that forcefulness of character and "spirit" owed its essence in great part to much in the total cultural, or spiritual inheritance of our civilization from pre-capitalist ages, which the culture produced by modern capitalism has been "doing away with." His faith in heredity in the biological sense did not go *so* far as to discount "environment" where the driving will, etc., are concerned. Beliefs or lack of them, absorbed from the cultural environment or "climate," matter here. But neither did he, as to this, desert the "economic interpretation"; *back of* beliefs and attitudes, ultimately, though it can be rather far back in history, lie the objective life situations and requirements which originally formed them. Now the stern requirements which confronted the feudal lords in early times, when they were a warrior class and as long as they had great functions or until they declined into mere courtiers in the age of absolute monarchy, bred in them the outlook and vigor of will, etc., which, along with their abilities, made for great achievements and the maintenance of a great class position. Likewise later, in the early phases of industrial capitalism, the requirements of their tasks, as well as the partial persistence still of some heroic feeling and thought in western culture, made heroes or giants of the great entrepreneurs. The essay on social classes is very largely about the decline of the feudal nobility; and there is a partial parallel with the author's theory of the decline of capitalism. Stern conditions and big tasks inspire great deeds; these produce a great or splendid social system and civilization; but the very achievements alter the conditions unfavorably for continuance of the same level of achievement or the will toward it; and the great class with the great world it has made decline. If there is a theory of life cycles of civilizations in Schumpeter's system, it is of this order. Classes, and in one sense dominant classes, but not oppressor classes, play a role in it — but through what they do in time to themselves, not through what they do to the lower classes and the resulting "struggles."

I have done no justice to the essay on social classes and would like to say much more about it, but this article already is too long and must be ended. In summary, I think I have shown that there is indeed a large, coherent Schumpeterian system involving both economic and sociological theory; that these two essays are important parts of it, related to the better known major works and illuminating and illumined by them; and also, that the whole structure in all its parts is much more unlike than like that of Marx, despite the importance of what it does owe to the latter. The most decisive differences are due above all to Schumpeter's rejection of the theory of class domination, oppression, and struggle as the mainspring of history, and all that goes with that

— and the different ideas used to fill that role. The main thing he shared with Marx was the economic interpretation of history; but without the Marxian supplement (class struggle) and with the others used instead, the economic interpretation became in Schumpeter's hands a quite different tool, and fruitful of quite other results.

12

THE FUTURE OF ECONOMIC LIBERALISM[1]

❧

Perhaps the best way to describe my humble offering is to call it a piece of tentative, general philosophizing on a very broad front. It is full of the highly fallible, subjective element of my personal views — the views merely of one liberal economist and citizen. They are views that involve, in addition to my limited and imperfect knowledge, beliefs or judgments in a realm of faith beyond strict knowledge, which I hold with conviction but also with humility and not as dogmatic certitudes. Having that character, then, my discourse is about not only the future of economic liberalism but also, and first of all, what economic liberalism itself is to my mind, and some points concerning its past and present, some internal problems, and the historical process and continuing task involved in its development.

On the first question, what it is, let me say at once that I personally reject every exclusive identification of all economic liberalism with any single, fixed, precise ideal and body of doctrine. What I think of, in the realm of doctrine, is a family of numerous, somewhat differing, and changing ways of thinking, which are versions of the common, developing, general outlook. And in the real world of practice, what I think of is a family, or international community of differing and changing, national varieties or approximate realizations of something like the free way

[1] This article first appeared in the May 1952 issue (*Proceedings*) of the *American Economic Review* and is reprinted here by permission from the American Economic Association.

of life in its economic aspect. To identify the latter a bit further, let me also call it liberal capitalism or the system of free enterprise.

Using the two latter expressions as synonymous and without any hesitation at all, I do want to make one point clear. Any at all nearly absolute idealization of anything actual is always, I think, to be avoided. Every national form of more or less liberal capitalism is always, through time, coming to need many new, not radical but not unimportant, modifications of many elements of its outer, legal and institutional framework, internal structure and more of operation, and the prevailing private and public policies and practices. Continually new modifications are required to enable the system to better realize its own better possibilities of all-around service to the people generally. It is true, I think, that the present and the visible future is above all a time for conserving and even, where possible, to some extent restoring important features of the system that have been impaired by unwise so-called "reforms." Even so, this itself, I think, calls for persistent, careful efforts to improve in order to conserve, not indiscriminate resistance to every kind of novel change. Still in the main I am not making a reformer's speech, but only urging care to avoid the kind of inflexible thinking which results from confusing an ideal that in its true meaning never can achieve any one at all perfect or permanent realization in the world of practice, with any one existing or historic approximation.

In the proper, general, and flexible sense, liberal capitalism, according to my faith, in its various and ever changing approximate imperfect realizations, is a necessary part of all modern and hereafter possible, tolerably free, humane, and rational civilization. There are plenty of intelligent and well meaning people who believe in the possibility of a liberal socialism, but I cannot share their faith at all. Hence, feeling as of course we all do today a deep concern for the future of free civilization, I feel the same concern for the future of liberal capitalism, which I identify with economic liberalism in the world of practice. And this concern for a liberal future underlies and motivates all that I have to say. Nevertheless, I shall not attempt much in the way of prophecy. I do believe that neither despair nor hysterical fear nor any near approach to them as one extreme, nor any complacent, highly confident hopefulness leading to relaxation from endeavor in the liberal cause, is justified. Also as in a sense a further element of prophecy, all my thinking does have a background of mostly unexpressed, vague guesses about the uncontrollable, brute fact ingredients of continuing trends and prospective changes in our civilization, and their likely effects in modifying the shape of the task of rational labor in the liberal cause. But I cannot take the standpoint of trying mainly to predict or prophesy, or estimate the prospect, simply, as that might appear to a passive onlooker. For I am not in any full sense a historical determinist — not in that or any sense a fatalist. I believe that to a large extent all free men together have the future of the free way of life in its economic and other aspects in their own hands, to save or destroy. Hence to me it seems that the proper question to ask is not, simply, what lies ahead? Rather, it is the question, what, in our epoch and as we look ahead, are some of the main elements of the task of helping to bring about a revival and renewed spread and on-going development of economic liberalism?

In my own thinking I find it necessary to provide the liberal economic theory with a wider context. Economic liberalism, it seems to me, is not a self-sufficient or complete entity, but is one integral part of an all-around, complete, or comprehensive liberalism. I use the inclusive, single word, liberalism, not in any of the corrupted senses which have crept into its now most common uses in the intellectual and political worlds, but in a sense much nearer, at least, to my understanding of its older, traditional, or classical meaning. And I mean by it the philosophy and, where and insofar as this exists, the prevailing, approximate practice of the free way of life in all its aspects: economic, social, cultural and ethical, juridical, political, and economic. I deliberately mention the economic side twice — at the beginning and again at the end of the list. For I have a notion that something not too far from a sound development of the liberal economy is both, in one way, the required basis and yet also, in another way, the dependent outcome of a sufficiently sound development of all the other essential parts and qualities of the complete liberal society and civilization. The economy has to provide indispensable conditions: sufficient prevalence of sufficient degrees of the economic freedoms, market relations, opportunities, and enterprising, intelligent, and skilled activities, all leading to very widespread — on even the lowest levels tolerably decent — and generally rising real incomes and living standards. All that and, I think, also appropriate, generally prevailing features of economic society and its operation, affecting the peoples' emotional and mental, personal, and social lives as well as their incomes; adequate incomes and not unduly harassing, anxiety-producing conditions of life are, I think, required to enable the people generally to achieve and maintain something like the liberal, independent, tolerant, reasonable state of their minds and emotions and unformulated but effective working, practical philosophies of life. Only so then can they play their parts as participants in developing and soundly operating liberal democracy in the political sphere, a liberal system of legal justice, and liberalism or liberality in the arts and sciences and all high culture, along with the liberal economy. The economy has to provide indispensable conditions, but also is dependent for its own existence, continuation, and chance to function and develop at its best upon the support of a general predominance of the liberal character and spirit in all institutions and the main activities in all spheres of life. And nothing is any more fundamental than liberalism in all things of the spirit and as a prevailing state of the minds and emotions of the people.

Now ideas about the relation between the development through time of the economy and the objective circumstances of the peoples' lives and that of the prevailing state of all mental life and culture in the same society generally have tended, I think, to involve or lie too near to one or the other of two opposite, equally untenable, extreme, one-sided points of view. We cannot today, I think, retain all of that outlook which strongly influenced economic liberal thought in the period of its origin and early development: the full measure of faith that prevailed in the eighteenth-century "enlightenment," in the power of pure thought and study as carried on by the leading scholars in all fields, and education in the widest sense or public enlightenment, to entirely shape society and the course of history. But neither can we, I think, go to the other extreme and accept the doctrine of economic-historical determinism. Those two dissimilar, non-liberal men of genius, Karl Marx the radical socialist and Schumpeter who was an extreme conservative in a European, non-American sense but also a defeatist in his own cause, could and did develop and hold differing forms of the doctrine of economic-historical determinism. But I think no liberal can be a fatalist, and I am a liberal and not a fatalist. I do not believe, with the men of the "enlightenment," that the progress, diffusion, and applications of understanding of pure truth can entirely control the development of the real economy and society and the objective circumstances of the peoples' lives. But neither do I believe the other doctrine, that the evolution of the real economy is fated to proceed along a predestined path and as it does so, to engender and strictly determine, through the effects of the peoples' objective life-situations in society upon their emotional and mental lives, a concurrent series of inevitable changes of the state of all mental life and culture, applied criteria of truth or knowledge, and all political life and institutions. Liberal freedom is significant because men have, though not unlimited, substantial amounts of free will and are not automata entirely compelled by external conditions to feel, think, and act in specific ways. But peoples' objective life-situations in economic and general society do strongly tend to influence, through their emotional lives, their basic attitudes or values, outlooks, opinions, and behavior.

Proper recognition of the psychological facts of life in that matter does not, I think, lead at all to the conclusion that intellectual work at developing, diffusing, and applying the best possible scientific knowledge and understanding of the liberal society's requirements is entirely impotent by any means. Nor does it mean that such work is any less important than it seemed to optimistic scientific minds before Freud and others began to open up the study of the role of the nonrational, emotional parts of all human beings as affected by their life-situations, in affecting all their mental processes, conclusions, and behavior. But it is my impression that the facts of life in this area, as they are beginning to be understood, do mean that our traditional and proper, principal kind of intellectual work as specialized economists — the study of just the rational requirements for best fulfillment of the peoples' economic, utilitarian, sensible needs and wants — is, though necessary and important, by itself insufficient from the liberal standpoint. I think it needs to be supplemented by, and in a growing measure in the future reciprocally adjusted to and with, the investigative work that is beginning to be done by other specialists in the newer, modern psychological, and social sciences, concerned to a great extent with study of the required conditions of best fulfillment of the peoples' emotional, social, and cultural needs, for emotional and mental health, a not too unsatisfied acceptance of their roles or functions in society, a sufficient measure of social, cultural, and moral agreement or community of feeling, and a resulting, relative stability of the entire society or social system. At the end of this paper I shall touch again on those matters which seem to me important. But of course our own field of work as liberal economists, concerned with the rational, economic requirements of the liberal society for its best development, is important, too; and for the bulk of my remaining time I take up now a topic in this field that is on all minds: the vogue and character of so-called "Keynesianism," and the question of what it portends, for good or ill or both, for the future of economic liberalism and liberal capitalism.

It is necessary to distinguish analysis from policy, in discussing Keynesianism. What it represents in the field of analysis, in my opinion, is not a revolution entirely or even largely replacing an old with a new, complete analysis. It is only an addition to the previously developed modes of economic analysis in the liberal tradition, modifying them to some extent but chiefly supplementing them with a new analysis of a different problem from that with which they were chiefly concerned. Economic theory or analysis of the conditions of best allocation of all resources and productive efforts in a suitably changing, self-adjusting, well-balanced, and efficient pattern of employment, properly related to the changing pattern of demands for different kinds of goods and services, has not lost its importance and needs continuing attention and development as one essential part of economics. And the newer analysis of the conditions of approximate stability of the economic system as a whole through time, in the

range of positions of neither too full employment nor severe
unemployment, needs careful development as not at all a substitute for the other allocation or particular supplies and demands
analysis, or an all-absorbing novelty withdrawing all attention
from that; but simply a new piece of analysis of a further problem, requiring integration with the other body or part of all
economic theory, in a new well-balanced and thoroughly, internally adjusted synthesis. The working out of such a synthesis,
incorporating the Keynesian analysis and giving it its due but
putting it in its place as only one part of economic analysis,
seems to me an important still to be completed task of economic
science.

Having said that, I pass on now to the vexed matters of policy
and politics. I believe that the Keynesian kind of monetary-fiscal,
continuous, relatively full employment, stabilization policy can
be a sound, useful, and quite important addition to and modification of the traditional program of economic liberalism. That is
to say, in itself it is capable of being what I think it should be —
a quite limited departure, only, from *laissez faire;* a new piece of
limited, state intervention or action upon economic conditions,
through public monetary and fiscal policy, entirely consistent
with liberal capitalism or the system of free enterprise; and
operating not at all to subvert it but on the contrary to strengthen
and preserve it. If properly developed and carried out in practice, this relatively stabilizing policy can, I think, enable the
free economy to serve all the people well, more steadily, and
thus help to reduce political demands and pressures for other,
radical changes really dangerous or injurious to the system. But
while there is this possibility and it is important to work to realize
it, I do think, also, on the other hand, that there are some potential, fairly serious dangers for liberal capitalism or economic
liberalism in the world of practice, in much so-called "Keynesian"
thinking together with general tendencies in the political world
which are interacting with it.

The dangers lie, I think, not as much in the strictly Keynesian
analysis and stabilization policy in themselves, as in other elements, not necessarily connected therewith, of the total tendencies of thought of a good many of the more idealistic and

enthusiastic, "left of center," combined Keynesian and welfare economists. I would even add that they lie not as much in all of the ideas and proposals of those economists themselves as in other, different, independently existing, widespread, popular, emotional, and resulting political tendencies toward expansion and multiplication of governmental controls and irrational policies, more likely to be realized in practice than the more rational proposals of economists, but with much incidental though unintentional help from them. I think the most serious and most common unwise tendency of mind to which all or most of us in our profession — and I do not exempt myself — have our liabilities, is our tendency to be, as political economists or policy advocates, overoptimistic idealists and political innocents; naïve in our judgments about the real psychological and political forces which are bound to interact with and change our proposals if and as they get applied in practice; in short, more or less blind to the more unattractive and intractable facts of life about human nature as it generally functions in and through the political process. I am not here agreeing at all, either, with the other extreme kind of outlook in this matter — the cynical or hardboiled or utter pessimism which too often passes for political realism. What I think we need to get as close to as we can is a true political realism or real understanding, equally remote from that and from any at all utopian or blue-sky, idealistic overoptimism.

Let me in this connection now refer to the brilliant, excellent, very interesting and suggestive essay by Arthur Smithies on Schumpeter and Keynes which appeared in the Harvard memorial book of essays pertaining to Schumpeter. In that essay Smithies pointed out, I think correctly, the basic contrast and issue between the standpoints of Keynes and Schumpeter, not in economics so much as in this other field or psychological and general social and political judgments or presuppositions. Keynes, by this account, stood in not a strict but a loose sense in the general, Benthamite, utilitarian tradition of nineteenth-century British liberalism; and shared in consequence the high optimistic faith, always inherent in that tradition, in the ability of an enlightened political democracy to develop and carry out, as such, rational policies well designed to serve the common interest of

all the citizens. Schumpeter, on the contrary, despised Benthamism and had as we all know — and here I go beyond the description of his attitude in Smithies' essay — a nondemocratic and non-
liberal aristocratic or *élitist* point of view, an extremely pessimistic
estimate of the mental and moral capacities of most human beings,
bitter hatred for all politics and politicians, and a gloomy conviction of the inability of political democracy to produce anything
but irrational and destructive public economic policies, if allowed
to make any breaches in capitalism's defense wall of strict *laissez
faire*. I am not going anywhere near to all-around agreement with
Schumpeter, and will not have time to discuss his well-known
views in this connection. I think my own position and its great
differences from his will become clear enough in the course of
my remarks on Keynes and Benthamism. In offering these I go on
beyond anything suggested in Smithies' essay, presenting views of
my own which he probably does not agree with.

I do on the whole agree with Smithies on the point that Keynes
himself was chiefly a liberal in the general traditional sense and
no socialist, and meant his new analysis and policy proposals to
aid, not subvert, liberal capitalism. Yet I am not fully reassured
about him in that connection by the fact of his link with Benthamism. For I think it is relevant and very significant about
the latter that while the original Benthamites were laissez-faire
liberals, in a later period of British history the Fabian socialists
were also Benthamites; and were so, I think, with entire consist-
ency as far as the essentials of Benthamism are concerned. I believe that in the hands of Bentham himself and the main group
of his early disciples, Utilitarian liberalism was made liberal in
the laissez-faire sense or direction only by their addition to or
inclusion in it of some more specific *ad hoc* judgments that were
not at all inherent or necessarily implied in its fundamental doctrines.

Utilitariansim is a comprehensive theoretical system of psychology and ethics, sociology, and social philosophy, jurisprudence or legal philosophy, political philosophy and theory, and
political economy. It has strong attractions and real merits and
has rendered much service in the development of the modern
Western rational and practical civilization and societies. But I

think it is partly vitiated, to a serious extent, throughout, by a basic radical error. That error is the presupposition that what is in principle the scientific kind of rationality — the logico-empirical way of solving problems and arriving at decisions — should and can be and tends to be or become universally dominant and fully effective in all human thinking and the guidance or direction of all human behavior in "enlightened" societies. The root of Benthamism is a mistaken faith that something close to ideally scientific, pure, and applied rationality can, and in the course of human progress will, become generally prevalent and controlling in all human thinking and behavior. Scientific reason is to solve all problems, not only in the realms of the pure and applied strict sciences, technology, and the economic thinking and behavior of the people in severally managing their own private economic affairs, but also in the realms of search for sound moral and other value judgments and the thinking and behavior of all or most citizens, politicians, legislators and public officials, and lawyers and judges, in forming and acting on their views on all questions of justice, political economy, and all public issues. Utilitarianism is a theory and program of applied scientific, democratic, and rational planning of all institutions, the legal order, and private or public planning of all activities, to perfect the harmony of all human interests and insure a simultaneous, well-balanced, rational and optimal satisfaction of them all.

Now as to public or collective democratic planning, the original Benthamites did not go beyond the idea of what may be called "framework planning" — scientific legislation to so construct the framework of well-enforced rules of legal justice surrounding the free areas of private conduct, that all the citizens would be able freely to pursue their own respective ends or interest, but only in the mode of exchanging services without injury or injustice to anybody. And the vision was that within its legal framework, the otherwise free and universally competitive and fluid private enterprise and free market economic society would operate or function in a way insuring optimal satisfactions of all interests. The democratic political society or state through its organ, the government, would design, develop, and maintain the correctly engineered framework of general laws, but treat all or most economic decisions as the internal business of economic society and not interfere with them. And within its own sphere the economic democracy of the free market and price system would insure a continuous reciprocal adjustment of all private economic decisions and activities, such that they would all be rational, not only in the self-interests of those concerned, but, also, in fact, in the common interest of all in the society. All this, of course, is one principal historic version of the classical *laissez faire*, economic liberalism in the realm of doctrine. What I am criticizing in the Benthamite version is the assumption or expectation of a generally prevailing, very high degree of applied or practical rationality of the same uniform kind or quality, not only in the sphere of all private economic decisions and adjustments, but also and equally in that of all the political, popular, legislative, and governmental decisions involved in the supposedly essentially scientific rational planning of the institutional and legal outer framework of the free economy.

On that assumption, there was and is no compelling reason for confining democratic, collective, and governmental planning to framework planning. The original expectation that the laissez-faire system, assigning one sphere and task to political democracy and the other to the economic democracy of the free market system, would be and remain so satisfactory to all or the great majority that after getting firmly established and pretty well perfected in its way it never would be challenged proved to be mistaken. And the Fabian socialists, rejecting the specific conclusions of original Benthamism but retaining as their own inspiration its radical optimism about the capacity of political democracy for scientific rational planning, consistently built upon that their dream of democratic scientific governmental planning of the entire pattern of all economic activities.

The Utilitarian way of thinking is thus politically ambivalent; and so too, I think, are Keynesian thinking and the tradition of what is called "welfare economics." And the source of the ambivalence in all cases is nonrecognition of the essential difference between the natures of economic life, on the one hand, and moral and political life, on the other hand. In the sphere of economic decisions and policies, there can and should be a fairly marked relative predominance of the role of an applied rationality having much in common, at least, with that which is called "scientific." But all moral and political life or feeling, thought, and action necessarily involve to a much greater relative extent emotions or feelings of all kinds, passions, imagination, sympathies, and antipathies, intuitive feelings ranging all the way from elements of the worst fanaticisms to some of the finest of all human insights, and the moral reasonableness which must sufficiently prevail to make possible a tolerably free and just society, and can be achieved by all sound, healthy minds but is not of the same nature with scientific, technical, or economic rationality. A liberal political democracy with an enlightened electorate, constitutional protections of all vital individual and minority rights from any majority and its government, and an independent judiciary make up by far the best instrument for developing the approximate moral consensus and legal order of a free society. But while political democracy in that form or with those accompaniments is supremely the right system for its task, it is, I think, suited only for its vitally important primary task and not too much beyond that; and is not at all well suited for extensive participation in making or controlling economic decisions.

For it is the political system's nature to function in all connections in the manner appropriate to its primary task: through a rather free play and interplay of the emotions as well as the rational minds of all concerned, and intimate blends of feeling and thinking which are inevitable and in every sense necessary in what is the essence and meaning of all politics — the search or struggle for approximate justice in the clashes and compromises among group interests, greeds, and passions. Moral reasonableness has to prevail as fully as possible, through and over and in spite of the turmoil of irrational passions which must be as far as possible moderated and induced to submit to reasonable compromises, but cannot be abolished or more than very partially tamed, nor made entirely consistent or compatible with entirely rational decisions. Such is the essential nature — which in its sphere is not the wrong but the right nature — of the entire political and governmental process, except insofar as the latter can properly include, within the limits of what is consistent with democracy, the work of a bureaucracy or civil service of nonpolitical experts, partially sheltered from political pressures and given limited amounts of authority and discretion.

With the help of that instrument, the political society or state and government can and must take on, in addition to its main task of developing — with the aid of the judiciary — the legal order of general justice, a fair amount and variety of additional, useful, and necessary public work of a different, more scientific-rational or technical kind, including the work of developing and carrying out the necessary public economic policies. But the more the state expands, well and then far beyond the limits set by strict *laissez faire*, the sum of its undertakings to take over and handle matters in the field of economic affairs and decisions, the more serious become two tendencies, and the dilemma between them. Insofar as politics shape the policies applied, there is a tendency to make or bring about irrational economic decisions harmful to the economy and the economic interests of the people generally; and the alternative is to expand the bureaucracy and the discretionary powers of its heads and members, eventually to the point or too far in the direction of replacing democracy with a government by experts, who may be experts in their technical jobs but cannot be experts in general justice. Democratic political government with all its inevitable imperfections is morally necessary, precisely because there can be no experts in quite that same sense or at all beyond rather narrow limits, in the work of getting as near as possible to ensuring justice to and among all the people. The members of the bar and bench are experts of the appropriate, special kind within this field. But in dynamic, rapidly changing, increasingly complex societies, legislation and statute law inevitably become increasingly important; and political democracy is the only method at all sufficiently compatible with the rightful liberties of all the people for developing this. And it is the best and right method just because it does not enthrone the relatively superior rationality of any group of superior minds, who would lack access to more than a small part of all the relevant experience; but enables all of the relevant, private experiences of all citizens, including all their feelings and desires as well as their knowledge and intelligence, to be consulted and given possible chances to count in the joint determination, through the turmoil of politics, of the more or less fair compromises that emerge as legislative additions to the legal order of general justice. But this process — the best for its purpose — is, beyond rather narrow limits, the worst for the different purpose of determining the pattern of economic activities. That pattern can be far more rational and efficient if determined, in the main, within the limits set by the legal order, by private managements of households and enterprises, and a continuous interadjustment of all the private economic decisions through the economic democracy of a reasonably free, competitive, and fluid market and price system.

Strict *laissez faire* does not follow from my argument and is not, I think, a tenable ideal for the present and future. A limited number of limited policies of state intervention to help in solving special problems are necessary, because not all of the results urgently needed in the common interest of all the people can be accomplished sufficiently by just the market mechanisms operating under actual or achievable conditions. I think a proper, careful development in practice of the Keynesian relative stabilization policy is in this category of sound and needed limited interventions. But it needs careful, conservative handling and safeguarding both from political pressures and from the visionary enthusiasms of some of the relatively socialistic or politically ambivalent Keynesian economists. I do not use those epithets with any intention of censuring the economists in question in any bitter or dogmatic spirit; I am only expressing my personal judgment. And I have in mind not only their tendencies to want to make the stabilization policy itself a too ambitious one, finance it with too little regard to debt expansion and excessive or unwise taxation dangers, and use it for more than stabilization, adding a use of "public investment" to take over and redirect much economic development. I have in mind also the numerous other independent interventions and reforms suggested now in various economics textbooks and other public writings, growing out of not only Keynesian but welfare economics; theories in the latter, showing on various ethical assumptions the theoretical desirabilities of various public measures to produce changes of the allocation of resources or the distribution of wealth and income. Significant judgments about welfare involve ethical value judgments which cannot be scientific, and I think the whole concept of a strict science of welfare is an absurdity redolent of Benthamism. My feeling is that economists should think about welfare problems indeed, even more than they do, but in doing so, fully develop their carefully considered personal ethical value judgments as such and express and argue for them, all in an avowedly and unmistakably nonscientific way, not confused at all with economic science. The emotional elements in all evaluations and in all ethics, politics, and jurisprudence, and the larger role that can and should be played in the practical management of economic affairs by a not unethical but not primarily ethics-preoccupied, mainly logico-empirical, nearly scientific, practical, business rationality — these considerations, I think, make it vitally important for the economic and political future of free society to recognize and properly develop the different characters and functions and mainly separate, not too deeply intersecting, spheres of liberal democracy and liberal capitalism; and not do anything to encourage a varied deluge of irrational political interventions into the economic sphere, by disseminating an endless variety of pseudo-scientific economic-ethical theories and proposals.

I think I have now made sufficiently clear my general position about all this and its great differences not only from the Benthamite tradition, overzealous Keynesianism, and welfarism, but also from the extreme opposite, entirely pessimistic, views of Schumpeter. I do not, with the latter, despair of the future of liberal capitalism, nor regard all democratic governmental interventions whatsoever as bound in practice to be irrational and destructive. And I base my sense of the limitations of democracy as an instrument for controlling economic affairs, not at all on any distrust of it even in its own main field nor on any low opinion of the mass of the people, but on the difference of the political and economic tasks and subject matters, the more emotional character of one and properly, relatively scientific-rational character of the other.

It is a familiar argument that growth of state direction of economic affairs tends to become cumulative and roll on with growing momentum to full socialism. The basis of the truth in that idea is, I think, the fact that irrational management of economic affairs creates conditions that create new demands for new interventions. And I attach great importance to this, because it seems evident to me that overexpansion of the power and sphere of authority of the political state, in the direction of full totalitarianism, is about the greatest evil and danger everywhere in the world in the twentieth century; and also that political democracy as an institution is no adequate safeguard against that danger, and is itself endangered by it. But our greatest task of all in the years now ahead, it seems to me, in working to help to preserve and properly develop liberal capitalism and democracy is to make new progress in understanding and learning how to cope with the modern widespread psychological, social, and political forces that oppose all we stand for. What conditions have been and are engendering the adverse emotional and political tides in great sectors of public opinion and behavior everywhere, and what might help to make them subside a bit?

I cannot believe that — within this country or any of the relatively prosperous truly liberal capitalist countries — the main causes of wide prevalence and high intensities of extreme oppositional or obstructure attitudes threatening and hampering liberal capitalism lie at all in its economic imperfections; or any imperfections, even with respect to distribution or instability or anything else, of its great and growing output of economic benefits reaching very much the greater part of all the people. For all its faults — and any human system would have many faults — liberal capitalism or the system of free enterprise, wherever it really exists and has a chance to function, is on the whole unmistakably a very excellent economic system with respect to its service to the economic welfare of the people generally — by far the best in this respect that the world has ever known or knows today. And I cannot believe that more than a small part of the mass of grievances and hatreds for it which can be found in all classes and among all kinds of people springs from any economic deprivations or lacks experienced by the people concerned. Yet I do not conclude that those attitudes are uncaused or in every sense entirely groundless. I think it is not in the economic respect but in other respects, primarily, that our capitalist economic and general society as it is, but need not remain with no modifications, has traits and a mode of operation tending to engender widespread emotional attitudes and views and forms of behavior inimical to it. The problem, as I sense it, is very difficult because precisely the qualities of the system which are economic virtues are causes of trouble of this other kind, if I am not mistaken. The progressive dynamism, the relative fluidity of migrations and adjustments of people and resources out of declining into newly opening fields of opportunity, the prevalence of keen or intense competition, the uncertainties inseparable from change and progress — all are bound up with the system's splendid and improving economic performance. But they all have emotional effects in people's lives, with repercussions on the system, that I think we need to explore. The pressures of and for intensely competitive enterprisingness and repeated change of routines of work and life and geographic and occupational locations, and difficult personal readjustments, and uncertainties and anxieties of people over their economic and general futures — all this works, I think, to breed not the calm, rational, decent, competitive behavior and behavior in one's rationally conceived economic interest, that our theory assumes; but aggressive passions stirred up by anxiety and resentment of pressure, and turning competition into fights or struggles, and group efforts to contrive monopolistic strongholds and to some extent avoid competition and change. And in other quarters, the sense of living in a world full of conflict and relative chaos produces demands that the state shall take matters in hand and produce order and stability and general security; while the groups striving to stabilize and retain their local economic and social positions in the face of external competition and pressures for adaptive change, add to their own efforts demands for state subsidies and assistance with local and occupational stabilization schemes.

My suggestion is that there lies behind all this something else beyond or beneath peoples' economic interests and often false ideas of how best to further their economic interests. The fundamental causes lie, I suspect, in excessive frustrations of peoples' noneconomic and nonrational but inevitable natural, human, and legitimate emotional needs; for sufficient, tolerable degrees of relative stability, continuity, and security, not of their incomes alone but of their local, personal, family, and group and community ways of life. Whether consciously or not, most people, I think, have natural yearnings and emotional needs for not too frequently disturbed roots in local, occupational, and institutional pasts; durations of familiar and valued interpersonal relations, and the sense of belonging in familiar places, lines of work, communities, neighborhoods, and intimate groups; and freedom from excessive anxieties, competitive pressures, pressures for recurrent, difficult change and adjustment, and feelings of necessity for continual high concentration on the struggle to maintain sufficient, that is their accustomed or better, incomes. Frustration of emotional needs of this sort produces a dim sense of living in an ugly, greedy, quarrelsome, hostile world; and the hatred produced by fear is directed at capitalism, the competitive system, big business as the source of the innovations necessitating change or adjustment and disturbance everywhere, and the supposed absence of sufficient public control as the explanation of the felt and hated qualities of the social environment. In short, my notion is that we need to collaborate with the investigators in the young psychological and social sciences that try to study the emotional side of individual and social life; and try in joint efforts to learn what conditions of life are required for tolerable emotional health and contentment or serenity, and how prevailing practices in free economic society might better provide or permit such conditions, without undue interference with economic requirements. I had hoped to develop my own amateur notions about this further, but there is no time left. The future of liberal capitalism, let me say as a concluding expression of my faith, is not safe but also is not hopeless, if all who believe in it will collaborate with fully awake but not overexcited and flexible minds, and in the study of all sides of the many-sided task of preserving it with the necessary adjustments and improvements.

INDEX

INDEX